THE ENCYCLOPEDIA OF SUSHI ROLLS

Ken Kawasumi

Translated by Laura Driussi

GRAPH-SHA / Japan Publications

Sushi rolls are a three-way taste experience: the fragrance and texture of the nori, the delicate sweetness of the rice, and the intense flavor of the fillings — all wrapped together in a single delicious package. Every type of roll is covered in this book, including the picturesque decorative rolls, which are wonderfully rewarding to slice and display.

Published by Graph-sha Ltd.,
1-26-26 Higashi, Shibuya-ku, Tokyo, 150-0011
Japan
Translated by Laura Driussi

First printing: October 2001

Distributors:
UNITED STATES: Kodansha America, Inc. through Oxford University Press, 198 Madison Avenue, New York, NY 10016.
CANADA: Fitzhenry & Whiteside Ltd., 195 Allstate Parkway, Markham, Ontario L3R 4T8.
UNITED KINGDOM and EUROPE: Premier Book Marketing Ltd., Clarendon House, 52 Cornmarket Street, Oxford OX1 3HJ, England.
AUSTRALIA and NEW ZEALAND: Bookwise International Pty Ltd., 174 Cormack Road, Wingfield, South Australia 5013, Australia.
ASIA and JAPAN: Japan Publications Trading Co., Ltd., 1-2-1 Sarugaku-cho, Chiyoda-ku, Tokyo, 101-0064 Japan.

ISBN 4-88996-076-7
Printed in Japan

Contents

Hosomaki
(Thin Rolls)

Temaki (Hand Rolls)

Uramaki (Inside-Out Rolls)

Kazarimaki
(Decorative Rolls)

Chinese Zodiac

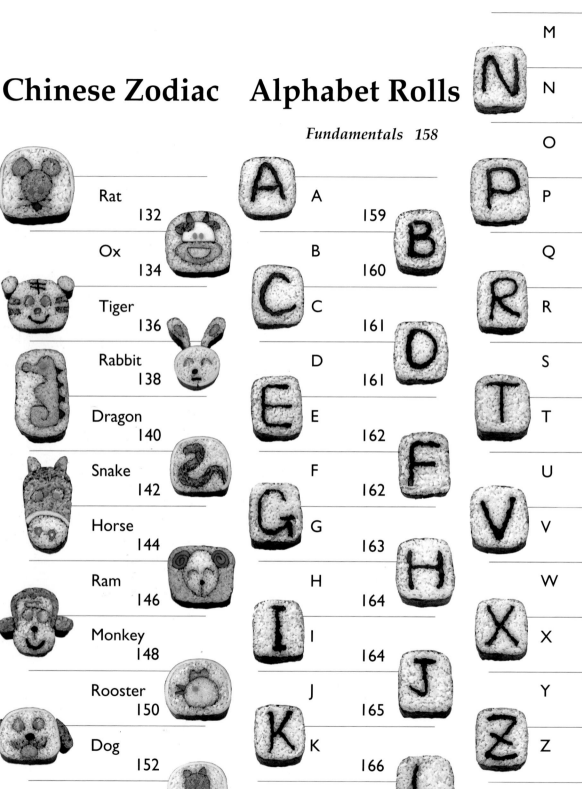

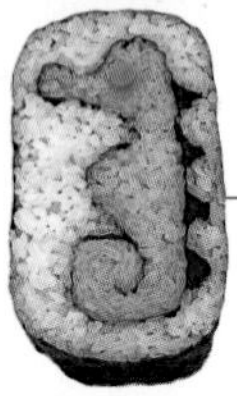

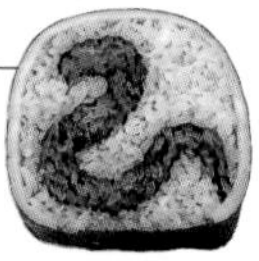

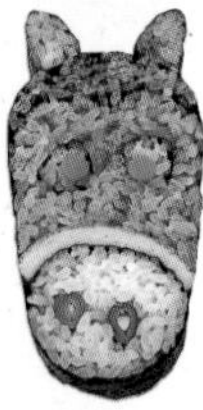

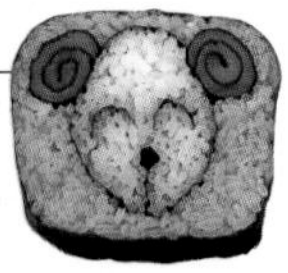

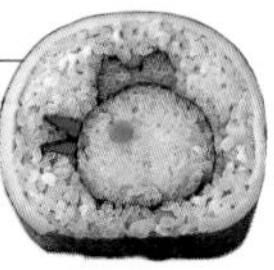

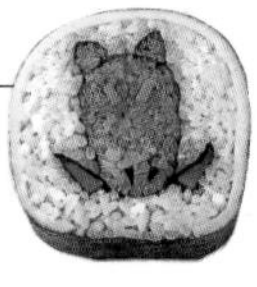

Alphabet Rolls

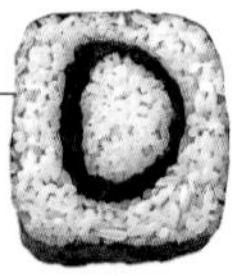

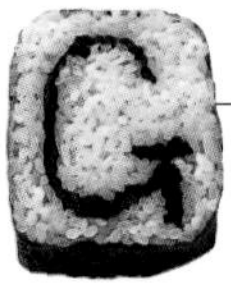

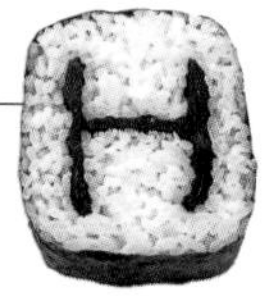

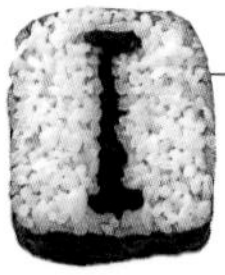

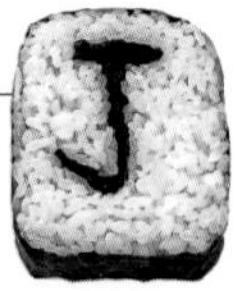

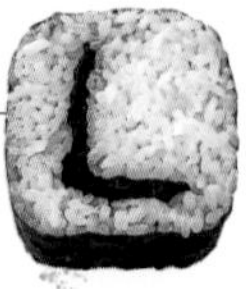

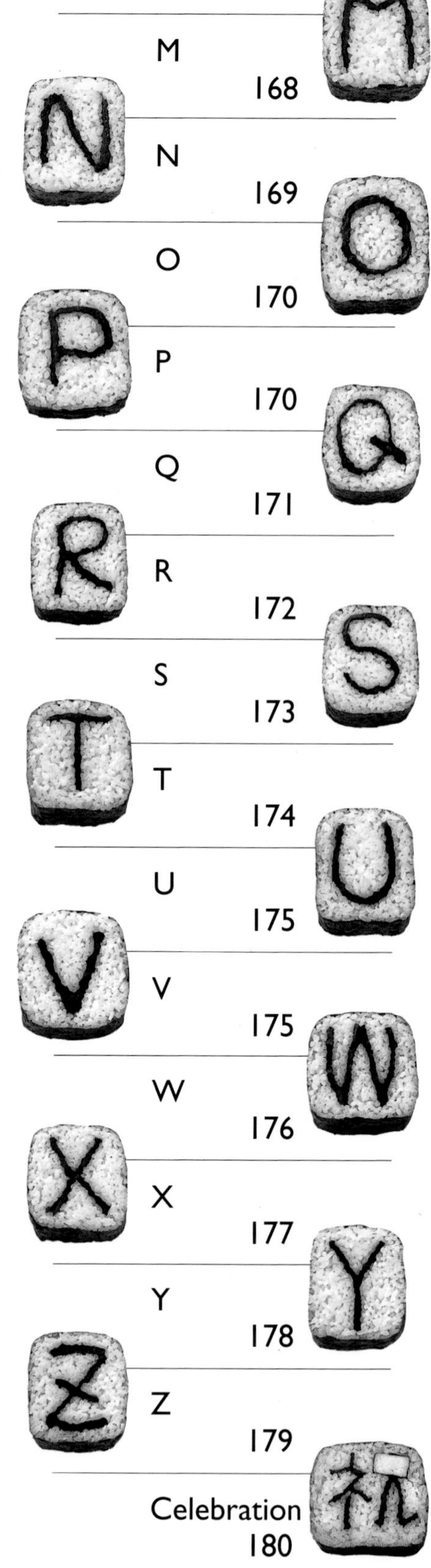

Metric Conversion Table:

1 Tbsp (tablespoon) = 15 cc
1 tsp (teaspoon) = 5 cc
1 cup = 200 cc
Sushi rice 1 cup = 180 cc

Sake, *Mirin*, and *Dashi stock* are essential to Japanese cooking.

Sake (rice wine) mellows food, tones down raw taste or smells and improves flavor. Dry sherry can be a substitute for *sake*.

Mirin (sweet cooking rice wine) is used to improve flavor and give food glaze and sweetness. *Mirin* may be substituted with 1 tablespoon *sake* and 1 teaspoon sugar. Both *sake* and *mirin* are now manufactured in the U.S.A.

Dashi stock is made from konbu and bonito flakes. You may also use commercial *dashi stocks*.

Japanese products have become widely available in recent years. Oriental import stores, health food stores and even some larger supermarkets carry a variety of Japanese foods.

If, however, the vegetable based ingredients cannot be acquired, be creative in substituting local alternatives. Try to match color and flavor wherever possible.

Raw fish, on the other hand, should be handled with care and these recipes should be followed closely.

Fundamentals

Making Sushi Rice

3 cups (540 cc) rice
3 cups (540 cc) water

(for rice and water, the cup used is a 180-cc rice measure from a rice cooker)

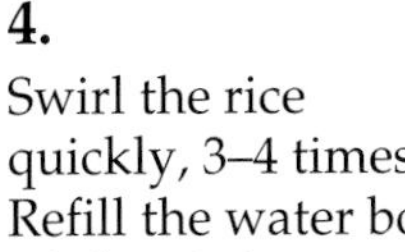

4–5 Tbsp rice vinegar
3–5 Tbsp sugar
$^{2}/_{3}$–1 Tbsp salt
1 piece kombu (1"(3cm) square)

1.
Fill a wooden sushi barrel with water and let stand for 30 minutes. Drain. Swab the interior with a cloth dipped in vinegar.

2.
Measure the rice into the pan of the rice cooker. Have a large bowl of water nearby.

3.
Pour the water from the bowl into the rice. (Do not use water from the tap —the slow filling allows the rice to sit in its particles too long before rinsing. The particles give the rice a raw flavor.)

4.
Swirl the rice quickly, 3–4 times. Refill the water bowl while stirring.

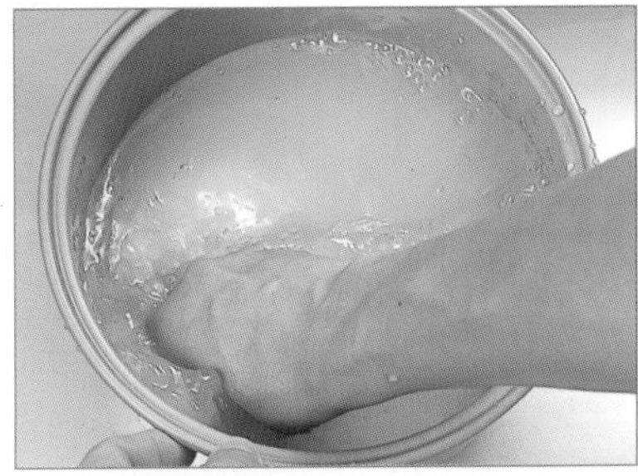

5.
Quickly pour off the cloudy water.

6.
Rub the rice between your fingertips as if to polish them, moving around the pan.

7.
Rinse the rice 4–5 more times, until the water stays clear. Drain one last time.

8.
Add the 3 cups of water. Let stand for 20–30 minutes. Place the pan in the rice cooker and start it. After the cooker stops, complete the steaming by leaving the rice in the cooker, unopened, for 20–30 minutes.

9.
While the rice cooks, make slits in the kombu and place in a saucepan with the sugar, salt, and vinegar.

10.
Heat the vinegar mixture, stirring to dissolve the sugar and salt.

11.
Just before the boiling point, remove the pan from the heat and discard the kombu. (Kombu will spoil the vinegar if left in too long.)

12.
Empty the steamed rice all at once into the sushi barrel. If the steaming period was too short, there will be hard cores inside the rice grains. If it was too long, the rice will not fully absorb the vinegar, leading to sogginess.

13.
Holding a rice paddle against the edge of the pot, pour the vinegar mixture evenly over the rice.

14.
First, gently push apart the rice with the back of the rice paddle, breaking up the cylinder.

15.
Next, holding the rice paddle as you use a knife, spread the rice out to cover the bottom of the sushi barrel, turning the barrel as you go.

16.
Push the rice over to one side of the barrel.

17.
With a cutting motion, spread the rice out again.

18.
Push the rice over to one side of the barrel once more.

19.
Again, spread the rice out with a cutting motion. These movements ensure that the vinegar mixture is evenly absorbed by the rice.

20.
Fanning as you go, turn the rice over in paddlefuls. The air helps the rice absorb the vinegar and gives the rice a polished look. After all the rice has been turned once, repeat the turning process.

21.
Gather all the rice on one side. Use a vinegar-dipped cloth to gather up the stray grains of rice on the paddle and in the barrel.

22.
Rinse the cloth with water and squeeze well. Cover the rice with the cloth, letting it rest until it reaches skin temperature. If the rice is too hot when rolling, the fillings may be bruised; if it is too cold, it is difficult to spread and the nori will not seal.

TIPS ON MAKING SUSHI RICE

What Kind of Rice?

Sushi is most delicious when the rice has just the right amount of stickiness. If the rice is not sticky enough, the sushi tastes dry. If it is too sticky, it is difficult to spread and has a mushy texture. In particular, "new crop" rice (*shinmai*) has too much water content for sushi. (To use new-crop rice, drain it in a strainer after step 7 and let stand 20–30 minutes. Then put it back in the rice cooker, add the cooking water, and cook. Continue with the last sentence of step 8.) Experiment with different brands to find your own favorite.

Professional sushi chefs make their own rice blends, using combinations of older or drier rice and new-crop or stickier rice

How Much Water?

Because you will be adding the vinegar, the rice should be cooked slightly harder than usual. The standard proportion for sushi is equal parts water and rice, but you should use about 10 percent less water for new-crop rice and about 10 percent more water for older rice.

Which Kind of Vinegar?

Grain vinegar
(kokumotsusu)
Nearly colorless, this mild vinegar is made from corn, grain, or rice.

Rice vinegar (komesu)
This yellowish vinegar, made from rice and alcohol, is the standard vinegar used for sushi.

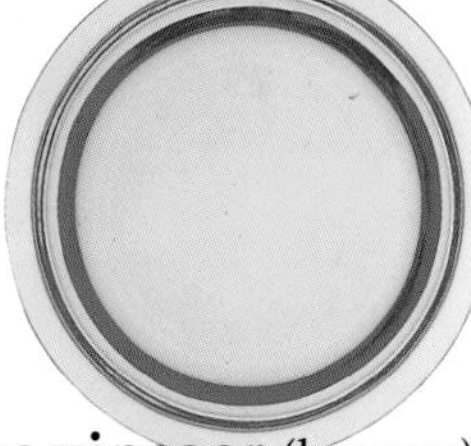

Sake-lees vinegar (kasuzu)
This vinegar, made from sake lees, is slightly stronger than the others. Because of its reddish color, it is also known as *akazu* (red vinegar).

Nori

Choosing Nori

The most widely available Japanese nori comes from three locations: Tokyo Bay (Chiba Prefecture), Kobe Bay (Hyogo Prefecture), and Ariake Bay (Saga Prefecture).

Kobe nori is thicker, while nori from Ariake Bay is made up of more delicate leaves (fragrance similar to aonori). From any of these locations, look for nori with uniform thickness, good fragrance, crisp texture, and sheen. If you can see holes in the nori, or if the nori has no fragrance, it is of lower quality.

For futomaki, choose a thicker, shiny sheet. This avoids breakage when rolling. For hosomaki, a more delicate, fragrant sheet is best. For temaki, select a thick sheet that has been well roasted for maximum flavor. For decorative sushi, thicker sheets are less likely to break, but if the sushi requires many sheets, avoid nori that is too thick.

Be sure to store nori in a cool place, well sealed. To roast nori, place two sheets together, shiny side inside, and roast high above a strong flame, starting from the four corners and turning when ready. Nori turns green when it is roasted.

Tokyo Bay (Chiba Prefecture)

Kobe Bay (Hyogo Prefecture)

Ariake Bay (Saga Prefecture)

Slicing Nori

Place the nori on a dry board. Press the tip of a chef's knife into the far edge of the nori and then rock the knife downward to slice through the near edge. Dragging the knife across the nori will lead to breakage.

Sushi Rolling Mats

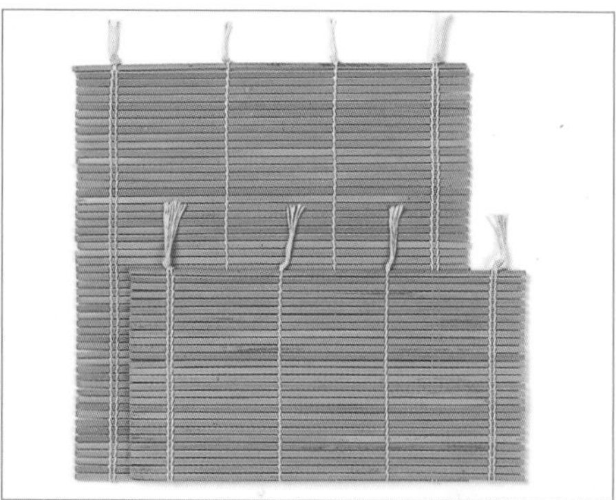

Rolling mats come in two sizes: futomaki (large roll) size and hosomaki (thin roll) size. Choose rolling mats that are tightly woven, knotted on one side only. Place the bamboo-bark side up when rolling. After use, wash carefully and dry completely to avoid mold.

Sushi Barrels

A well-prepared sushi barrel absorbs the excess liquid, giving the rice a glossy look. To keep the rice from sticking to the barrel, fill it with water and let it stand before use. After use, clean all the way into the corners. Let it dry completely. Store it upside down to keep the bands from loosening.

Maki-zushi

FUTOMAKI
Large Rolls

Fillings

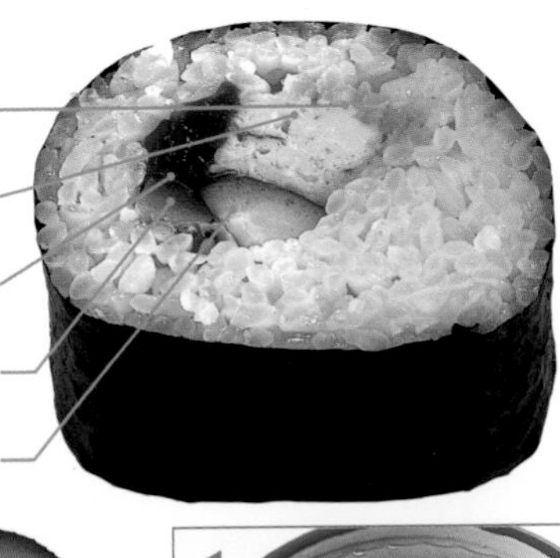

Simmered Gourd

(for 3 futomaki rolls)

$^{7}/_{8}$ oz (25g) kampyo (dried gourd strips)
1 tsp salt
1 cup dashi stock
5 Tbsp sugar
1 Tbsp sake
1 Tbsp mirin
4 Tbsp soy sauce

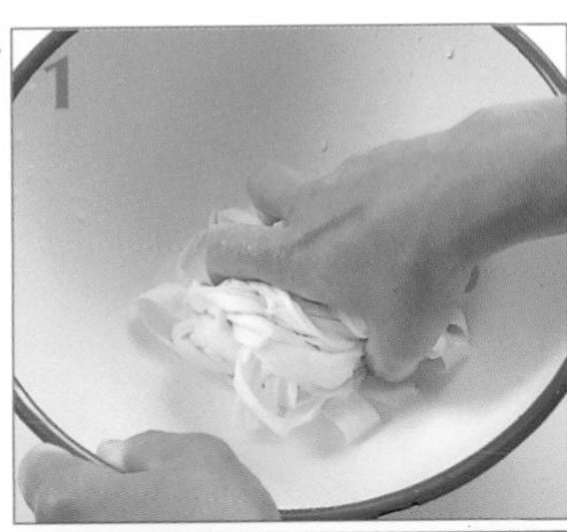

1. Rinse the kampyo and rub with the salt to soften (Fig. 1). Rinse again, then soak for 10 minutes in fresh water.
2. Boil 15–20 minutes, or until you can pierce the gourd with a fingernail (Fig. 2). Drain, let cool, and squeeze well.
3. Return the gourd to the pot with all remaining ingredients and stir (Fig. 3).
4. Bring to a boil. Partially cover, or use a wooden lid that fits inside the pot (*otoshibuta*; Fig. 4). Reduce the heat to a simmer.
5. Stirring occasionally, continue simmering until the liquid is reduced by three-quarters. Remove from heat and let cool in the liquid (Fig. 5).

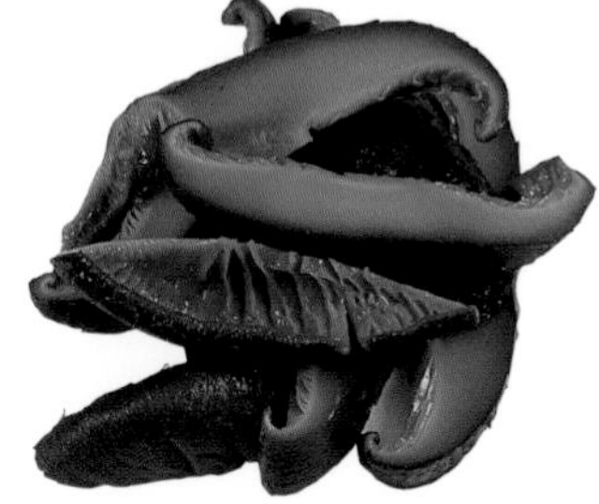

Simmered Shiitake

(for 3 futomaki rolls)

10 small dried shiitake mushrooms
3 Tbsp sugar
1 Tbsp sake
1 Tbsp mirin
4 Tbsp soy sauce
$^{1}/_{2}$ tsp salt

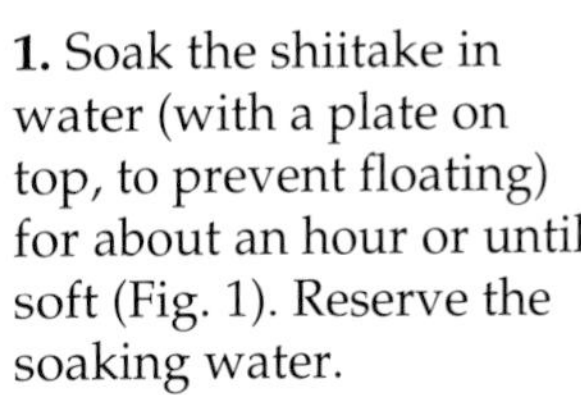

1. Soak the shiitake in water (with a plate on top, to prevent floating) for about an hour or until soft (Fig. 1). Reserve the soaking water.
2. Remove the stems and place in a pot with the remaining ingredients (Fig. 2) and $1^{1}/_{2}$ cups of the soaking water.
3. Bring to a boil. Carefully scoop out the foam (Fig. 3).
4. Partially cover, or use a wooden lid that fits inside the pot (*otoshibuta*; Fig. 4). Reduce the heat to a simmer and continue cooking for about 30 minutes, or until the liquid has reduced. (Fig 5).
5. Remove from heat. Let cool in the liquid. Slice thin.

Oboro Sprinkles

(for 3 futomaki rolls)

3 pieces cod (8 $^1/_2$ oz; 240 g)
1 tsp salt
Red food coloring
1 Tbsp sake
1 Tbsp sugar
1 tsp mirin
Pinch salt

1. Bring a pot of water to boil and add the salt and the cod (Fig. 1). Cook until the cod flakes easily and is no longer translucent. Drain.

2. Remove the skin and bones and dark flesh (Fig. 2). Chop finely (Fig. 3).

3. Grind well in a mortar (Fig. 4) or food processor.

4. Wrap in a cloth and rinse under cold water to remove the fat (Fig 5). Squeeze well. Wash out the mortar.

5. Return the cod to the mortar. Combine the sake and food coloring and pour over the cod (Fig. 6). Grind again until the color is evenly distributed (Fig. 7).

6. Place in a pot over medium heat and stir with 4–5 chopsticks (Fig. 8). When the sprinkles are dry (Fig. 9), remove from heat.

7. Spread out in a baking dish to cool (Fig. 10).

Note: Try using sea bream, red snapper, flathead, or other white fish instead of the cod. Prawns work well also.

Omelet *(for one omelet in an 8 1/4" (21 cm) -square omelet pan)*

180 cc dashi stock
4 1/2 Tbsp sugar
1 Tbsp sake
1 Tbsp mirin
Pinch salt
7–8 eggs
Cooking oil

1. Heat the stock, sugar, sake, mirin and salt in a pot, stirring until the sugar is dissolved (Fig. 1). Let cool.
2. Beat the eggs. Stir in the stock mixture (Fig. 2).
3. Soak a piece of cloth in the oil and wipe the pan with it (Fig. 3). Over medium heat, pour in a quarter of the egg mixture (Fig. 4). Pop any air bubbles with chopsticks (Fig. 5). When the surface begins to dry, fold it in thirds (Fig. 6).
4. Push the folded egg to one end of the pan. Pour another fourth of the egg mixture all around the pan, underneath the cooked egg as well (Fig 7), and fold in thirds again when ready. Repeat until all the egg is cooked.
5. Shape the egg using the corners of the pan (Fig. 8).

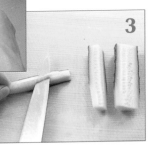

Cucumbers

1. Trim the ends and remove any tough sections of the peel (Fig.1).
2. Rub with salt (Fig. 2) to soften the peel. Rinse off the salt and pat dry.
3. Cut into 4 1/3"(11 cm) lengths for crosswise-nori recipes or in 3 1/2"(9 cm) lengths for lengthwise-nori recipes. Slice into quarters. If there are a lot of seeds, trim them off (Fig. 3).

How to Roll Futomaki

1 Prepare the fillings. Pat any wet fillings dry (such as shiitake and kampyo).

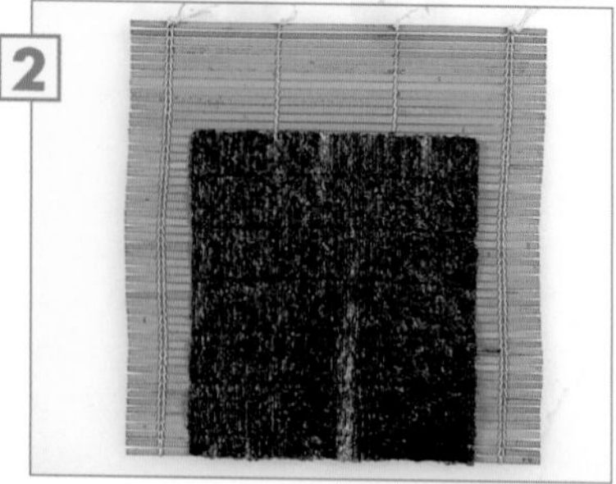

2 Place the mat flat side up, with the knots away from you. Place the nori on the mat shiny side down, lining up the short side with the bottom edge of the mat.

3 Gather the rice loosely into two 4 1/4 oz (120 g) portions. Two portions are easier to spread.

4 Leaving about 1 1/2"(4 cm) of nori at the top and bottom, place the portions on the nori. Using the pads of your fingers, spread the rice evenly, beginning with the left and right edges (*above left*). Next, pull the middle portion toward you (*above right*).

5 Spread the rice of the second portion, pushing it all the way to the left and right edges and closing up the gap between the two portions. There should be 1"(3 cm) of nori left at the top.

6 • For large amounts of filling, create a ridge with an additional 2 oz (60 g) of the rice. The ridge prevents the filling from spilling forward.

7 Line up the fillings in the center of the rice. Sprinkles and other loose fillings should go toward the top, so that the ridge can hold them in place.

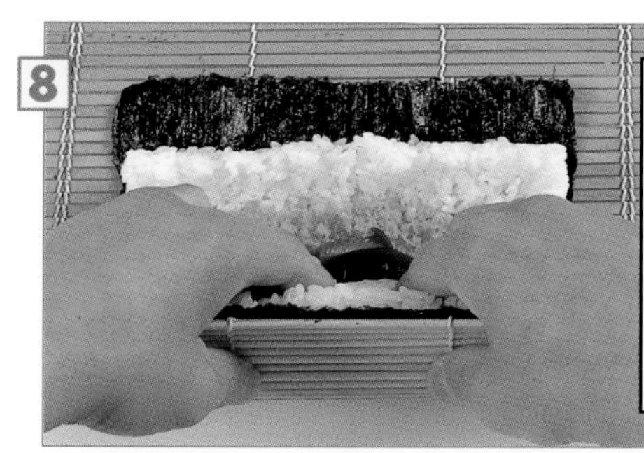

Side view

Holding down the filling with your fingers, lift the mat with your thumbs, rolling forward until the edge of the mat touches the top of the ridge.

At this point, firmly squeeze the mat by curling your fingertips toward you (see arrow). If the roll is not squeezed here, the fillings will remain loose in the roll even after you squeeze it again in step 11.

Now, pull up the top edge of the mat and continue rolling forward with the heels of your hands until the seam of the nori is at the bottom of the roll.

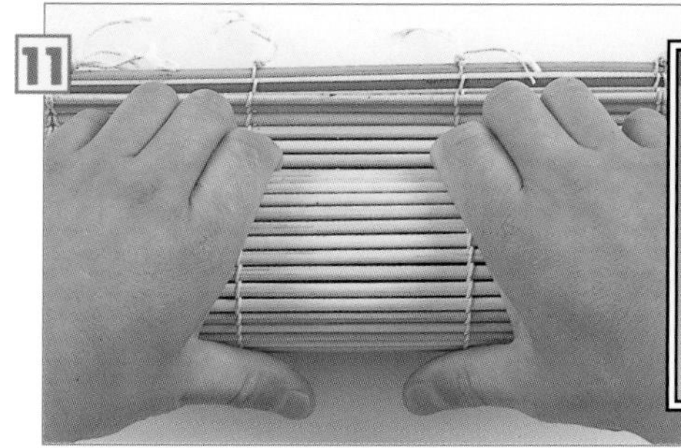

Rounding your hands into a tunnel shape, squeeze again with your thumbs and fingertips at the base of the roll. Avoid pushing the top—this will force the fillings out at the ends.

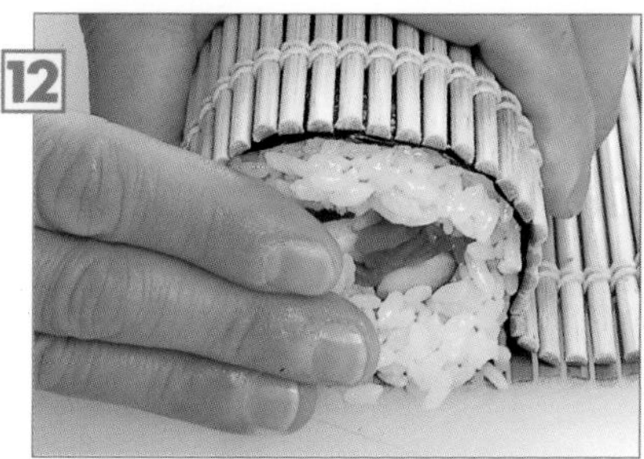

Slide the roll to the right edge of the mat and flatten the end, then repeat on the left side.

Cut into eight pieces. Wipe your knife with a damp towel after each slice.

Vegetarian Roll

(*for 1 roll*)

- 10 1/2 oz (300 g) sushi rice (p. 9)
- 1 sheet roasted nori
- 3 simmered shiitake
- 1/2 bunch mitsuba (honewort)
- 35" (90 cm) simmered gourd
- Takuan pickles
- 2/3 piece simmered tofu

1. Prepare the simmered shiitake and the simmered gourd as on page 17. Thinly slice the shiitake. Cut the gourd into 7" (18 cm) lengths.
2. Prepare the simmered tofu as at right. Squeeze almost all the liquid out of the tofu and slice into thirds.
3. Blanch the mitsuba, rinse in cold water, and squeeze out the liquid. Julienne the takuan into 4" (10 cm) lengths.
4. Spread the rice as on page 20, using 8 1/2 oz (240 g) of the rice plus 2 oz (60 g) for the ridge. Place the fillings on the rice as shown. Roll as on page 21. Flatten the ends and cut into 8 slices.

Simmered Tofu

(*3 pieces*)

- 3 pieces freeze-dried tofu
- 2 cups dashi stock
- 2 Tbsp sugar
- 1 tsp sake
- 1 tsp mirin
- 3 Tbsp light soy sauce

1. Soak the tofu until very soft in warm water, with a plate on top to prevent floating (Fig. 1).

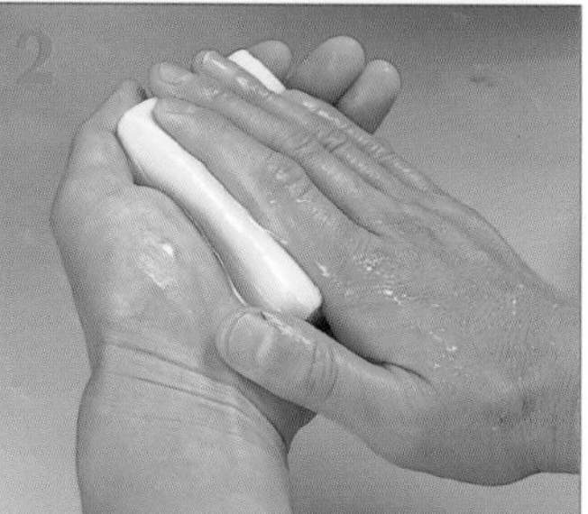

2. Rinse quickly. Press between your hands to remove excess water (Fig. 2).

3. Bring the remaining ingredients to boil in a saucepan. Add the tofu (Fig. 3).

4. Partially cover, or use a wooden lid that fits inside the pot (*otoshi-buta*; Fig. 4) and simmer for 10 minutes.

5. Remove from heat. Let stand until cool to absorb the flavors (Fig. 5).

Omelet Roll (Datemaki)

Omelet Sheet

(for 1 omelet in a 8 1/4" (21 cm)-square omelet pan)

4 Tbsp dashi stock
2 Tbsp sugar
1/2 Tbsp sake
1/2 Tbsp mirin
1 tsp light soy sauce
1/2 tsp salt
4 eggs
1 Tbsp cornstarch
3 1/2 oz (100 g) cooked white fish
2 oz (60 g) poi or yamato-imo
Cooking oil

1. Bring the stock, sugar, sake, mirin, soy sauce, and salt to a boil, then let cool.
2. Beat the eggs in a bowl. Stir in the stock mixture. Add the cornstarch, mixed with 1 Tbsp *water* (Fig. 1).
3. Grind the fish well in a mortar and gather in the center. Grind the poi on the upper edges of the mortar (Fig. 2) and stir into the fish.
4. Add a quarter of the egg mixture at a time, grinding to a smooth paste (Fig. 3).
5. Heat the oil in the omelet pan. Pour in the egg mixture (Fig. 4) and cook over very low heat. To prevent uneven browning, shift the position of the pan.
6. When the top of the omelet begins to dry out, lift it with a chopstick and turn it over (Fig. 5). Cook for 2–3 minutes. Remove and cool on a wire rack.

(for 1 roll)

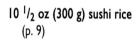

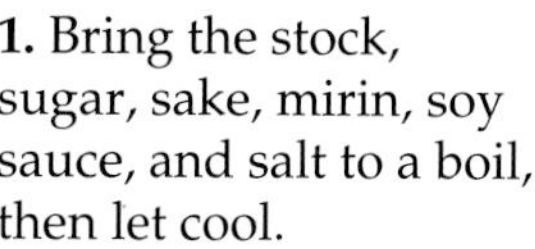

10 1/2 oz (300 g) sushi rice (p. 9)
1 sheet omelet
3 Tbsp oboro sprinkles (p. 18)
41 1/4" (105 cm) simmered gourd
Takuan pickles
Cucumber slices
1/2 piece grilled anago
5–6 pieces mibuna pickles
Roasted sesame seeds

1. Prepare the omelet sheet as at right. Prepare the gourd as on page 17 and cut into 5 equal lengths.
2. Cut the grilled anago (conger eel) to match the width of the omelet.
3. Julienne the takuan and cucumber into 4 1/3" (11 cm) lengths. Squeeze the mibuna pickles and cut into 1/2" (1.5 cm) lengths.

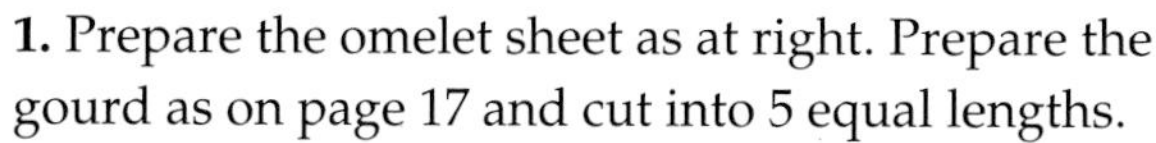

4. Spread 8 1/2 oz (240 g) of the rice on the omelet, plus 2 oz (60 g) ridge. Place the fillings with sesame seeds on the rice as shown. Roll as on page 21 and then flatten the ends. With the seam side down, slice into 8 pieces.

Rolled Eel Roll

(for 1 roll)

10 1/2 oz (300 g) sushi rice (p. 9)
1 sheet roasted nori

1 rolled conger eel

1. Prepare the rolled conger eel as at right. Reduce the cooking liquid to a sauce and set aside.
2. Place the nori lengthwise on the mat. Spread the rice as on page 20, leaving 1" (3 cm) of nori at the top. Use all of the rice in the two portions, because the ridge is not used for this roll.
3. Roll as on page 21. Flatten the ends and cut into 8 slices. Brush the sauce on the slices.

Note: The eel may also be rolled with roasted sesame seeds, green shiso leaves, or mitsuba (honewort).

Rolled Conger Eel

(for 1 roll)

7" (18 cm) burdock root
Dash vinegar
4 conger eels (anago)
1 tsp salt
3 cups dashi stock or water
6 Tbsp sugar
2 Tbsp sake
4 Tbsp mirin
3/4 cup soy sauce

1. Scrape the burdock root and quarter lengthwise, leaving one end uncut. Boil until tender in water with the vinegar.
2. Scrape both sides of the conger eel with a chef's knife, discarding any giblets (Fig. 1).
3. Rub with the salt to remove the stickiness (Fig. 2). Rinse and pat dry.
4. Lay the eel fillets flat and place the burdock root crosswise at one end (Fig. 3). Roll by hand. Secure the finished roll with bamboo skewers.
5. Combine the remaining ingredients in a pan and bring to a boil. Add the skewered eel roll and partially cover. Cook over medium-low heat (Fig. 4).
6. Cook for 20 minutes, turning once, until the liquid is reduced by half.
7. Remove from heat and let the roll cool in the liquid (Fig. 5).

1

2

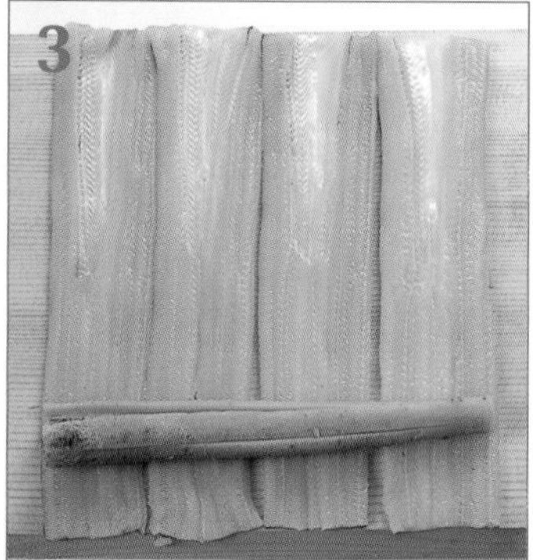
3

4

5

Simmered Squid

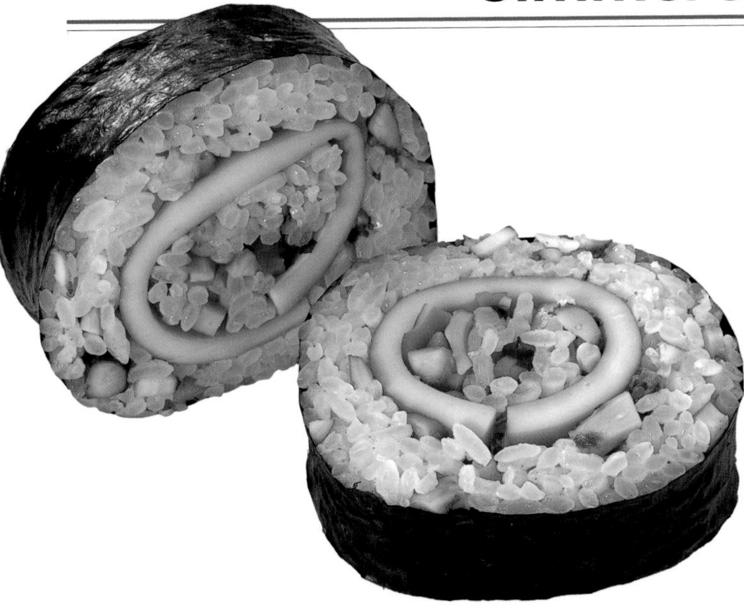

(for 1 roll)

12 $^{1}/_{2}$ oz (350 g) sushi rice (p. 9)
1 sheet roasted nori
2 simmered squid
2 green shiso leaves
Takuan pickles

1. Prepare the simmered squid as at right. Slice to match the width of the nori.
2. Slice the shiso leaves in half lengthwise. Julienne the takuan into 4" (10 cm) lengths.
3. Leaving 1" (3 cm) of nori at the top, spread 7 oz (200 g) of the squid rice (Fig.5) on the nori.
4. Slice open the cooked squid. Pack with the remaining rice and place the shiso leaves and takuan in each as shown.
5. Roll as on page 21. Flatten the ends and slice into 8 pieces.

Simmered Squid

(for 1 roll)

2 squid (surume-ika)
3 cups water
2 Tbsp sugar
1 Tbsp sake
1 Tbsp mirin
4 Tbsp soy sauce
Pinch salt
$^{1}/_{2}$ tsp ginger juice

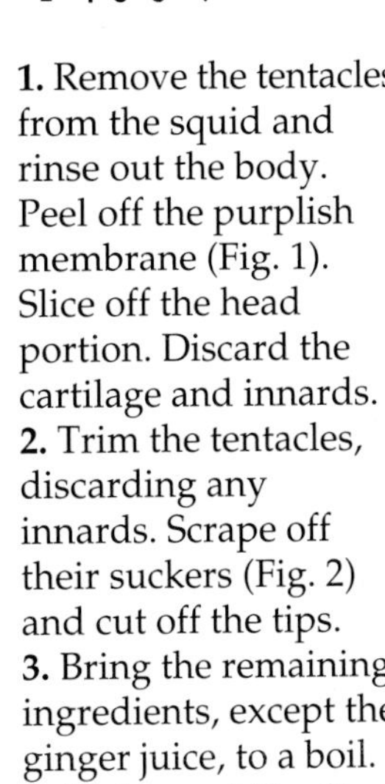

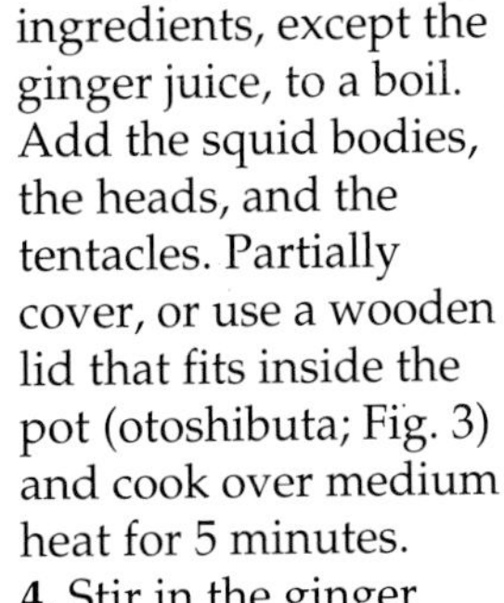

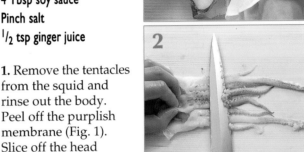

1. Remove the tentacles from the squid and rinse out the body. Peel off the purplish membrane (Fig. 1). Slice off the head portion. Discard the cartilage and innards.
2. Trim the tentacles, discarding any innards. Scrape off their suckers (Fig. 2) and cut off the tips.
3. Bring the remaining ingredients, except the ginger juice, to a boil. Add the squid bodies, the heads, and the tentacles. Partially cover, or use a wooden lid that fits inside the pot (otoshibuta; Fig. 3) and cook over medium heat for 5 minutes.
4. Stir in the ginger juice (juice from grated ginger; Fig. 4) and remove from heat. Let cool in the liquid, then drain well.
5. Mince the tentacles and head. Gently stir 1 oz (30 g) of the chop-ped squid into the sushi rice(Fig.5).

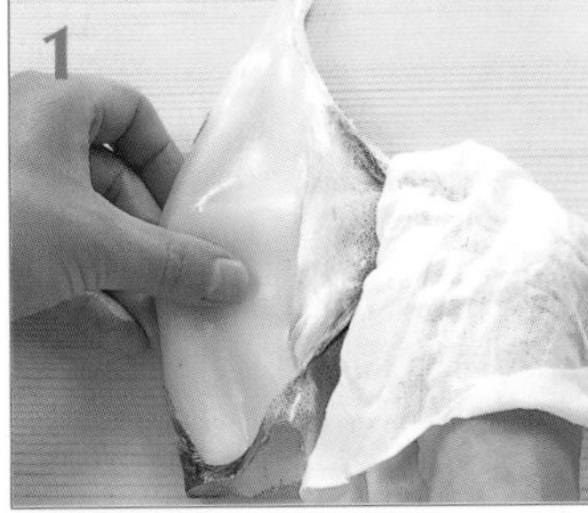

1

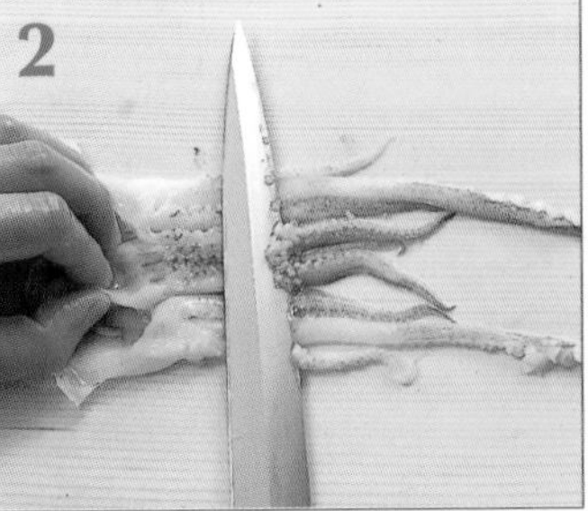

2

3

4

5

Mackerel Roll (Shime-saba)

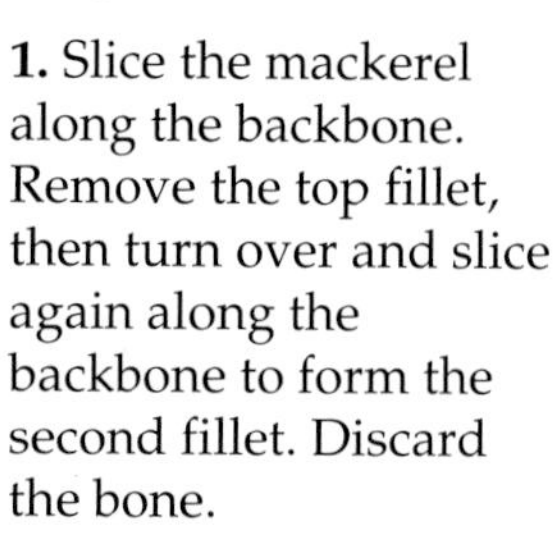

(for 1 roll)

8 ½ oz (240 g) sushi rice (p. 9)
1 sheet roasted nori
1 marinated mackerel
2 green shiso leaves
¾ oz (20 g) pickled ginger
Roasted sesame seeds

1. Prepare the mackerel as at right.
2. Slice the shiso leaves into thirds lengthwise. Squeeze the excess liquid from the ginger and slice.
3. Place the nori lengthwise on the mat (short side close to you). Lay the mackerel on the nori so that there is ⅜" (1 cm) of nori showing at the bottom and 1 ½" (4 cm) at the top.
4. Leaving ⅜" (1 cm) at the top and bottom, spread the rice on the mackerel. Sprinkle with the sesame seeds. Place the shiso and ginger in the center of the rice.
5. Roll as on page 20, ending with the seam side down. Flatten the ends and cut into 8 slices.

Marinated Mackerel

(for 1 roll)
1 mackerel
Salt
Vinegar

1. Slice the mackerel along the backbone. Remove the top fillet, then turn over and slice again along the backbone to form the second fillet. Discard the bone.
2. Sprinkle plenty of salt on both fillets and place in a bamboo strainer (Fig. 1). Let stand one hour.
3. Rinse off the salt and pat dry. Marinate in vinegar for 40 minutes (Fig. 2).
4. With tweezers, remove the small lateral bones (Fig. 3). Peel off the outer membrane, starting at the head (Fig. 4).
5. Holding your knife parallel to the board, slice each fillet across. Arrange the four pieces as Fig.5 in a square about 7" (18 cm)-wide and 6" (15 cm)-long.

Note: To serve mackerel raw, choose the freshest possible meat. The eyes should be clear and the skin should have a silvery color. The flesh should be firm and the gills should have a fresh, red appearance.

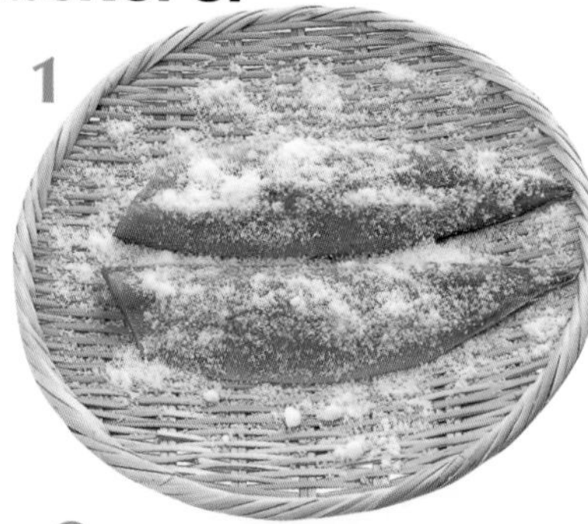

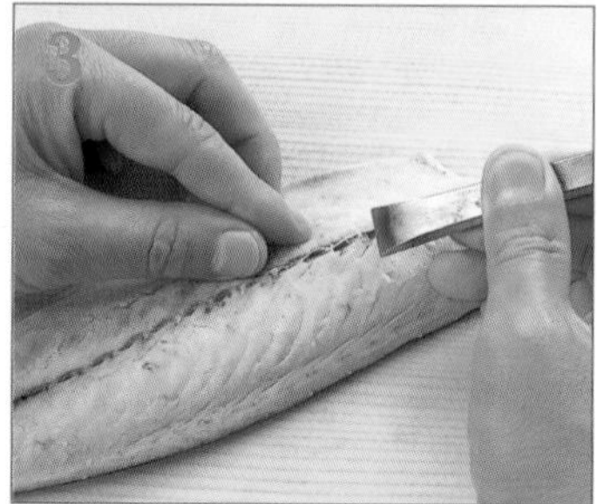

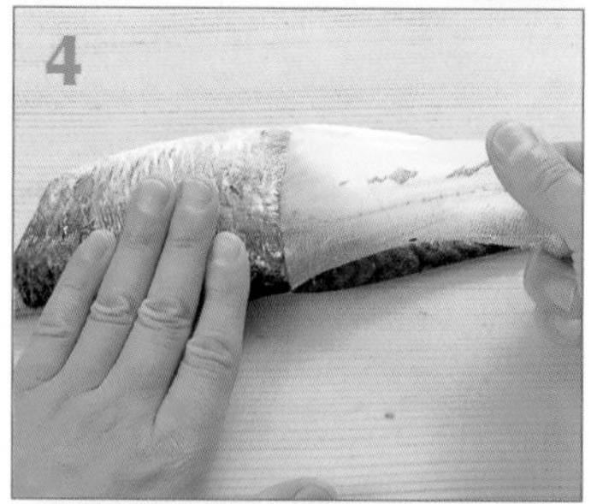

Salmon Miso Sauté

Salmon-Miso Sauté

(for 2 rolls)

1 salmon steak
1 leaf cabbage
$^1/_6$ onion
$^1/_2$ green pepper
$^1/_3$ oz (10 g) carrots
$^3/_4$ oz (20 g) bean sprouts
2 Tbsp miso
1 Tbsp sugar
1 tsp sake
1 tsp mirin
1 Tbsp cooking oil

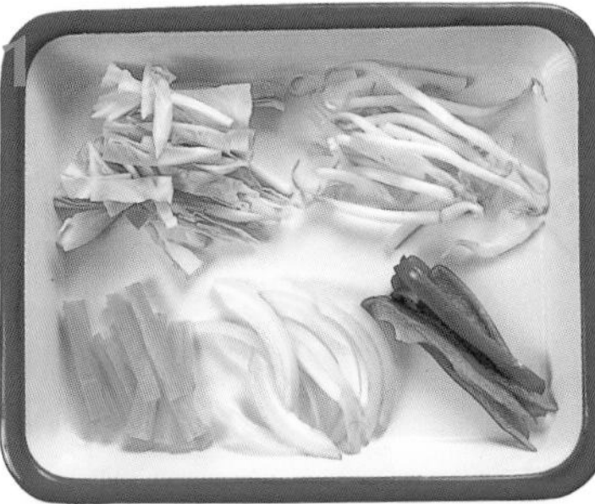

1. Chop the cabbage, julienne the onion and green pepper, and cut the carrots into 1 $^1/_2$" (4 cm) matchsticks (Fig. 1).
2. Combine the miso, sugar, sake, and mirin.
3. Fry the salmon in the oil until both sides are lightly browned (Fig. 2). Remove the bones and skin.
4. Push the salmon to one side and add the vegetables (Fig. 3).
5. When the vegetables are tender, stir the salmon in, breaking it into pieces (Fig.4).
6. Stir in the miso mixture (Fig. 5) and transfer to a plate to prevent overcooking.

(for 1 roll)

10 $^1/_2$ oz (300 g) sushi rice (p. 9)
1 sheet roasted nori

This salmon miso dish is a traditional fisherman's recipe from northern Japan. When served on the beach, the salmon is cooked whole in an iron pan, the vegetables are stirred in, and miso is added for flavor.

1. Prepare the salmon mixture as at right.
2. Place the nori lengthwise on the mat (short side toward you). Spread the rice evenly, leaving 1" (3 cm) of nori at the top.
3. Place the salmon mixture in the center of the rice as shown and roll as on page 21, ending with the seam side down. Flatten the ends and cut into 8 slices.

Marinated Smelt

(for 1 roll)

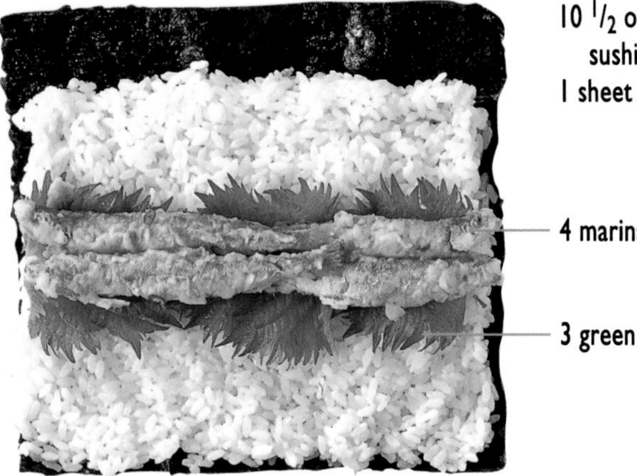

10 $^1/_2$ oz (300 g) sushi rice (p. 9)
1 sheet roasted nori

4 marinated smelt

3 green shiso leaves

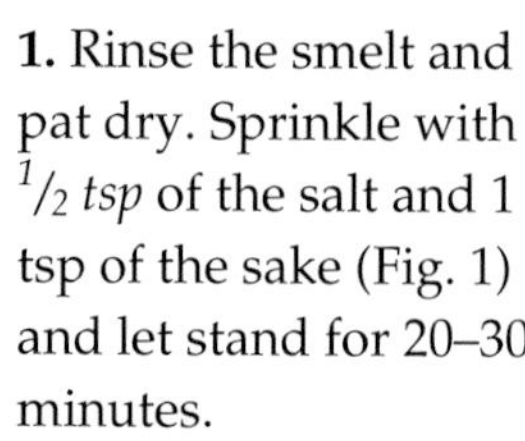

1. Prepare the marinated smelt as at right.
2. Place the nori crosswise on the mat (long side toward you). Leaving 1" (3 cm) at the top, spread the rice evenly (no ridge for this roll).
3. Place the shiso leaves in the center of the rice as shown. Drain the smelt and place on top of the shiso.
4. Roll as on page 21, ending with the seam side down. Flatten the ends and slice into 8 pieces.

Marinated Smelt

(for 3 rolls)

12 smelt
1 tsp salt
1 tsp sake
1 dried red chili pepper
2 Tbsp vinegar
1 cup dashi stock
1 Tbsp sugar
1 tsp light soy sauce
Pastry flour
Cooking oil for deep frying

1. Rinse the smelt and pat dry. Sprinkle with $^1/_2$ *tsp* of the salt and 1 tsp of the sake (Fig. 1) and let stand for 20–30 minutes.
2. Remove the seeds from the chili pepper and slice into thin rounds. Place in a saucepan with the remaining salt and vinegar, the dashi stock, the sugar, and the soy sauce. Bring to a boil (Fig. 2) and remove from heat.
3. Dredge the smelt in the flour, shaking off the excess (Fig. 3).
4. Deep fry at 340° F (170° C) (Fig. 4).
5. When golden, remove from the pan and place in the vinegar mixture(Fig.5). Allow to cool in the liquid.

Seared Bonito Roll

(for 1 rolls)

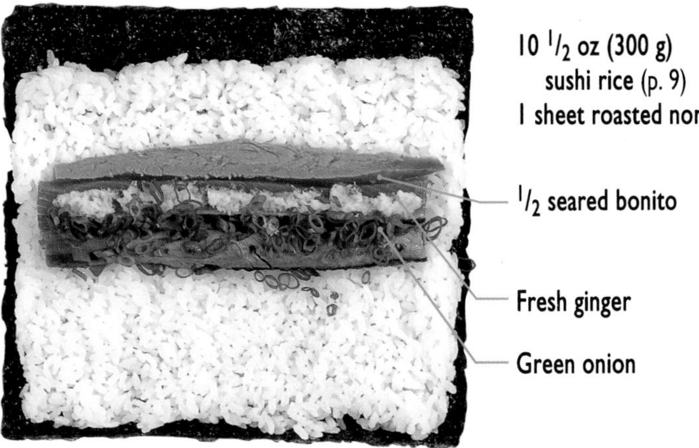

1. Prepare the seared bonito as at right.
2. Grate the ginger. Chop the green onion.
3. Place the nori crosswise on the mat (long side toward you). Spread the rice on the nori evenly, leaving 1" (3 cm) at the top. (No ridge in this recipe.)
4. Drain the bonito and pat dry. Place on the rice with the ginger and green onion on top.
5. Roll as on p. 21, leaving the seam side down. Flatten the ends and slice into 8 pieces.

Seared Bonito

(for 2 rolls)

I cup dashi stock
I Tbsp sake
$^1/_2$ Tbsp mirin
3 Tbsp soy sauce
I bonito fillet (katsuo)

1. Bring the stock, sake, mirin, and soy sauce to a boil and remove from heat.
2. Skewer the bonito on 5 metal skewers. Pierce the skin all over with toothpicks (Fig. 1).
3. Hold the bonito skin-side down over a flame until brown (Fig. 2). Turn over and sear the flesh side just until the color changes.
4. Plunge in ice water to stop the cooking (Fig. 3). Pat dry.
5. Cut to a length that matches the nori. The fillet should make 6–8 julienne slices (Fig 4).
6. Marinate in the dashi mixture for 30 minutes (Fig. 5).

Note: Piercing the skin keeps it from separateing from the flesh or splitting during the searing. It also helps the bonito cook more quickly.

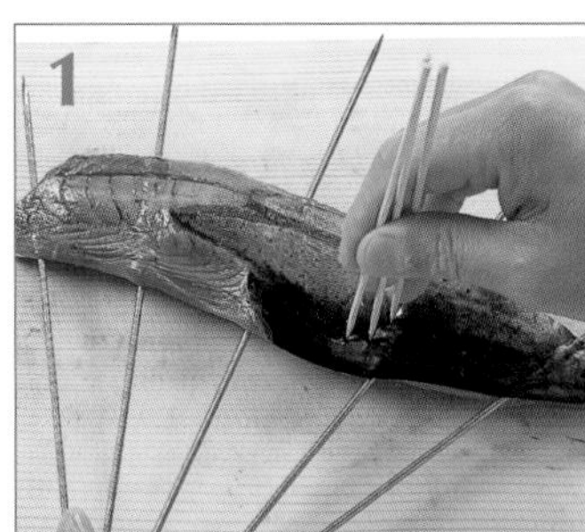

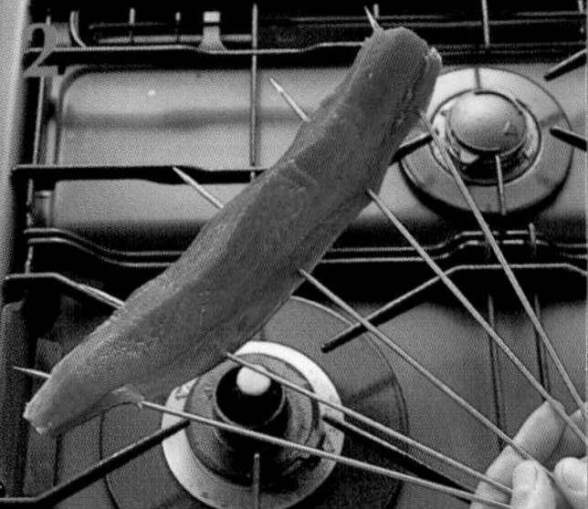

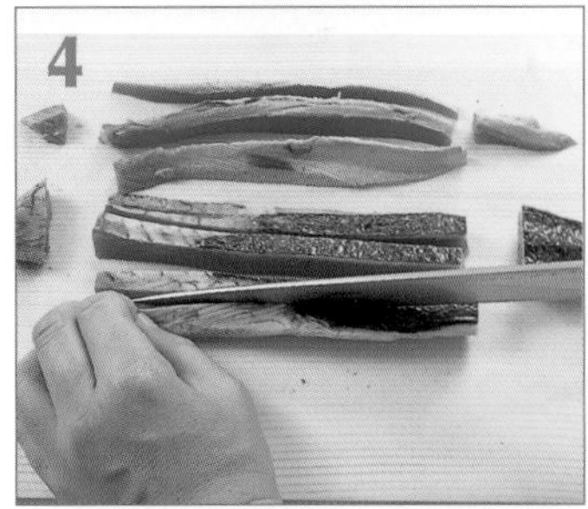

Double-Rolled Corned Beef

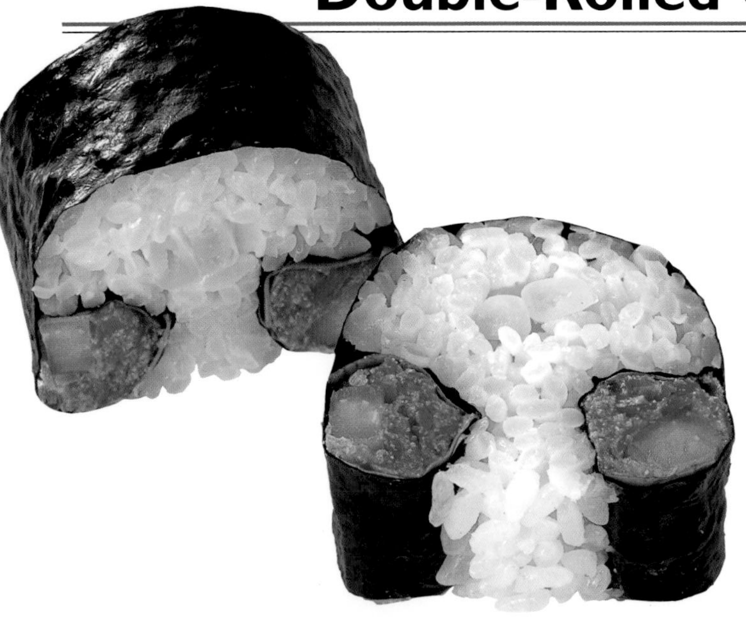

(for 1 roll)

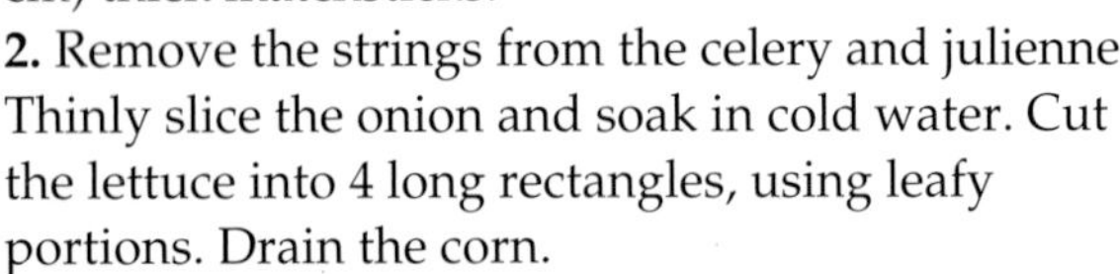

1. Cut cooked (or canned) corned beef into $^{1}/_{2}$" (1.5 cm) thick matchsticks.
2. Remove the strings from the celery and julienne. Thinly slice the onion and soak in cold water. Cut the lettuce into 4 long rectangles, using leafy portions. Drain the corn.
3. Place the nori lengthwise on the mat (short side toward you). Spread 3 $^{1}/_{2}$ oz (100 g) of the rice evenly in a 2 $^{3}/_{4}$" (7 cm) stripe in the center of the nori. Arrange the corn in a line as shown.
4. Place the lettuce, corned beef, onion, and celery at the top and bottom of the nori as shown.
5. Roll as shown at right. Slice into 8 pieces, wiping the blade with a damp cloth after each slice.

How to Roll

1. Pressing the front filling with your fingers, lift the mat.

2. Roll tightly until the mat touches the rice. Squeeze into position and unroll the mat.

3. Turn the mat around and make another the small roll in the front.

4. Place the mat in the palm of your hand. Round your hand so that the small rolls nearly touch each other. Place the remaining 1 oz (30 g) rice in the space between the rolls.

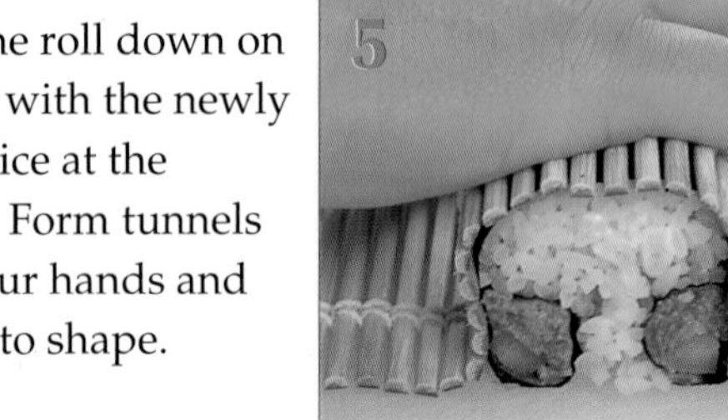

5. Put the roll down on a board with the newly added rice at the bottom. Form tunnels with your hands and press into shape.

Double Roll with Smoked Ham

(for 1 roll)

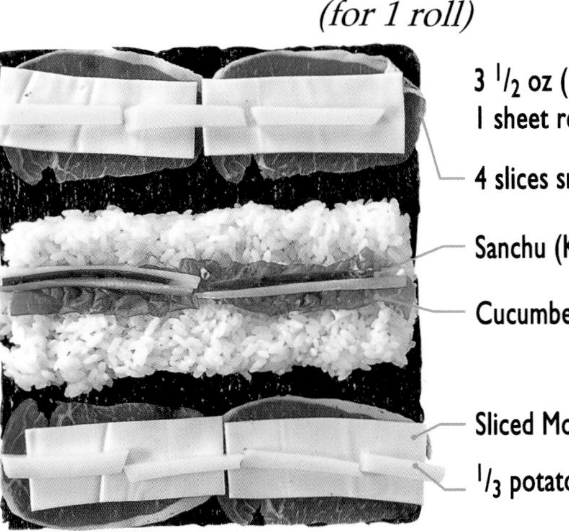

$3\ ^{1}/_{2}$ oz (100 g) sushi rice (p. 9)
1 sheet roasted nori
4 slices smoked ham
Sanchu (Korean lettuce)
Cucumber
Sliced Monterey Jack cheese
$^{1}/_{3}$ potato

1. Cut the potato into $^{1}/_{4}$" (7 mm)-thick matchsticks and parboil in salted water.
2. Cut the cheese into rectangles. Cut the lettuce into strips about $^{3}/_{4}$" (2 cm) wide. Cut the cucumber into 4" (10 cm) julienne.
3. Place the nori lengthwise on the mat (short side toward you). Spread the rice in a strip about $2\ ^{3}/_{4}$" (7 cm) wide. Place the lettuce and cucumber on top as shown.
4. On the front and back ends of the nori, stack the ham, cheese, and potato sticks as shown.
5. Roll as described on p. 30 except that no additional rice is added between the small rolls. Form a tunnel with your hands and press into shape. Slice into 8 pieces.

Note: Prosciutto may be substituted for the smoked ham.

Tricolor Fancy Roll

(for 1 roll)

7 oz (200 g) sushi rice
1 oz (30 g) bonito flakes
1 sheet roasted nori
4" (10 cm) cucumber
2 artificial crab sticks
1 strip thin omelet ($^{3}/_{4}$ x 8 $^{1}/_{4}$"; 2 x 21 cm)

1. Stir the bonito flakes (katsuobushi furikake) into the rice.
2. Rub the cucumber with salt. Cut into quarters lengthwise. Save two of the quarters for another use.
3. Place the nori crosswise on the mat (long side toward you). Stack the egg, crab sticks, and cucumbers about $^{3}/_{8}$" (1 cm) from the near edge. Form the rice into a tube and place it a bit past the center of the nori.
4. Holding down the front filling with your fingers, roll up the mat and squeeze once, then continue rolling until the small roll touches the rice.
5. Lift the edge of the mat again, this time rolling up the entire roll as on page 21.
6. Finish with the seam side down. Flatten the ends and cut into 8 slices.

Tricolor Seafood Roll

(for 1 roll)

10 1/2 oz (300 g) sushi rice (p. 9)
1 sheet roasted nori
Freshly grated wasabi
1 oz (30 g) fresh tuna
1 oz (30 g) large squid body
4 1/3" (11 cm) cucumber

1. Cut the tuna into a long stick, 1/2" (1.5 cm) thick. Julienne the squid.
2. Rub the cucumber with salt and rinse. Cutting into quarters lengthwise, use two quarters per roll.
3. Place the nori crosswise on the mat (long side toward you). Spread the rice evenly, leaving 1" (3 cm) at the top.
4. Spread the wasabi on the rice. Arrange the fillings in the middle of the rice.
5. Roll as on page 21, ending with the seam side down. Flatten the ends and slice into 8 pieces.

Eel-Egg Roll

(for 1 roll)

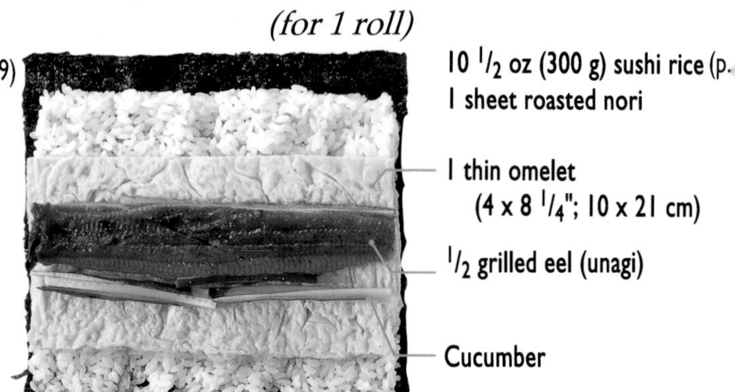

1. Cut the eel at an angle into two pieces, to avoid slippage during rolling.
2. Rub the cucumber with salt, then cut into 4" (10 cm) julienne.
3. Place the nori crosswise on the mat (long side toward you). Leaving 1" (3 cm) of nori at the top, spread the rice evenly.
4. Place the omelet in the middle of the rice. Reassemble the pieces of eel on top. Place the cucumber in front of the eel.
5. Roll as on page 21, ending with the seam side down. Flatten the ends and slice into 8 pieces.

Round Clam Roll

(for 1 roll)

- 10 1/2 oz (300 g) sushi rice (p. 9)
- 1 sheet roasted nori
- 3/4 oz (20 g) chrysanthemum flowers
- 3–4 stalks chrysanthemum leaves
- 8–10 shelled round clams (aoyagi)

1. Pluck the chrysanthemum petals and blanch. Drain well and cool completely. Squeeze out the liquid and marinate in a mixture of *vinegar*, *sugar*, and *dashi stock*.
2. Blanch the chrysanthemum leaves (shungiku), drain, and squeeze well.
3. Place the nori crosswise on the mat (long side toward you). Spread the rice evenly, leaving 1" (3 cm) at the top.
4. Place the chrysanthemum leaves in the center. Place the round clams in an overlapping row in front. Squeeze the chrysanthemum petals and place them in a row in back.
5. Roll as on page 21, ending with the seam side down. Flatten the ends and slice into 8 pieces.

Seafood Medley

(for 1 roll)

- 10 1/2 oz (300 g) sushi rice (p. 9)
- 1 sheet roasted nori
- Freshly grated wasabi
- Cucumber
- 2 Tbsp bay scallops
- 2 sacs herring roe
- 1 oz (30 g) fresh tuna
- 3 shrimp
- 2 Tbsp flying-fish roe
- 6 Tbsp salmon roe

1. Soak the herring roe in water and remove the outer membrane. Devein and boil the shrimp, peel them, and remove the tails. Rinse the scallops in salted water. Slice the tuna into matchsticks.
2. Rub the cucumber with salt, rinse, and cut into 4" (10 cm)-lengths julienne.
3. Place the nori crosswise on the mat (long side toward you). Spread the rice evenly, leaving 1" (3 cm) at the top. Spread the wasabi in a line, then sprinkle the two kinds of roe over the rice. Place the remaining fillings as shown.
4. Roll as on page 21, ending with the seam side down. Flatten the ends and slice into 8 pieces.

Beef Roll

(for 1 roll)

10 1/2 oz (300 g) sushi rice (p. 9)
1 sheet roasted nori
3/4 oz (20 g) bean sprouts
4 Tbsp beef sprinkles

1. To make the beef sprinkles, fry 3 1/2 *oz (100 g) ground beef in cooking oil*. Stir in *1 Tbsp sugar* and *1 Tbsp soy sauce*. Use 4 Tbsp of this mixture per roll.
2. Blanch the bean sprouts in salted water. Drain and let cool, then squeeze out the liquid.
3. Place the nori crosswise on the mat (long side toward you). Spread the rice evenly, leaving 1" (3 cm) at the top.
4. Place the fillings as shown. Gather the bean sprouts in back to prevent the beef sprinkles from scattering when you roll.
5. Roll as on page 21, ending with the seam side down. Flatten the ends and slice into 8 pieces.

Tempura Roll

(for 1 roll)

10 1/2 oz (300 g) sushi rice (p. 9)
1 sheet roasted nori
2 shrimp
1/3 bunch mitsuba (honewort)

1. Peel and devein the shrimp. Dip in tempura batter and deep fry.
2. Blanch the mitsuba, plunge in cold water, and squeeze out the excess liquid.
3. Place the nori crosswise on the mat (long side toward you). Spread the rice evenly, leaving 1" (3 cm) at the top.
4. Place the shrimp and mitsuba as shown.
5. Roll as on page 21, ending with the seam side down. Flatten the ends and slice into 8 pieces.

Kalbi Roll

(for 1 roll)

- 10 1/2 oz (300 g) sushi rice (p. 9)
- 1 sheet roasted nori
- 1/2 oz (15 g) kimchee
- 2 oz (60 g) kalbi beef

1. Cook the beef slices to taste, Korean kalbi-style. Coat with *yakiniku sauce*.
2. Gently squeeze the liquid from the kimchee.
3. Place the nori crosswise on the mat (long side toward you). Spread the rice evenly, leaving 1" (3 cm) at the top.
4. Place the kalbi and kimchee as shown.
5. Roll as on page 21, ending with the seam side down. Flatten the ends and slice into 8 pieces.

Note: Lettuce or sanchu (Korean lettuce) may be added to the roll. If the roll is not going to be served immediately, allow the kalbi to cool before rolling.

Chicken Tenderloins

(for 1 roll)

- 10 1/2 oz (300 g) sushi rice (p. 9)
- 1 sheet roasted nori
- Freshly grated wasabi
- 2 chicken tenderloins
- 4–6 stalks rape blossoms (na-no-hana) or broccoli rabe

1. Ask for very fresh chicken tenderloins. Pull off the white tendon. Poach quickly in boiling water just until the outer surface changes color (or, cook them through for safer servings). Plunge in cold water. Pat dry.
2. Trim the tough bottoms of the rape blossoms. Blanch, plunge in cold water, and squeeze out the liquid.
3. Place the nori crosswise on the mat (long side toward you). Spread the rice evenly, leaving 1" (3 cm) at the top.
4. Spread the wasabi on the rice. Place the fillings as shown.
5. Roll as on page 21, ending with the seam side down. Flatten the ends and slice into 8 pieces.

Gyoza

(for 1 roll)

10 1/2 oz (300 g) sushi rice (p. 9)
1 sheet roasted nori
4 potstickers
2 garlic stems

1. Fry the potstickers until well browned.
2. Chop an 8 1/4" (21 cm) length of garlic stem in half and blanch. Drain well.
3. Place the nori crosswise on the mat (long side toward you). Spread the rice evenly, leaving 1" (3 cm) at the top.
4. Place the fillings as shown.
5. Roll as on page 21, ending with the seam side down. Flatten the ends and slice into 8 pieces.

Note: If the sushi will not be served immediately, allow the potstickers to cool before rolling.

Asparagus Roll

(for 1 roll)

10 1/2 oz (300 g) sushi rice (p. 9)
1 sheet roasted nori
Mayonnaise
4 slices Japanese bacon
1 stalk asparagus

1. Cut the bacon into 4 3/4" (12 cm) lengths.
2. Trim the asparagus. Blanch, drain, and let cool.
3. Place the nori crosswise on the mat (long side toward you). Spread the rice evenly, leaving 1" (3 cm) at the top.
4. Place the bacon lengthwise on the rice. Spread with a line of mayonnaise and place the asparagus on top. Roll the bacon tightly by hand, leaving it in a tube in the center of the rice.
5. Roll as on page 21, ending with the seam side down. Flatten the ends and slice into 8 pieces.
Note: Japanese bacon is similar to Canadian bacon and is fully cooked. Try substituting thin slices of ham.

Ginger Pork Roll

(for 1 roll)

- 10 1/2 oz (300 g) sushi rice (p. 9)
- 1 sheet roasted nori
- 3/4 oz (20 g) bean sprouts
- 2 oz (60 g) ginger pork

1. To prepare the ginger pork, sauté 2 oz (60 g) of thinly sliced pork in *cooking oil* with *juice from grated ginger*, sake, *mirin*, and *soy sauce*. Transfer to a plate to cool.
2. Sauté the bean sprouts in *cooking oil* with *salt* and *pepper* to taste. Transfer to a plate to cool.
3. Place the nori crosswise on the mat (long side toward you). Spread the rice evenly, leaving 1" (3 cm) at the top.
4. Place the fillings as shown.
5. Roll as on page 21, ending with the seam side down. Flatten the ends and slice into 8 pieces.

Broiled Saury

(for 1 roll)

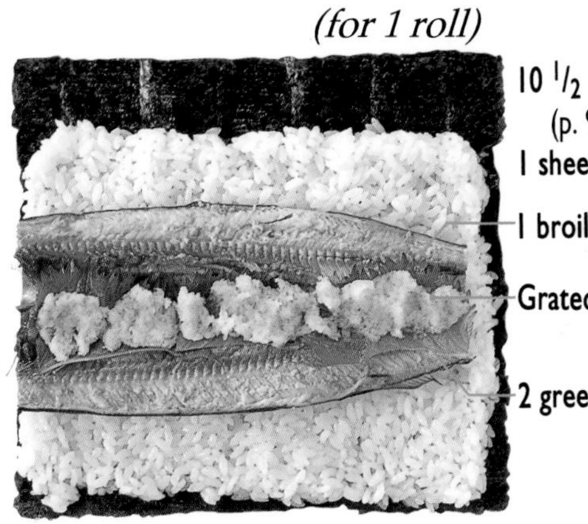

- 10 1/2 oz (300 g) sushi rice (p. 9)
- 1 sheet roasted nori
- 1 broiled saury
- Grated daikon
- 2 green shiso leaves

1. Sprinkle the saury with salt and broil on both sides until cooked through. Remove the head and tail. Butterfly the fish, removing the bones and giblets.
2. Cut the shiso leaves in half lengthwise. Grate the daikon and squeeze well.
3. Place the nori crosswise on the mat (long side toward you). Spread the rice evenly, leaving 1" (3 cm) at the top.
4. Place the butterflied saury on the rice with the shiso leaves and daikon atop. Fold the saury back together.
5. Roll as on page 21, ending with the seam side down. Flatten the ends and slice into 8 pieces.

Sunrise Roll

(for 1 roll)

10 1/2 oz (300 g) sushi rice (p. 9)
Yukari sprinkles
1 sheet roasted nori

1 large chikuwa (fish-cake tube)

7 quail eggs

1. Hard-boil the quail eggs and plunge in cold water. Let stand until cool, then peel.
2. Open the chikuwa by slicing it lengthwise on one side.
3. Place the sushi rice in a bowl and stir in the yukari (minced dried beefsteak leaves).
4. Place the nori crosswise on the mat (long side toward you). Spread the rice evenly, leaving 1" (3 cm) at the top.
5. Tuck the quail eggs into the chikuwa as shown.
6. Roll as on page 21, ending with the seam side down. Flatten the ends and slice into 8 pieces.

Chicken Salad

(for 1 roll)

10 1/2 oz (300 g) sushi rice (p. 9)
1 sheet roasted nori

1 3/4 oz (50 g) chicken-burdock-root salad

Sanchu (Korean lettuce)

1. Boil pieces of boneless chicken in salted water. Remove to a plate to cool. Peel a small length of *burdock root* and julienne. Boil in water with a splash of *vinegar*, then drain and cool. Combine with the chicken, some *roasted sesame seeds*, and your choice of *salad dressing*.
2. Place the nori crosswise on the mat (long side toward you). Spread the rice evenly, leaving 1" (3 cm) at the top. Cut the sanchu into 3 rectangles and place on the rice. Add the chicken salad.
3. Roll as on page 21, ending with the seam side down. Flatten the ends and slice into 8 pieces.

Octopus Roll

(for 1 roll)

10 1/2 oz (300 g) sushi rice (p. 9)
1 sheet roasted nori
4 pieces of octopus
2–3 leaves sai choy

1. Chop cooked octopus into bite-size pieces, sprinkle with *salt* and a splash of *sake*, and dredge in *cornstarch*. Deep fry until just golden.
2. Blanch the sai choy leaves. Plunge in cold water, and squeeze out the liquid.
3. Place the nori crosswise on the mat (long side toward you). Spread the rice evenly, leaving 1" (3 cm) at the top.
4. Spread out the leaves along the center of the rice and place the octopus on top. Sprinkle with *shichimi togarashi* (seven-spice chili powder) or lemon juice to taste.
5. Roll as on page 21, ending with the seam side down. Flatten the ends and slice into 8 pieces.

Bamboo Shoots

(for 1 roll)

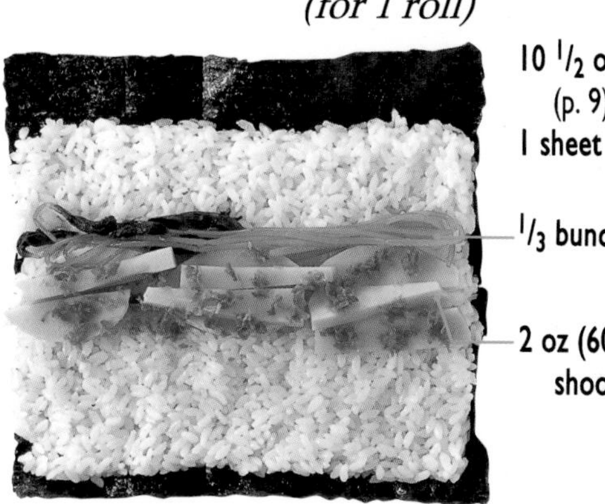

10 1/2 oz (300 g) sushi rice (p. 9)
1 sheet roasted nori
1/3 bunch mitsuba (honewort)
2 oz (60 g) cooked bamboo shoots

1. Cut a small boiled bamboo shoot (5 1/4 oz; 150 g) into 2"(5 cm)-long matchsticks. Boil in *1 cup dashi stock, 2 Tbsp sugar, 1 Tbsp sake, 2 Tbsp mirin*, and 4 *Tbsp soy sauce*. When reduced by two-thirds, sprinkle with *1/5 oz (5 g) shaved bonito*. Use about a third of this mixture per roll.
2. Blanch the mitsuba, plunge in cold water, and squeeze out the liquid.
3. Place the nori crosswise on the mat (long side toward you). Spread the rice evenly, leaving 1" (3 cm) at the top. Place the fillings as shown.
4. Roll as on page 21, ending with the seam side down. Flatten the ends and slice into 8 pieces.

Special Futomaki

For a change of pace, try these unusual sushi made with other starches in place of the sushi rice.

Mashed Potato

(for 1 roll)
1 sheet roasted nori

4 small potatoes
Curry powder

2 slices ham

1 stalk asparagus

1. Peel the potatoes and cut into bite-size pieces. Boil until tender. Drain, mash, and stir in the curry powder.
2. Trim the asparagus. Blanch and drain.
3. Place the nori crosswise on the mat (long side toward you). Spread the potato mixture evenly, leaving 2" (5 cm) at the top. Place the ham and asparagus as shown.
4. Roll as on page 21. Flatten the ends and slice into 8 pieces.

Soba

(for 1 roll)
1 sheet roasted nori

3 oz (80 g) dried soba

2 oz (60 g) nagaimo (Chinese yam)

3/4 oz (20 g) sansai (preserved mountain vegetables)

1. Divide the soba (buckwheat noodles) into 5 bunches and tie one end of each bunch with thread.
2. Holding the tied end with tongs or chopsticks, shake each bunch under boiling water until just tender. Rinse in cold water and squeeze out the excess water with chopsticks.
3. Peel the nagaimo and cut into 1/4" (7 mm)-thick matchsticks.
4. Place the nori lengthwise on the mat (short side toward you). Cut off the tied ends of the soba bunches and spread evenly on the nori, leaving 2" (5 cm) at the top.
5. Place the nagaimo and sansai on top as shown and roll as on p. 21. Cut into 8 pieces. Serve with soba

Spaghetti

(for 1 roll)
1 sheet roasted nori

3 oz (80 g) spaghetti
1 sac cod roe

Kaiware (daikon sprouts)

1. Boil the spaghetti in salted water. Drain in a colander.
2. Remove the roe from the sac and stir into the hot spaghetti. Cool.
3. Place the nori lengthwise on the mat (short side toward you). Spread the spaghetti mixture evenly, leaving 2" (5 cm) at the top.
4. Trim the ends of the kaiware and place as shown. Roll as on p. 21 and slice into 8 pieces.

HOSOMAKI
Thin Rolls

How to Roll Hosomaki

1

Cut the nori in half lengthwise. Place the nori on the mat, uncut edge toward you. Place 3 oz (80 g) of sushi rice toward the top edge of the nori *(above left)*. Leaving $^3/_8$" (1 cm) of nori at the top and $^1/_5$" (5 mm) at the bottom, spread the rice evenly with the tips of your fingers *(above right)*. To keep the filling in the center, make a small ridge at the top and a very slight indent in the center.

2

Place the filling in the center of the rice. Wasabi should be spread underneath the filling.

3

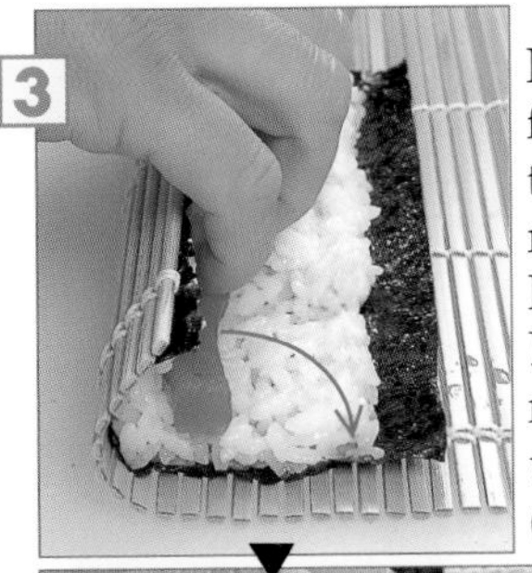

Pressing the filling with your fingers, lift the mat with your thumbs *(left)* and roll until it meets the far end of the rice. Press into place *(below left)*. Lift the mat away from the nori and continue rolling until the seam side is down *(below right)*.

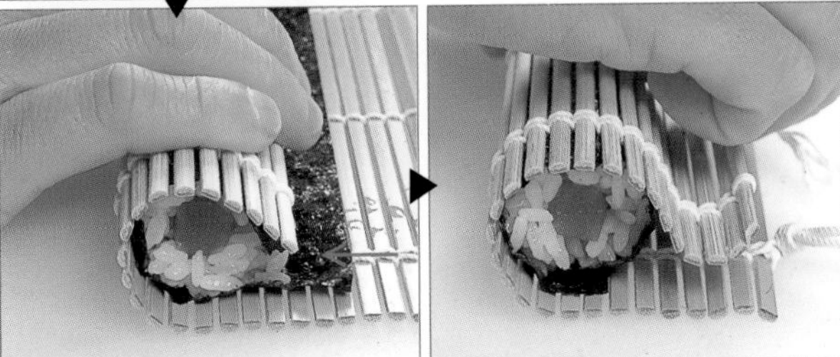

4

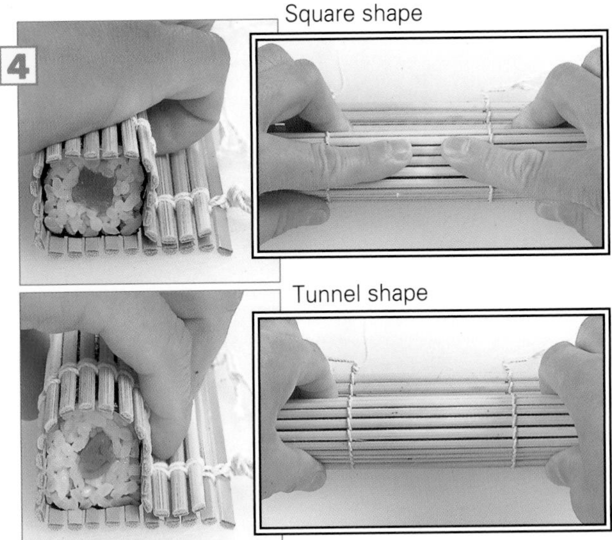

Shape into either a square or a tunnel as shown. Traditionally, hosomaki rolls with gourd are served in the tunnel shape and others are served in the square shape, but the choice is yours. Slide the roll to each end of the mat and flatten the ends.

5

Each roll can be cut into 4 or 6 pieces. In either case, first cut the roll into two equal lengths and place the lengths side by side. For variety, you can cut the first third normally and then cut the remainder at an angle *(left)*.

Gourd

1. Fold the gourd strip into thirds and twist into a rope.
2. Spread the rice and roll as on p. 43.

Note: Twisted gourd is easier to roll in hosomaki.

Takuan

1. Julienne the takuan as on p. 52. Slice the shiso leaves lengthwise.
2. Spread the rice as on p. 43, add the fillings as shown, and roll.

Cucumber

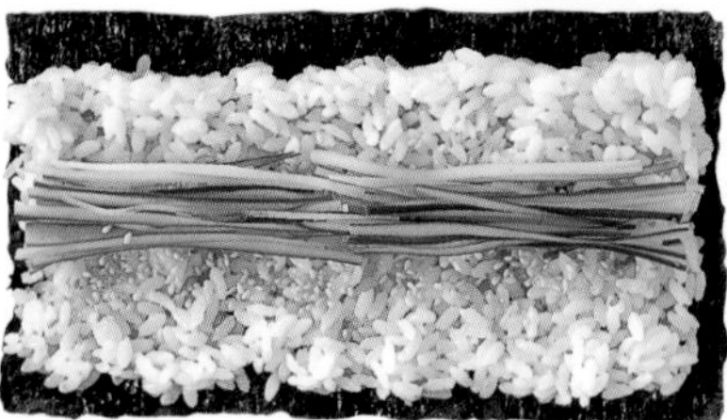

1. Julienne the cucumber into 4" (10 cm) lengths.
2. Spread the rice and roll as on p. 43.

Ume

Note: Add a few drops of mirin to the minced umeboshi for a smoother flavor.

1. Finely mince the flesh of the umeboshi. Cut the shiso leaves into 3/8" (1 cm)-wide strips.
2. Spread the rice as on p. 43, place the fillings as shown, and roll.

Natto

(for 1 roll)

1. Stir the natto with a dash of salt until threads form. Chop the green onions.
2. Spread the rice as on p.43, add the natto and onion as shown, and roll.

Kombu

(for 1 roll)

1. Spread the rice as on p. 43.
2. Place the fillings as shown and roll as on p. 43.

Uni

(for 1 roll)

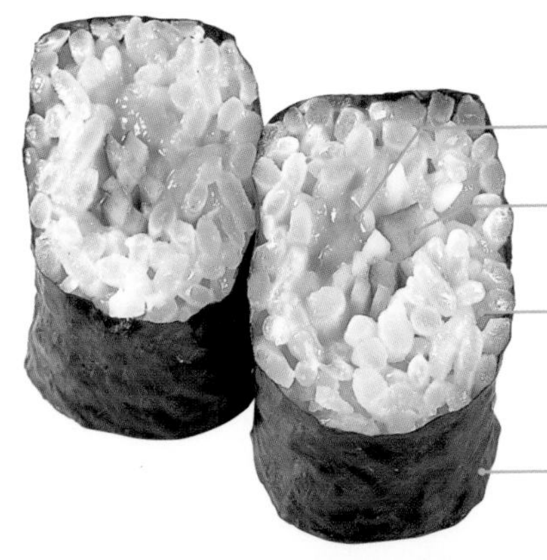

1. Julienne the cucumber in 4" (10 cm) lengths.
2. Spread the rice as on p. 43, add the fillings as shown, and roll.

Takuan and Tuna

(for 1 roll)

1. Cut the toro into sticks. Julienne the takuan as on p. 52.
2. Spread the rice as on p. 43. Place the toro and takuan on the rice, sprinkle with the sesame seeds, and roll.

Chicken

(for 1 roll)

1 chicken tenderloin

3 oz (80 g) sushi rice (p. 9)

Freshly grated wasabi

$^1/_2$ sheet roasted nori

1. Trim the chicken. Poach quickly (or cook through) and plunge in ice water. Drain and slice lengthwise.
2. Spread the rice as on p. 43. Spread the wasabi on the rice, place the slices of chicken as shown, and roll.

Cheese

(for 1 roll)

1 $^1/_2$ oz (45 g) white cheese

3 oz (80 g) sushi rice (p. 9)

$^1/_2$ sheet roasted nori

1. Cut the cheese into $^3/_8$" (1 cm)-thick sticks.
2. Spread the rice as on p. 43, place the cheese as shown, and roll.

Greens

(for 1 roll)

4–5 stalks seri (Japanese parsley) or spinach

Shaved bonito

3 oz (80 g) sushi rice (p. 9)

$^1/_2$ sheet roasted nori

1. Trim the seri and blanch. Plunge in cold water, then squeeze out the liquid.
2. Spread the rice as on p. 43, add the fillings as shown, and roll.

Jellyfish

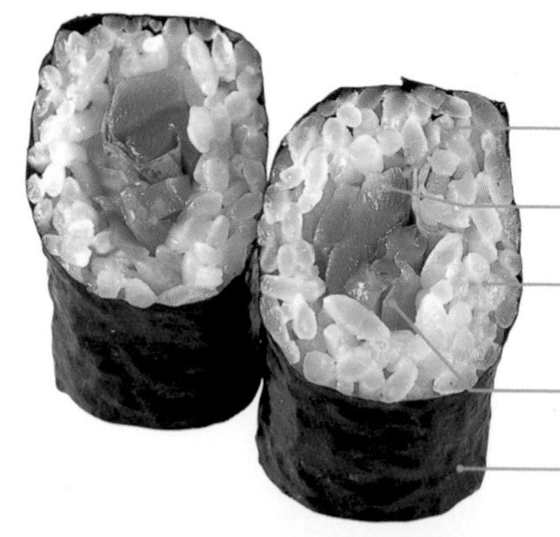

(for 1 roll)

1 lettuce leaf

1 oz (30 g) menma (pickled young bamboo)

3 oz (80 g) sushi rice (p. 9)

$^1/_3$ oz (10 g) salted preserved jellyfish

$^1/_2$ sheet roasted nori

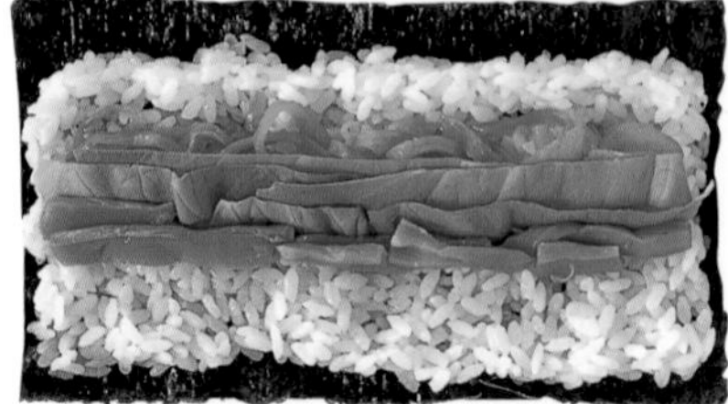

Note: Marinate the jellyfish in sugar, soy sauce, and sesame oil for added flavor.

1. Soak the jellyfish in water to reduce the saltiness. Slice the lettuce into $^3/_8$" (1 cm)-wide strips.
2. Spread the rice as on p. 43, add the fillings as shown, and roll.

Smelt

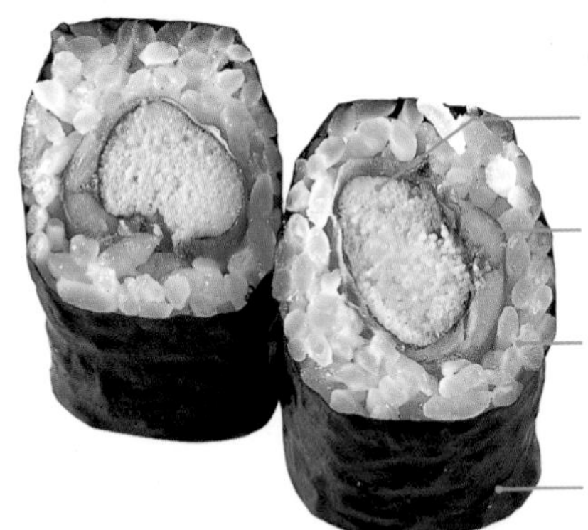

(for 1 roll)

- 2 smelt (shishamo) with egg sac
- Mayonnaise
- 3 oz (80 g) sushi rice (p. 9)
- 1/2 sheet roasted nori

1. Broil the smelt until cooked through. Discard the head and tail.
2. Spread the rice as on p. 43, add the fillings as shown, and roll.

Shirasu

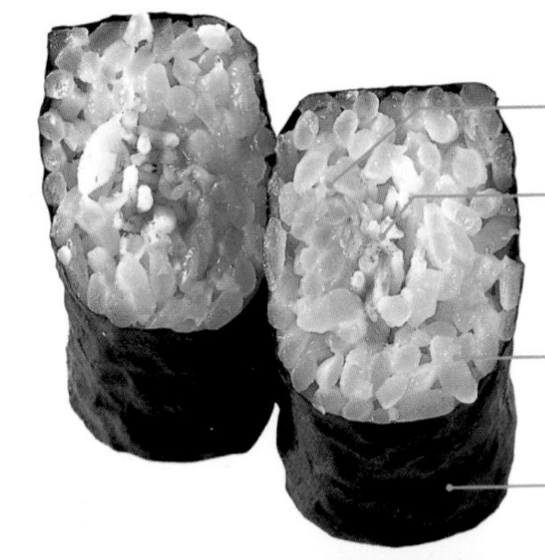

(for 1 roll)

- 1/2 tsp umeboshi paste
- 1 Tbsp shirasu (dried young sardines)
- 3 oz (80 g) sushi rice (p. 9)
- 1/2 sheet roasted nori

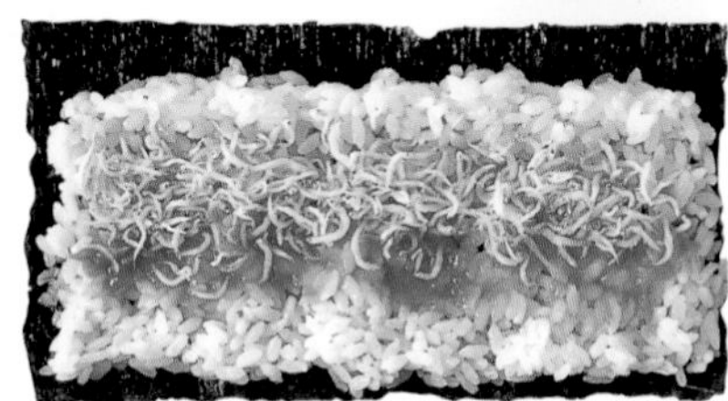

1. Spread the rice as on p. 43.
2. Spread with the umeboshi and arrange the shirasu as shown. Roll as on p. 43.

Kimpira

(for 1 roll)

- 1 oz (30 g) kimpira (simmered burdock root and carrot)
- 3 oz (80 g) sushi rice (p. 9)
- 1/2 sheet roasted nori

1. To make kimpira, sauté julienned burdock root and carrot in oil with *sake, sugar, mirin,* and soy sauce until the liquid is absorbed.
2. Spread the rice as on p. 43, add the fillings as shown, and roll.

Shrimp and Greens

(for 1 roll)

- 1/8 cucumber
- 3/4 oz (20 g) large squid body
- 3 boiled, peeled shrimp
- 3 lettuce leaves
- Kaiware (daikon sprouts)
- Mayonnaise
- 1/2 sheet roasted nori

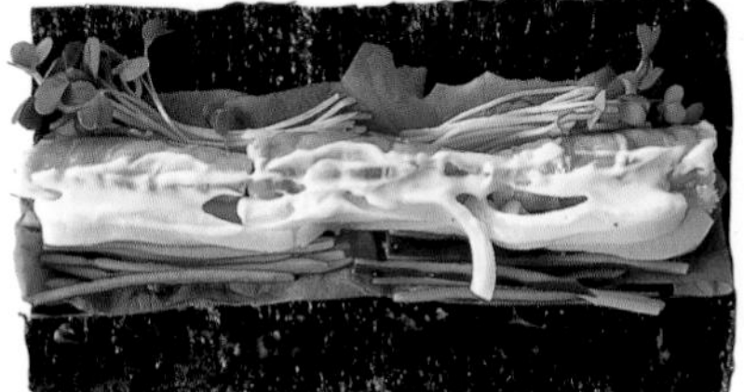

1. Julienne the squid and cucumber. Trim the kaiware.
2. Spread the lettuce on the nori as shown. Arrange the fillings on top and spread with mayonnaise. Roll as on p.43.

Ark Shells

1. Julienne the ark shell meat and cucumber.
2. Spread the rice as on p. 43. Spread the wasabi on the rice, arrange the fillings as shown, and roll.

Roasted Shiitake

(for 1 roll)

- Myoga (Japanese ginger)
- 1 large fresh shiitake
- 3 oz (80 g) sushi rice (p. 9)
- 1/2 sheet roasted nori

1. Discard the stem of the shiitake. Broil on a rack and thinly slice. Thinly slice the myoga and soak in water.
2. Spread the rice as on p. 43, add the fillings as shown, and roll.

Marinated Tuna

1. Mince 1 oz (30 g) of fresh tuna. Stir in *1/2 tsp each mirin, soy sauce,* and *sesame oil,* and *chopped scallions (white part),* and make the marinated tuna.
2. Spread the rice as on p. 43, add the fillings as shown, and roll.

Uni and Jellyfish

1. Julienne the cucumber into 4" (10 cm) lengths.
2. Spread the rice as on p. 43, add the fillings as shown, and roll.
Note: Uni-jellyfish mix (uni-kurage) is available in jars at specialty stores.

Sweet Wasabi

(for 1 roll)

Freshly grated wasabi
Sugar
Pickled ginger
3 oz (80 g) sushi rice (p. 9)
1/2 sheet roasted nori

1. Trim the wasabi root and shave off the outer skin.
2. Grate the wasabi with a fine grater (such as a shark-skin grater) in a circular motion, without using force. If your grater is too rough, cover the surface with aluminum foil (Fig. 1).
3. Cut in the sugar (Fig. 2) and pound the mixture. Pounding activates the sugar, making the wasabi milder and fragrant. Julienne the ginger.
4. Spread the rice as on p. 43, add the fillings as shown, and roll.

Fried Rice

(for 1 roll)

4–5 leftover nigiri sushi
1 egg, beaten
Salt and pepper
1 Tbsp butter
1 Tbsp cooking oil
1/2 sheet roasted nori

1. Mince the nigiri toppings.
2. Scramble the egg in *cooking oil.*
3. Add the minced toppings to the pan (Fig. 1) and sauté just until the raw ingredients change color.
4. Melt the butter in the pan and stir in the rice from the nigiri (Fig. 2). When the grains of rice have separated, add the salt and pepper.
5. Spread the fried rice as on p. 43 and roll.

Squid and Natto

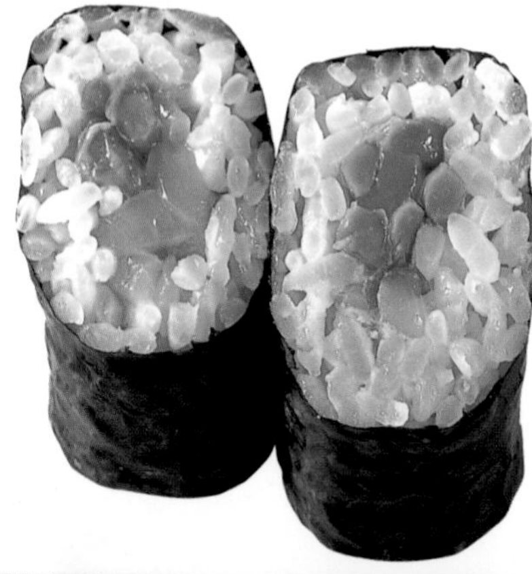

(for 1 roll)

$^3/_4$ oz (20 g) large squid body
1 Tbsp natto
Salt
$^1/_2$ scallion (white part)
$^1/_2$ green shiso leaf
3 oz (80 g) sushi rice (p. 9)
$^1/_2$ sheet roasted nori
Freshly grated wasabi

1. Ask for skinless sashimi-grade squid. Slice into short julienne strips. Chop the scallion and shiso.
2. Sprinkle the salt on the natto (Fig. 1) and stir well until threads form. The salt makes the threads form more quickly.
3. Stir the scallion and squid into the natto (Fig. 2). Add the shiso and mix thoroughly.
4. Spread the rice as on p. 43. Spread the wasabi in a line in the center. Place the squid mixture on the wasabi and roll. Cut into 6 pieces.

Miso Sardines

(for 1 roll)

1 sardine
1" (3 cm) white part of scallion
1 tsp miso
$^1/_2$ tsp ginger juice
$^1/_2$ green shiso leaf
3 oz (80 g) sushi rice (p. 9)
$^1/_2$ sheet roasted nori

1. Clean the sardine. Slice along the bone to make two fillets. Discard the bones, skin, head, and tail. Cut julienne.
2. Mince the scallion and scatter over the sardine pieces.
3. Spoon the miso and ginger juice over the sardine (Fig.1) and mince until well blended (Fig.2).
4. Spread the rice as on p. 43. Spoon the sardine mixture in a line in the center of the rice. Scatter chopped shiso on top and roll. Cut into 6 pieces.

Pressed Flounder

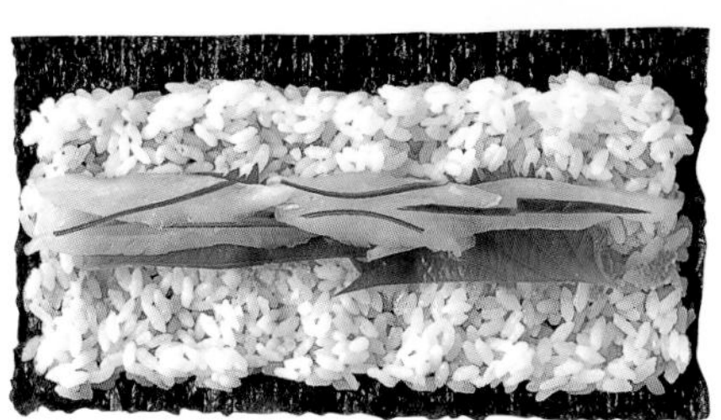

(for 1 roll)

- 1 oz (30 g) flounder
- Kombu
- Sake
- 1 green shiso leaf
- 3 oz (80 g) sushi rice (p. 9)
- 1/2 sheet roasted nori
- Freshly grated wasabi

1. Cut two pieces of kombu to match the size of the flounder fillet. Wipe with a cloth soaked in sake.
2. Place the flounder between the kombu pieces (Fig. 1) and wrap tightly in plastic wrap (Fig. 2). Refrigerate for 2–3 hours until the flounder has absorbed the kombu flavor.
3. Cut the flounder into sticks. Sliver some of the kombu; discard the rest.
4. Spread the rice as on p. 43. Spread the wasabi on the rise, and place the half-sliced shiso lengthwise and the remaining fillings as shown. Roll and cut into 6 pieces.

Simmered Clams

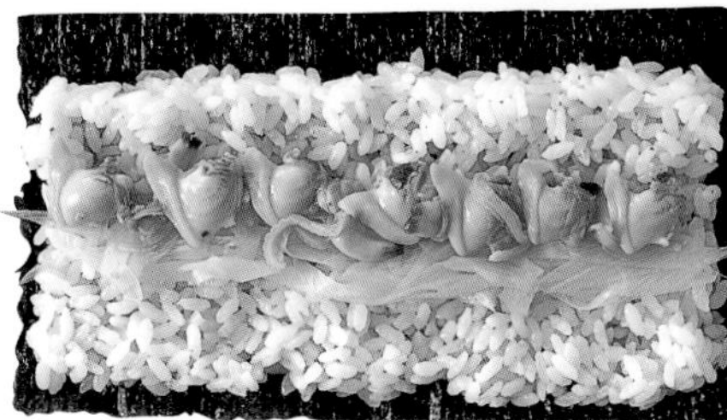

(for 1 roll)

- 1 oz (30 g) clam meat
- 2" (5 cm) scallion
- 1/2 cup dashi stock
- 1 tsp sugar
- 1 tsp mirin
- 1 tsp sake
- 1 tsp soy sauce
- 3 oz (80 g) sushi rice (p. 9)
- 1/2 sheet roasted nori

1. Rinse the clams and drain. Cut the scallion into diagonal rounds.
2. Heat the stock, sugar, mirin, sake, and soy sauce. Add the clams (Fig. 1). When the mixture boils, add the scallion (Fig. 2). Continue boiling until the clams puff up. Remove from heat and let stand until cool.
3. Spread the rice as on p. 43. Drain and squeeze out the clams and scallion and arrange on the rice as shown. Roll as on p. 43 and cut into 6 pieces.

Deluxe Hosomaki

In these recipes, multiple hosomaki rolls are combined to make new shapes. Add any of these deluxe hosomaki to your sushi platter for a decorative touch.

Flower *Triangular Petals*

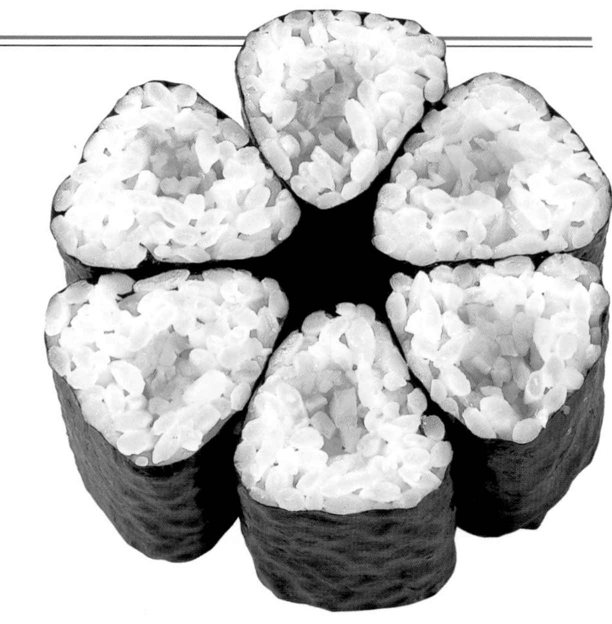

(for 1 roll)

$^{3}/_{4}$ oz (20 g) takuan pickles
3 oz (80 g) sushi rice (p. 9)
$^{1}/_{2}$ sheet roasted nori

How to Julienne Takuan Pickles

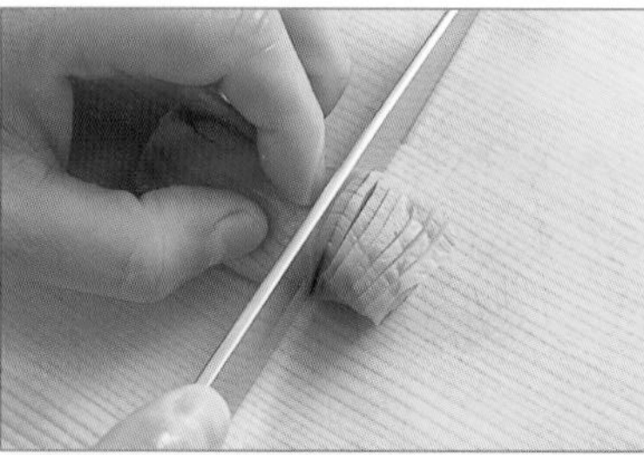

1. Make thin, deep slices in the takuan without cutting all the way through.

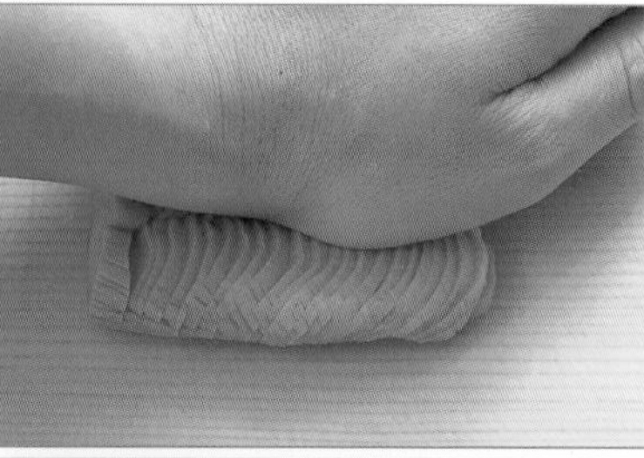

2. Flatten the takuan from the side in a domino pattern. The slices are held together by the bottom edge of the takuan, making them easier to cut.

3. Starting at the right edge, cut through the layers into thin julienne strips.

1. Julienne the takuan as at left.
2. Spread the rice as on p. 43 and add the takuan as shown.
3. Bring the mat up and over to meet the top edge of the rice (Fig. 1). Pull the edge of the mat away from the nori and continue rolling until the seam side is down (Fig. 2).
4. Shape the rice into a triangle (Fig. 3). Slice into 6 pieces and arrange into a flower shape.

Flower *Teardrop Petals*

(for 1 roll)
1 oz (30 g) fresh tuna
3 oz (80 g) sushi rice (p. 9)
$^1/_2$ sheet roasted nori
Freshly grated wasabi

1. Cut the tuna into sticks to fit the nori.
2. Spread the rice as on p. 43, spread with wasabi, and place the tuna as shown.
3. Bring the mat up and over to meet the top edge of the rice. Pull the edge of the mat away from the nori and continue rolling until the seam side is down.
4. Pinch one end of the roll to make a teardrop *(below)*. Slice into 6 pieces and arrange into a flower shape.

Wisteria

(for 1 roll)
Cucumber
2 Tbsp oboro sprinkles (p. 18)
3 oz (80 g) sushi rice (p. 9)
$^1/_2$ sheet roasted nori

1. Cut two julienne slices of cucumber, each 4 $^1/_3$" (11 cm) long.
2. Leaving $^3/_8$" (1 cm) of nori at the top and bottom, spread out the rice evenly. Place the sprinkles and the cucumber in the center.
3. Lift the bottom (front) edge of the mat up and over until the bottom edge of the rice meets the top edge of the rice (Fig. 1). Press together. Do not roll.
4. Curve the mat into a comma shape (Fig. 2). Slice into 8 pieces and arrange on the plate.

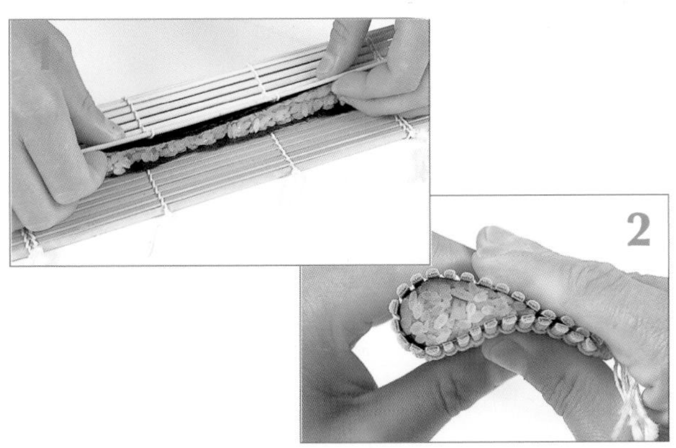

TEMAKI
Hand Rolls

How to Roll Temaki

Slice the nori in half lengthwise. Slice off $^{3}/_{4}$" (2 cm) from the end of each half piece. At sushi restaurants, the leftover strips are saved for other purposes, such as bands around egg sushi.

Gather a 2 oz (60 g) cylinder of rice and place it so that the bottom is at the center of the nori and the top is in the lefthand corner. Press the cylinder gently with your fingertips, spreading out the rice and making a well for the filling.

Place the filling in the well. Wasabi goes in a line in the well also.

As shown at far left, take the lefthand bottom corner of the nori and tuck it in at a spot in the middle of the nori, about $^{1}/_{3}$ of the way down from the top (see the markings on Fig. 3). Continue rolling into a bouquet shape (Fig 4, right side).

Hosomaki Style

The nori is re-roasted during the rolling process for a crisp texture.

1. Place the rice at one end of a full half sheet of nori (no trimming). Place the fillings in a well in the rice (Fig. 1).

2. Roll halfway (Fig. 2). Lightly roast the remaining nori over a flame (Fig. 3). Remove from heat and continue rolling.

Cod Roe

(for 1 roll)

$^{1}/_{2}$ small sac cod roe

1 green shiso leaf

2 oz (60 g) sushi rice (p. 9)

$^{1}/_{2}$ sheet roasted nori

Freshly grated wasabi

1. Trim the nori as on p. 55.
2. Place the rice on the nori and make a well. Add the wasabi, shiso leaf, and cod roe, then roll.

Squid

(for 1 roll)

$^{3}/_{4}$ oz (20 g) large squid body

$^{1}/_{2}$ green shiso leaf

Roasted sesame seeds

2 oz (60 g) sushi rice (p. 9)

$^{1}/_{2}$ sheet roasted nori

Freshly grated wasabi

1. Julienne the squid. Squid can be difficult to chew, so the pieces should be kept short.
2. Trim the nori as on p. 55. Place the rice on the nori and make a well. Add the wasabi, shiso, and squid. Sprinkle with sesame seeds, then roll.

Salmon Roe

(for 1 roll)

Cucumber

2 oz (60 g) sushi rice (p. 9)

1 Tbsp salmon roe

$^{1}/_{2}$ sheet roasted nori

Freshly grated wasabi

1. Cut the cucumber into 3" (8 cm)-long julienne.
2. Trim the nori as on p. 55. Place the rice on the nori and make a well. Add the wasabi, cucumber, and salmon roe, then roll.

Shrimp

1. Devein the shrimp, boil until just cooked, and peel off the shell and tail.
2. Cut the cucumber into 3" (8 cm)-long julienne.
3. Trim the nori as on p. 55. Place the rice on the nori and make a well. Add the mayonnaise, shrimp, and cucumber, then roll.

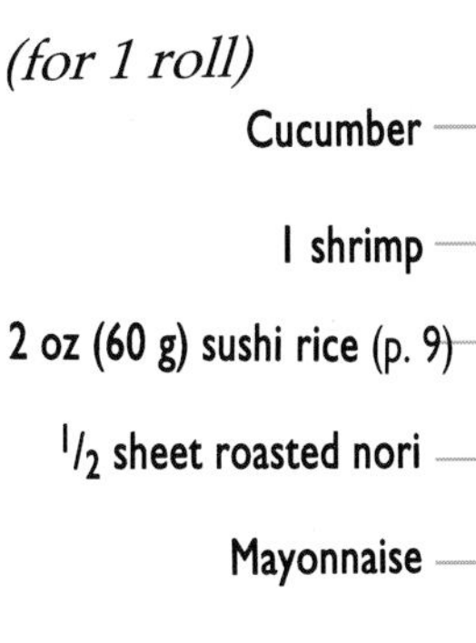

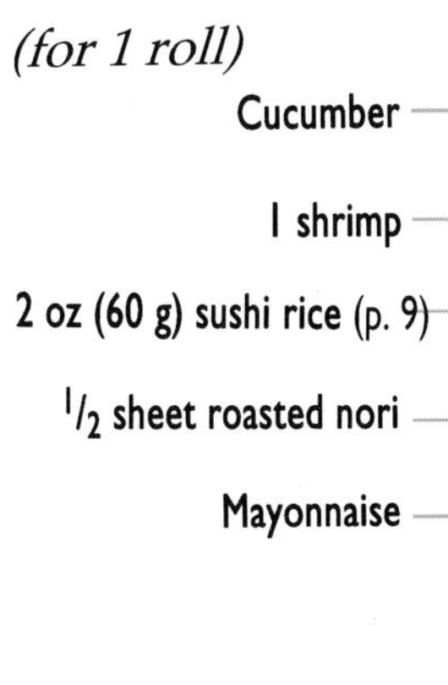

(for 1 roll)

Cucumber
1 shrimp
2 oz (60 g) sushi rice (p. 9)
$^1/_2$ sheet roasted nori
Mayonnaise

Broiled Scallop

1. Broil the scallop, brushing with a mixture of equal parts *soy sauce*, *sake*, and *mirin*. Slice into sticks.
2. Julienne the scallion. Soak in cold water, then drain.
3. Trim the nori as on p. 55. Place the rice on the nori and make a well. Add the wasabi, scallion, and scallop, then roll.

(for 1 roll)

White part of scallion
$^1/_2$ large scallop
2 oz (60 g) sushi rice (p. 9)
$^1/_2$ sheet roasted nori
Freshly grated wasabi

Roe Medley

1. Soak the herring roe in cold water to reduce the saltiness. Remove the membrane.
2. Trim the nori as on p. 55. Place the rice on the nori and make a well. Add the wasabi, shiso, herring roe, flying-fish roe, and salmon roe, then roll.

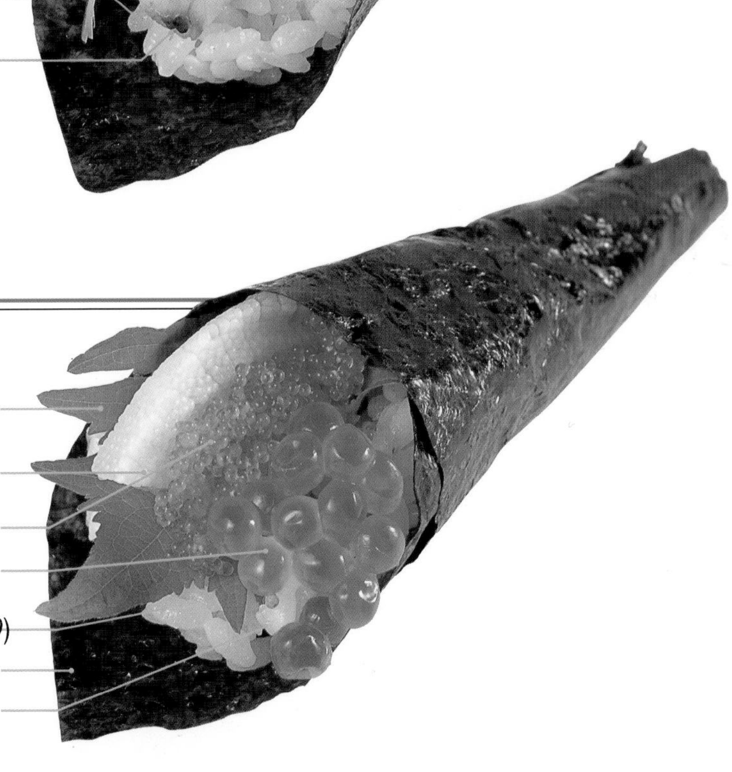

(for 1 roll)

1 green shiso leaf
1 small sac herring roe
1 tsp flying-fish roe
1 tsp salmon roe
2 oz (60 g) sushi rice (p. 9)
$^1/_2$ sheet roasted nori
Freshly grated wasabi

Pickles

(for 1 roll)

Misozuke yamagobo

Takuan pickles

Mibuna pickles

Roasted sesame seeds

2 oz (60 g) sushi rice (p. 9)

1/2 sheet roasted nori

1. Julienne the yamagobo (miso-pickled wild burdock root) and the takuan (yellow daikon pickles). Cut the mibuna (pickled greens) into 3" (8 cm) lengths.
2. Trim the nori as on p. 55. Place the rice on the nori and make a well. Add the pickles. Sprinkle with sesame seeds and then roll.

Shiokara

(for 1 roll)

1–2 tsp shiokara (seasoned squid entrails)

1 green shiso leaf

2 oz (60 g) sushi rice (p. 9)

1/2 sheet roasted nori

1. Trim the nori as on p. 55.
2. Place the rice on the nori and make a well. Add the shiso and shiokara, then roll.

Garnishes

(for 1 roll)

Cucumber

Murame (red shiso buds)

Daikon

Roasted sesame seeds

1/2 green shiso leaf

2 oz (60 g) sushi rice (p. 9)

1/2 sheet roasted nori

Freshly grated wasabi

This roll uses the "tsuma" and "ken"—complementary flavor garnishes—traditionally served with sashimi. With its crisp texture and fresh flavor, it is a delicious accompaniment to sake.
1. Cut the daikon, cucumber, and shiso into very fine julienne. Soak in cold water and drain.
2. Trim the nori as on p. 55. Place the rice on the nori and make a well. Add the wasabi and other fillings. Sprinkle with sesame seeds and then roll.

Sea Vegetables

1. Soak the seaweed mix in water and squeeze well.
2. Trim the nori as on p. 55. Place the rice on the nori and make a well. Add the wasabi and seaweed mix. Sprinkle with sesame seeds and then roll.

Note: Dried seaweed mix is available in specialty stores. For added flavor, add ponzu soy sauce, salad dressing, or cucumber.

(for 1 roll)

Dried seaweed mix
Roasted sesame seeds
2 oz (60 g) sushi rice (p. 9)
1/2 sheet roasted nori
Freshly grated wasabi

Ume

1. Finely mince the umeboshi. Stir in a little *mirin* to develop the flavor.
2. Peel the nagaimo and cut into medium-thick julienne strips.
3. Trim the nori as on p. 55. Place the rice on the nori and make a well. Spread the ume in the well and add the shiso and nagaimo, then roll.

(for 1 roll)

1/2 umeboshi
1/2 green shiso leaf
Nagaimo (Chinese yam)
2 oz (60 g) sushi rice (p. 9)
1/2 sheet roasted nori

Gingered Eggplant

1. Julienne the ginger and soak in water.
2. Thinly slice the eggplant and sauté in *cooking oil* with *freshly grated ginger, sake, mirin*, and *soy sauce*.
3. Trim the nori as on p. 55. Place the rice on the nori and make a well. Add the eggplant mixture and the ginger, then roll.

(for 1 roll)

Ginger
1/4 Japanese eggplant, sautéed
2 oz (60 g) sushi rice (p. 9)
1/2 sheet roasted nori

Tonburi (Cypress Caviar)

(for 1 roll)
1–2 tsp tonburi
1 green shiso leaf
Shaved bonito
2 oz (60 g) sushi rice (p. 9)
1/2 sheet roasted nori
Freshly grated wasabi

1. Trim the nori as on p. 55.
2. Place the rice on the nori and make a well. Add the wasabi, shiso, tonburi, and shaved bonito, and then roll.

Note: Tonburi, also known as Japanese caviar, are the seeds of the summer cypress (houki-gi). They have a unique texture and fragrance. Tonburi may also be flavored with sanbaizu (a vinegar/sugar/soy sauce mixture) before rolling.

Miso Cucumber

(for 1 roll)
Cucumber
1 tsp unrefined miso (moromimiso)
2 oz (60 g) sushi rice (p. 9)
1/2 sheet roasted nori

1. Slice the cucumber into a 3/8" (1 cm)-thick stick.
2. Trim the nori as on p. 55. Place the rice on the nori and make a well for the miso and cucumber, then roll.

Note: Moromimiso is a mild miso made with whole soybeans.

Daikon Pickles

(for 1 roll)
3/4 oz (20 g) daikon nukazuke
Roasted sesame seeds
1/4 myoga (Japanese ginger)
2 oz (60 g) sushi rice (p. 9)
1/2 sheet roasted nori

1. Thinly slice the daikon nukazuke (daikon pickled in salted rice-bran paste). Thinly slice the myoga and soak in cold water.
2. Trim the nori as on p. 55. Place the rice on the nori and make a well for the nukazuke and myoga. Sprinkle with sesame seeds, then roll.
Note: The nukazuke may also be flavored with green shiso leaves or ginger.

Chinese Pickles

1. Julienne the zaasai.
2. Make a thin omelet and slice into very thin strips.
3. Julienne the scallion. Soak in cold water, then drain.
4. Trim the nori as on p. 55. Place the rice on the nori and make a well. Place the omelet strips, pickles, and scallion on the rice and roll.

(for 1 roll)

Nori Tsukudani

1. Cut the takuan and cucumber into 3" (8 cm)-long julienne.
2. Trim the nori as on p. 55. Place the rice on the nori and make a well. Add the nori tsukudani, the takuan, and the cucumber, then roll.

Note: Nori tsukudani (sweet-simmered nori paste) is available in packaged form in specialty stores.

(for 1 roll)

Takuan pickles
Cucumber
1/2 tsp nori tsukudani
2 oz (60 g) sushi rice (p. 9)
1/2 sheet roasted nori

Tsukudani

1. Trim the nori as on p. 55.
2. Place the rice on the nori and make a well. Add the tsukudani. Sprinkle with sesame seeds, then roll.

Note: Kounago tsukudani is just one of many kinds of fish-based tsukudani available in packaged form in specialty stores. Use your favorite kind in this recipe.

(for 1 roll)

Mushroom

(for 1 roll)

- $^3/_4$ oz (20 g) sautéed shimeji and enoki mushrooms
- Parsley
- 2 oz (60 g) sushi rice (p. 9)
- $^1/_2$ sheet roasted nori

1. Separate the stalks of the mushrooms. Sauté in *butter* and season with *salt* and *pepper*.

2. Trim the nori as on p. 55. Place the rice on the nori and make a well. Add the mushroom mixture. Sprinkle with minced parsley, then roll.

Steak

(for 1 roll)

- Parsley
- 1 oz (30 g) cooked steak
- $^1/_2$ lettuce leaf
- 2 oz (60 g) sushi rice (p. 9)
- $^1/_2$ sheet roasted nori

1. Season the steak with *salt* and *pepper* and slice.

2. Trim the nori as on p. 55. Place the rice on the nori and make a well. Spread the lettuce in the well, then place the steak slices on top and tuck the parsley alongside. Roll.

Note: This roll may be flavored with lemon juice or with wasabi.

Beef Tongue

(for 1 roll)

- 2 oz (60 g) sushi rice (p. 9)
- 2–3 slices beef tongue
- $^1/_2$ lettuce leaf
- Lemon slice
- $^1/_2$ sheet roasted nori

1. Sprinkle the tongue with *salt* and grill over a flame. Slice into $^1/_2$" (1.5 cm)-wide strips.

2. Trim the nori as on p. 55. Place the rice on the nori and make a well. Spread the lettuce in the well and put the beef on top, with the lemon alongside. Roll.

Chinese Chicken

1. Boil the chicken in salted water and drain. Thinly slice the chicken and toss with *sesame-oil-flavored salad dressing.*
2. Trim the nori as on p. 55. Place the rice on the nori and make a well. Spread the lettuce in the well and add the chicken, then roll.

(for 1 roll)

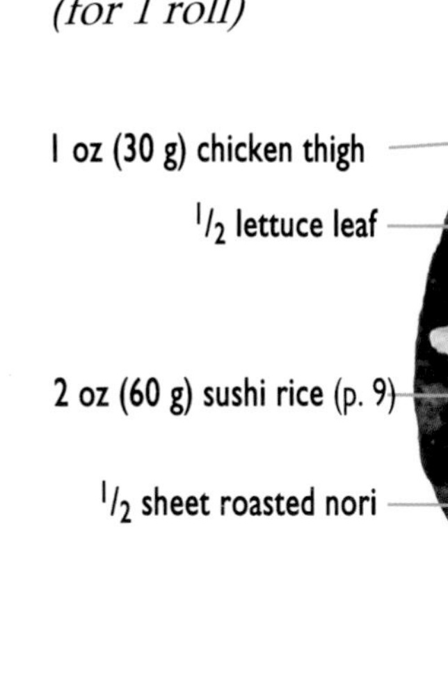

1 oz (30 g) chicken thigh
1/2 lettuce leaf
2 oz (60 g) sushi rice (p. 9)
1/2 sheet roasted nori

Tuna Salad

1. Stir *mayonnaise* into the tuna. Season with *pepper*.
2. Slice the cucumber into 3" (8 cm)-long julienne.
3. Trim the nori as on p. 55. Place the rice on the nori and make a well. Put the lettuce in the well and top with the tuna mixture and the cucumber, then roll.

(for 1 roll)

Cucumber
1 Tbsp canned tuna
1/4 lettuce leaf
2 oz (60 g) sushi rice (p. 9)
1/2 sheet roasted nori

Wasabi Pickles

1. Blanch the wasabi flowers in salted water and plunge in cold water. Squeeze well and cut into 2 or 3 lengths.
2. Trim the nori as on p. 55. Place the rice on the nori and make a well. Add the wasabi flowers and the wasabi pickles, then roll.

(for 1 roll)

1 stalk wasabi flower
1/2 tsp wasabizuke
2 oz (60 g) sushi rice (p. 9)
1/2 sheet roasted nori

Note: Wasabi flowers are the young stalks of wasabi plants. They have a slightly spicy, slightly bitter flavor. Wasabizuke is wasabi leaves preserved in sake lees. Both items are available in specialty stores.

Minced Tuna

(for 1 roll)

1 oz (30 g) toro (fatty tuna)
White part of scallion
2 oz (60 g) sushi rice (p. 9)
1/2 sheet roasted nori
Freshly grated wasabi

1. With a spoon, scrape the meat from tuna slice (Fig. 1).
2. Julienne the scallion. Soak in cold water, then drain (Fig. 2).
3. Trim the nori as on p. 55. Place the rice on the nori and make a well. Add the wasabi, tuna, and scallion, then roll.
Note: This recipe is a good use for fibrous toro. Toro that is free of tough fibers is best enjoyed as sashimi; fibrous toro can be scraped and used in hosomaki and temaki.

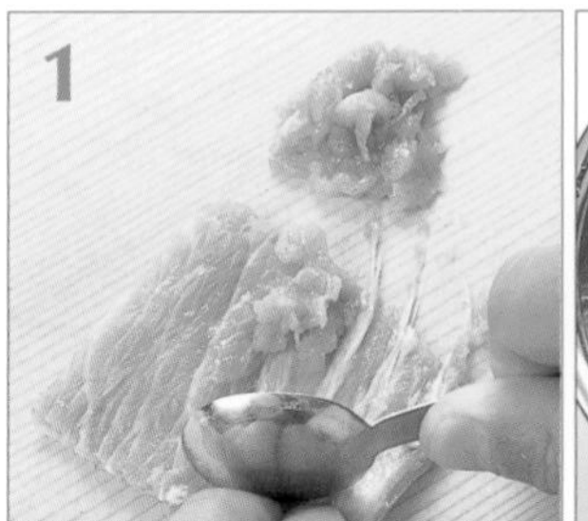

Miso Scallops

(for 1 roll)

8–10 bay scallops
Salted wakame
1 Tbsp white miso
1/2 Tbsp sugar
1/2 tsp mirin
1 Tbsp vinegar
Japanese mustard
2 oz (60 g) sushi rice (p. 9)
1/2 sheet roasted nori

1. Rinse the scallops in salted water. Rinse the salt from the wakame and soak in cold water. Remove any thick fibers and chop.
2. Put the miso, sugar, mirin, and vinegar into a mortar (Fig. 1) and grind well. Stir in the mustard (Fig. 2).
3. Stir in the scallops and the wakame.
4. Trim the nori as on p. 55. Place the rice on the nori and make a well, spoon the filling on top, and then roll.

Grilled Tuna

(for 1 roll)

1 oz (30 g) toro (fatty tuna)
Salt and pepper
Soy sauce
White part of scallion
2 oz (60 g) sushi rice (p. 9)
$^1/_2$ sheet roasted nori
Freshly grated wasabi

1. Julienne the scallion. Soak in cold water, then drain.
2. Cut the toro into bite-size pieces and season with *salt* and *pepper* (Fig. 1).
3. Grill over a high flame. When the surface color changes, brush on the soy sauce (Fig.2) and continue grilling until the soy sauce is dry.
4. Trim the nori as on p. 55. Place the rice on the nori and make a well. Add the wasabi, toro, and scallion, then roll.

1

Crispy Sea Bream Skin

(for 1 roll)

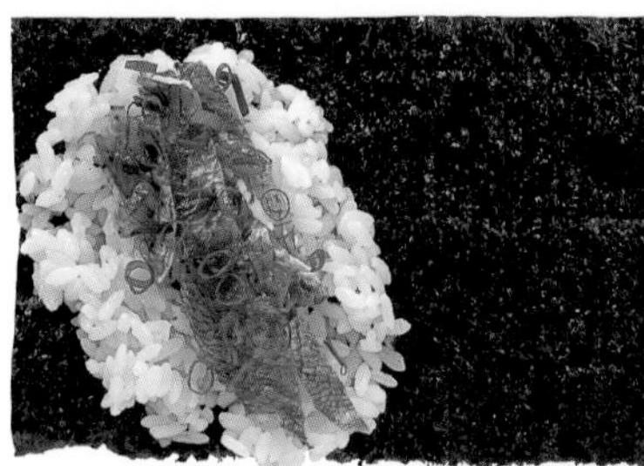

$^1/_2$ sea bream (tai) skin
Salt
Green onion
2 oz (60 g) sushi rice (p. 9)
$^1/_2$ sheet roasted nori

1. To skin the sea bream, lay it skin side down and slide a knife between the skin and the flesh at the tail end (Fig 1). Reserve the fillet for another use.
2. Sprinkle the skin with salt and grill over a flame (Fig. 2). When both sides are golden, cut into $^3/_8$" (1 cm)-wide strips.
3. Trim the nori as on p. 55. Place the rice on the nori and make a well. Add the crisp skin pieces and the green onion, then roll.
Note: For added flavor, drizzle the grilled skin with lemon or other citrus juices.

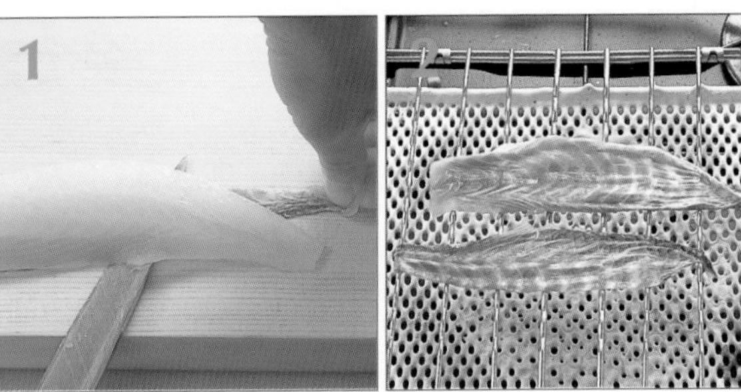
1

Uramaki
Inside-Out Rolls

How to Roll Uramaki

Place two $5^1/_4$ oz (150 g) portions of rice on the nori as shown *(above left)*.Using the pads of your fingers, spread the rice evenly *(above right)* to cover the nori. Note that the rolling mat is not used until step 5.

Sprinkle roasted sesame seeds or other coatings all over the rice. Press into place with the palm of your hand.

Turn the rice-covered nori over. Place the fillings at a point about $^1/_3$ of the way up the nori.

If the fillings are dark in color, spread 7 oz (200 g) of the rice, turn it over. Spread the remaining rice $3^1/_2$ oz (100 g) up to the halfway point *(left)* before placing the fillings. See the examples below.

No rice on the inside layer

Rice on the inside layer

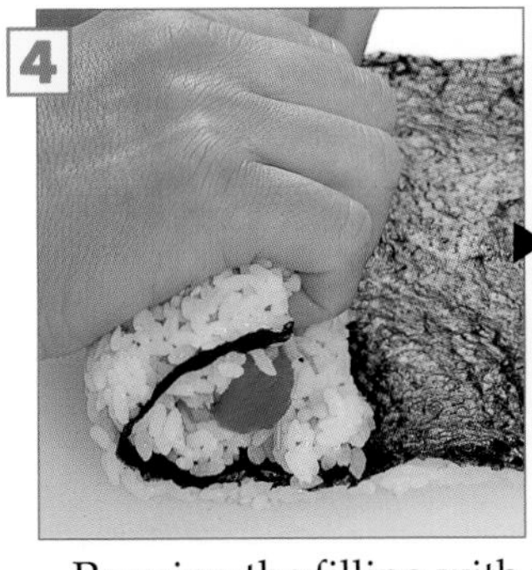

Pressing the filling with your fingers, roll the sushi by hand as for a jelly roll, ending with the seam side down.

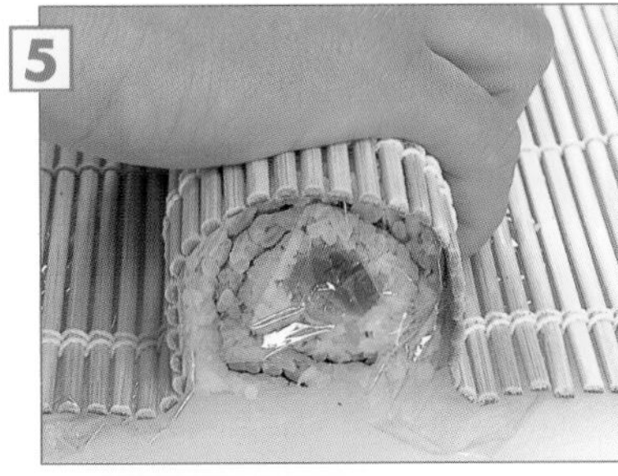

Cover the roll with plastic wrap and form a tunnel shape with the rolling mat on top. Slide the roll to the right edge of the mat and flatten the end, then repeat on the left side.

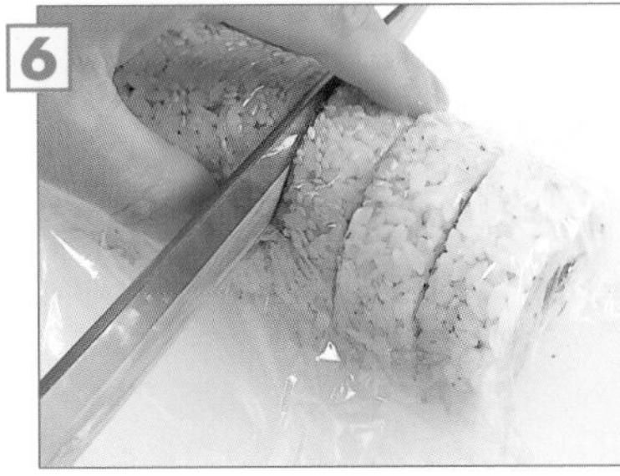

Leaving the wrap on the roll, slice into eight pieces. Wipe your knife with a damp towel after each slice. Remove the wrap before serving.

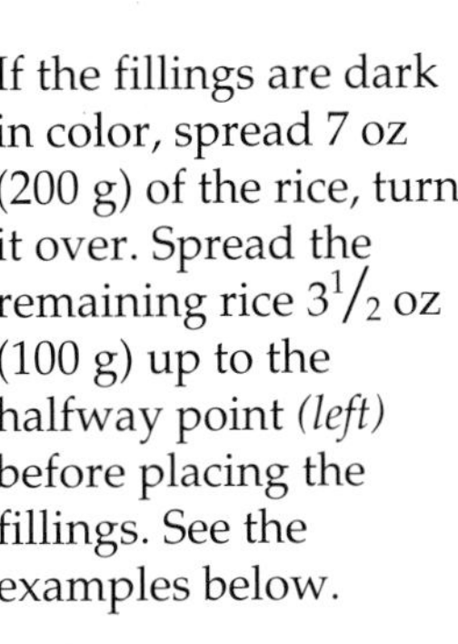

Sea Bream

(for 1 roll)

1 sheet roasted nori
10 1/2 oz (300 g) sushi rice (p. 9)
1–2 green shiso leaves

1. Ask for sashimi-grade sea bream (tai) without skin. Cut into sticks to fit the nori.
2. Julienne the scallion. Soak in cold water, then drain.
3. Blanch the mitsuba, plunge in cold water, then squeeze out the liquid.
4. Spread the rice on the nori as shown on p. 67, sprinkling julienned shiso leaves as the outer coating. Turn the rice and nori over, place the fillings as shown above, and roll.
5. With the seam side down, cover the roll in plastic wrap and press into a tunnel shape with a rolling mat. Flatten the ends and cut into 8 slices.

Crab

(for 1 roll)

1 sheet roasted nori
10 1/2 oz (300 g) sushi rice (p. 9)
1 tsp yukari sprinkles

1. Rinse the salt from the wakame and soak in cold water. Remove any thick fibers and chop.
2. Rub the himo with salt to eliminate the stickiness, then rinse.
3. Spread the rice on the nori as shown on p. 67, with the yukari (minced dried beefsteak leaves) as the outer coating. Turn the rice and nori over, place the fillings as shown above, and roll.
4. With the seam side down, cover the roll in plastic wrap and press into a tunnel shape with a rolling mat. Flatten the ends and cut into 8 slices.
Note: Himo is a skirtlike muscle that surrounds the scallop. Substitute with any firm-fleshed seafood, such as squid or shellfish, that contrasts with the crabmeat.

Sausage

(for 1 roll)

1. Make shallow 3/8" (1 cm) slits in the sausages to prevent splitting. Boil 3–4 minutes.
2. Thinly slice the onion, soak in water to soften the flavor, and squeeze well.
3. Spread the rice on the nori as shown on p. 67, sprinkling minced carrot as the outer coating. Turn the rice and nori over, place the fillings as shown above, and roll.
4. With the seam side down, cover the roll in plastic wrap and press into a tunnel shape with a rolling mat. Flatten the ends and cut into 8 slices.
Note: Lettuce and ketchup make tasty additions to this roll.

Pork Cutlet

(for 1 roll)

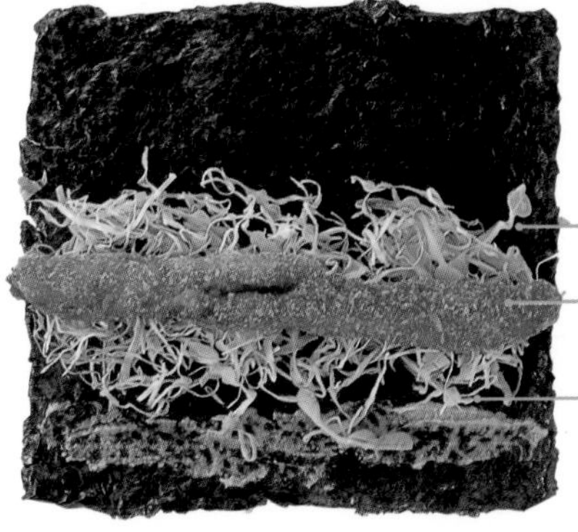

1. Cut the pork into two sticks. Season with *salt* and *pepper* and dip in *flour*, then *beaten egg*, and then *bread crumbs*. Deep fry until golden.
2. Remove ribs from the cabbage and slice thinly. Soak in water and then squeeze well.
3. Spread the rice on the nori as shown on p. 67, sprinkling shredded lettuce leaves as the outer coating. Turn the rice and nori over, place the fillings as shown above, and roll.
4. With the seam side down, cover the roll in plastic wrap and press into a tunnel shape with a rolling mat. Flatten the ends and cut into 8 slices.
Note: Breaded shrimp, chicken fingers, or hamburger may be used instead of the pork.

Salmon and Roe

(for 1 roll)

1 sheet roasted nori
$10\frac{1}{2}$ oz (300 g) sushi rice (p. 9)
1–2 green shiso leaves
$\frac{1}{3}$ potato
$\frac{1}{2}$ salmon fillet
2 Tbsp salmon roe

1. Peel the potato and cut into $\frac{1}{4}$" (7 mm)-thick matchsticks. Rinse and boil in salted water.
2. Season the salmon with salt and grill on a rack. Discard the skin and bones and break into 4 chunks.
3. Spread 7 oz (200 g) of the rice on the nori as shown on p. 67, sprinkling julienned shiso leaves as the outer coating. Turn the rice and nori over, place the remaining rice (to help break some of the roe) and the fillings as shown above, and roll.
4. With the seam side down, cover the roll in plastic wrap and press into a tunnel shape with a rolling mat. Flatten the ends and cut into 8 slices.

Fried Tofu

(for 1 roll)

1 sheet roasted nori
$10\frac{1}{2}$ oz (300 g) sushi rice (p. 9)
2 Tbsp roasted sesame seeds
$1\frac{1}{2}$ aburage (tofu puffs)
$\frac{1}{3}$ bunch mitsuba (honewort)
2 omelet sticks ($\frac{1}{2}$" (1.5 cm) square) (p. 19)
33" (84 cm) simmered gourd (p. 17)

1. Rinse the aburage with boiling water. Rub under running water to remove excess oil. Bring *1 cup water, 2 Tbsp sugar, 2 Tbsp mirin, 1 Tbsp sake,* and $2\frac{1}{2}$ *Tbsp soy sauce* to a boil and add the aburage. Cook until the liquid is absorbed. Trim off the edges and open flat.
2. Cut the gourd strips into $8\frac{1}{4}$" (21 cm) lengths. Blanch the mitsuba and plunge in cold water, then squeeze.
3. Spread the rice on the nori as shown on p. 67 and sprinke with the sesame seeds. Turn the rice and nori over, place the fillings as shown above, and roll.
4. With the seam side down, cover the roll in plastic wrap and press into a tunnel shape with a rolling mat. Flatten the ends and cut into 8 slices.

California

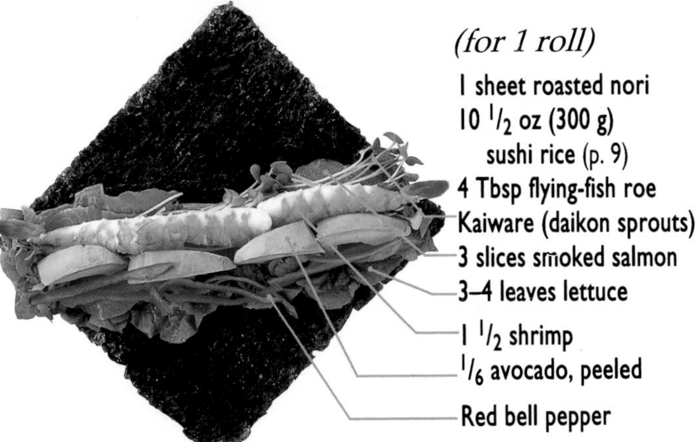

1. Devein the shrimp, boil until just tender, and peel, leaving the tail on. Slice in half lengthwise.
2. Cut the avocado piece into 4 slices. Julienne the bell pepper and trim the kaiware.
3. Spread the rice on the nori as shown on p. 67, using the flying-fish roe as the outer coating.
4. Turn the rice and nori over, pointing one corner toward you. Lay the lettuce on the nori, then the smoked salmon, and then the other fillings as shown above.
5. Roll as for a jelly roll, ending with the seam side down. Drape with plastic wrap and use a rolling mat to form into a tunnel shape. Cut into two pieces, then slice each piece into thirds. Remove the wrap.

Tuna Salad

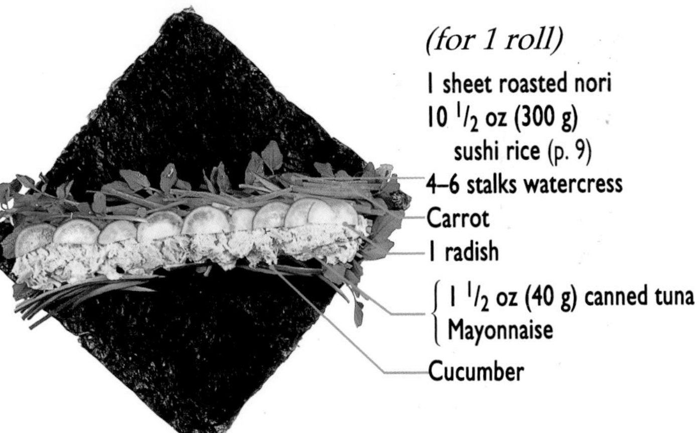

1. Drain and flake the tuna. Stir in the mayonnaise.
2. Julienne the carrot and the cucumber. Cut the radish into thin half rounds.
3. Spread the rice on the nori as shown on p. 67.
4. Turn the rice and nori over, pointing one corner toward you. Place the tuna first and arrange the other fillings as shown above.
5. Roll as for a jelly roll, ending with the seam side down. Drape with plastic wrap and use a rolling mat to form into a tunnel shape. Cut into two pieces, then cut each piece into thirds.

Two-Sided Roll

Fillings are placed at the top and bottom as well as at the center. Roll the top and bottom separately, then finish shaping the complete roll.

(for 1 roll)

- 1 sheet roasted nori
- 10 $\frac{1}{2}$ oz (300 g) sushi rice (p. 9)
- 2 Tbsp roasted sesame seeds
- 1 Tbsp oboro sprinkles (p. 18)
- Takuan pickles
- Mibuna pickles
- 4 $\frac{1}{3}$" (11 cm) cucumber

1. Julienne the takuan into 4 $\frac{1}{3}$" (11 cm) lengths. Squeeze the mibuna pickles (pickled greens) and chop. Quarter the cucumber lengthwise.
2. Spread the rice on the nori as shown on p. 67, using the sesame seeds as the outer coating.
3. Turn the rice and nori over. Place the oboro sprinkles, takuan, and mibuna pickles in the center. Place the cucumbers about 1" (3 cm) from the top and bottom.
4. Wrap the cucumbers into a tiny roll in front (Fig. 1). Turn everything around and make another tiny roll for the other cucumber quarters (Fig. 2).
5. Roll the tiny rolls together so that they meet in the center (Fig. 3).
6. Turn the roll upside down so that the seam is at the bottom. Drape with plastic wrap and use a rolling mat to form into a tunnel shape (Fig. 4). Flatten the ends and slice into 8 pieces.

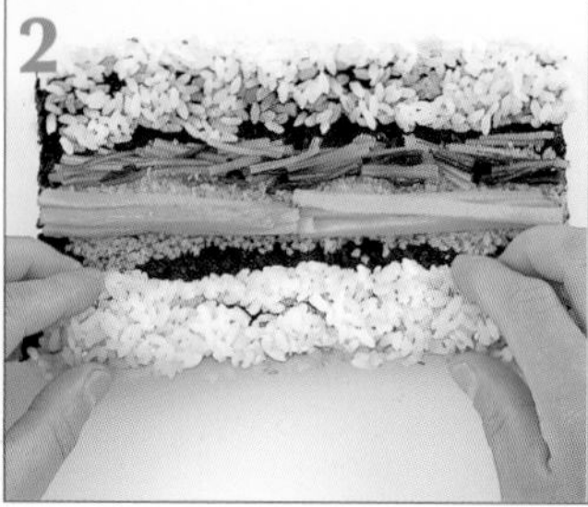

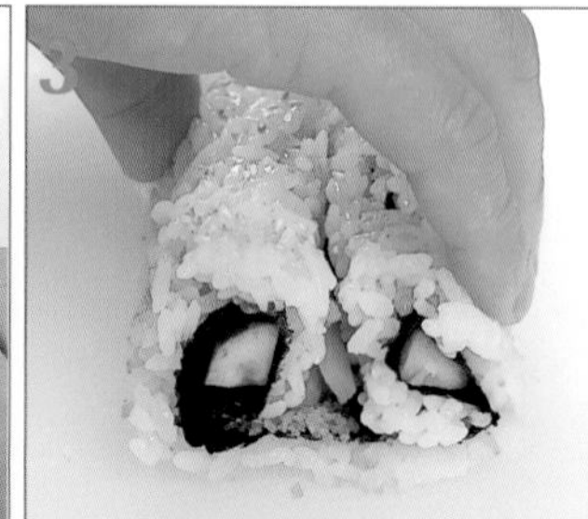

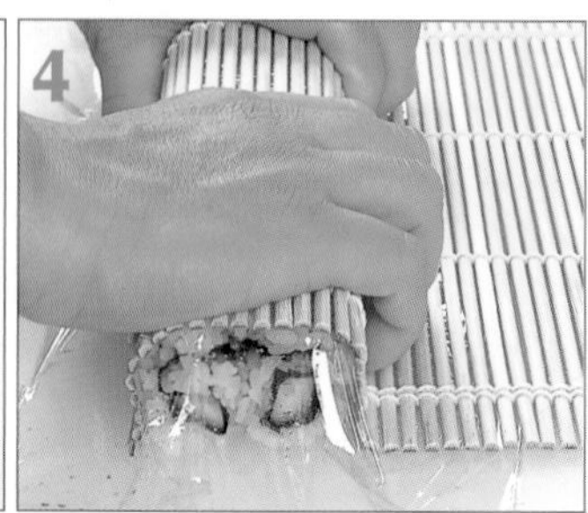

Onigiri Roll

This is a convenient way to make many onigiri (rice balls) at once. Place the different fillings side by side, roll into a triangle shape, and wrap with another sheet of nori.

(for 1 roll)

- 2 sheets roasted nori
- 10 1/2 oz (300 g) sushi rice (p. 9)
- 1/4 cod roe sac
- 2 umeboshi (pickled plums)
- 1/5 oz (5 g) shaved bonito
- Soy sauce
- 1/2 piece salted salmon

1. Broil the cod roe sac and the salmon. Flake the salmon into chunks, discarding the bones and skin.
2. Seed the umeboshi and chop into pieces. Stir soy sauce into the shaved bonito.
3. Spread the rice on the nori as shown on p. 67. Turn the rice and nori over and place the fillings so that each one occupies a quarter of the length of the nori.
4. Holding the fillings in place with your fingers (Fig. 1), roll as for a jelly roll, finishing with the seam side down.
5. Drape with plastic wrap. Form into a triangle with a rolling mat (Fig. 2).
6. Remove the wrap and roll with another sheet of nori. Flatten the ends and slice into 8 pieces, wiping the blade with a wet cloth after each slice.
Note: Instead of sushi rice, plain salted rice may be used for this recipe. Other fillings to try: tuna salad and kombu tsukudani.

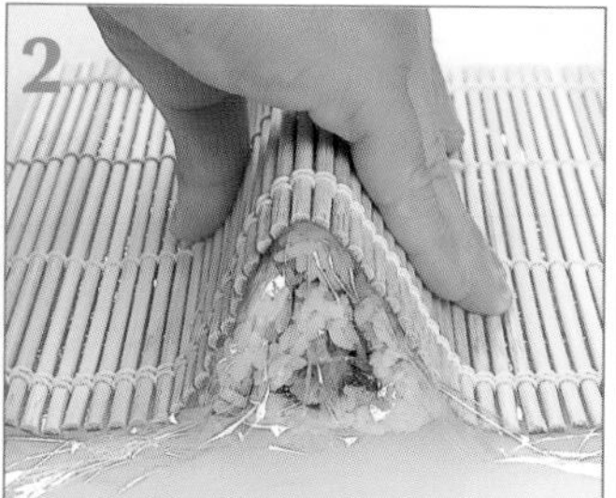

Cod Roe

(for 1 roll)

1. Separate the cod roe sacs.
2. Julienne the cucumber. Cut the daikon into thin strips about 3/8" (1 cm) wide. Soften in lightly salted water.
3. Spread 7 oz (200 g) of the rice on the nori as shown on p. 67, using the yukari sprinkles (minced dried beefsteak leaves) as the outer coating.
4. Turn the rice and nori over, spread the remaining rice on the bottom half, and place the fillings as shown above. Roll as for a jelly roll, ending with the seam side down.
5. Drape with plastic wrap and form into a tunnel shape with a rolling mat. Flatten the ends and slice into 8 pieces.

Ham and Egg

(for 1 roll)

1. Cut the ham into sticks to fit the nori.
2. To make the thin omelet, beat 1 egg, sprinkle with *salt*, and cook with *oil* in a large frying pan. Trim down to a 8 1/4 x 3 1/2" (21 x 9 cm) rectangle.
3. Peel the potato and cut into 1/4" (7 mm)-thick matchsticks. Rinse, then boil in salted water. Boil the bean sprouts in salted water and drain well.
4. Spread the rice on the nori as shown on p. 67 and sprinkle with the sesame seeds. Turn the rice and nori over, place the fillings as shown above, and roll, ending with the seam side down.
5. Drape with plastic wrap and form into a tunnel shape with a rolling mat. Flatten the ends and cut into 8 pieces.

Kazarimaki

Decorative Rolls

SUSHI

Techniques for Decorative Rolls

•Size of the Nori

For easier rolling, all of the recipes in this section use a horizontal half sheet of nori. Because some recipes call for fractions of this half sheet, this section uses the term *halfsheet* to represent this standard size, as in "$^{1}/_{3}$ of a halfsheet." When a full sheet is needed, the phrase a *full sheet of nori* is used, as in "the vertical half of a full sheet of nori."

Cutting the Nori

Cut the nori in half crosswise. Press the tip of a chef's knife into the far edge of the nori and then rock the knife downward to slice through the sheet.

1 halfsheet = 4" (10.5 cm) x 7" (18 cm)
$^{1}/_{2}$ halfsheet = 4" (10.5 cm) x 3 1/2" (9 cm)
$^{1}/_{3}$ halfsheet = 4" (10.5 cm) x 2 1/3" (6 cm)

•Coloring the Rice

Mix the colored ingredient into the rice thoroughly without crushing the grains of rice. Oboro sprinkles must be very well incorporated into the rice or the rice will separate after slicing.

• Spreading The Rice

Horizontally on nori

1. Turn the nori and mat so that the long edge is toward you. Place the rice in a tube in the center.

2. Using the pads of your fingers, spread the rice evenly in all directions.

3. Spread the rice all the way to the top and bottom edges. Each recipe will specify how much nori to leave at the left and right sides (which will be the top and bottom when you begin rolling).

In small shapes

For panda mouth, flower petals, and so on, shape the rice on a board before placing it on the rice.

• Symmetrical Parts

For butterfly wings, animal eyes, and other parts that are used twice in the same roll, make the part once using a full sheet of nori and then cut it in half. The two parts will then be identical.

• Small Fillings

To keep small fillings in place (e.g., the yellow flower of the tulip, p. 80), press them gently with a chopstick. The contrast will be sharper in the sliced sushi.

• Thin Rolls

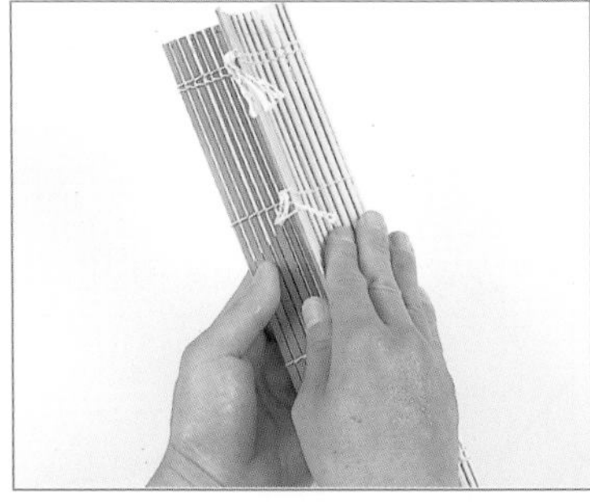

For very thin rolls (e.g., plum blossom petals, p. 84, or animal eyes), finish the roll by placing it in the middle of the mat and rubbing the two halves of the mat against each other.

• Putting Parts Together

For the Chrysanthemum Crest (p. 128) and other complex rolls, put the parts together at the edge of the mat rather than in the middle. It is easier to see the picture forming.

• Adding Rice after Rolling

Hold the mat in a U shape with your hand and place the additional rice on top. If your hands are small, try using containers to hold the mat in place *(left)*.

• Squares and Circles

Decorative sushi can be squares, tunnels, or circles. For squares and tunnels, finish rolling with the seam side down and press into shape with the rolling mat. For the circle, form the roll first, lift the mat, and then roll it up and down inside the mat.

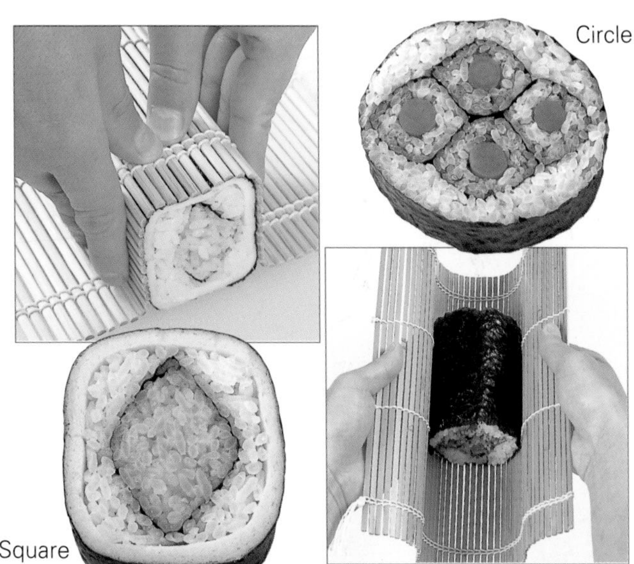

• Slicing

Wipe your blade with a wet cloth after each slice. Cut the roll little by little rather than pushing the knife through all at once.

Tulip

(for 1 roll)
2 tsp egg sprinkles
4 $^{1}/_{3}$" (11 cm) cucumber
7 $^{1}/_{2}$ oz (220 g) sushi rice
Roasted nori

Setup: Prepare the egg sprinkles as below. For different colors, try red pickled ginger (beni-shoga), oboro sprinkles (p. 18), or takuan pickles instead of the egg sprinkles.

How to Make Egg Sprinkles

1. Beat *1 egg* and *3 yolks*. Stir in *1 Tbsp sugar, 1 Tbsp sake, 1 Tbsp mirin*, and *1 tsp salt*. Pour into a saucepan and stir over low heat with 4–5 chopsticks.

2. When the egg has separated into small pieces, push them through a strainer.

3. Spread on a plate to cool and to evaporate the excess liquid.

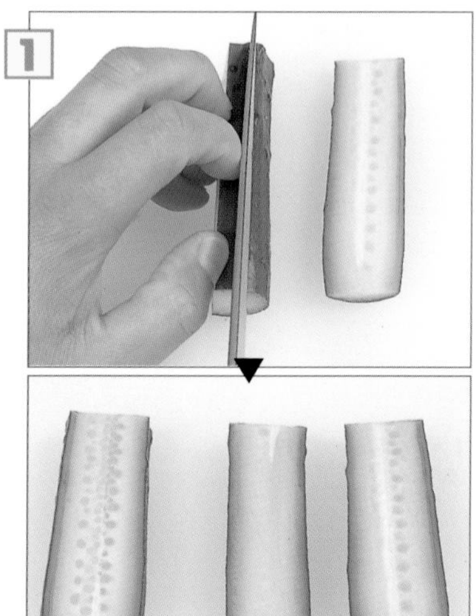

Choosing a straight part of the cucumber, slice off 2 sides (the two pieces on the right side of the lower photo).

These will form the leaves of the tulip.

Using 3 grains of rice, attach $^{1}/_{3}$ halfsheet to 1 halfsheet of nori (see p. 85, Fig. 4). Leaving 1" (3 cm) at both ends, spread 3 $^{1}/_{2}$ oz (100 g) of the rice on the strip. Place two 1 oz (30 g) ridges on the center of the rice.

3

Fold a $^{1}/_{2}$ halfsheet of nori in half and tuck it between the ridges, pressing it into place with a chopstick.

4

Spoon the egg sprinkles into the folded nori, pressing again with the chopstick *(left)*. The pressure compacts the sprinkles for a cleaner finished look. Next, fold the edges of the nori over the tops of the ridges *(below)*.

5

Now, press the two ridges together. The stem is formed by the two sides of the nori meeting in the middle.

6

Place the cucumber slices on the ridges as shown. Make two more 1 oz (30 g) ridges at the edges of the rice.

7

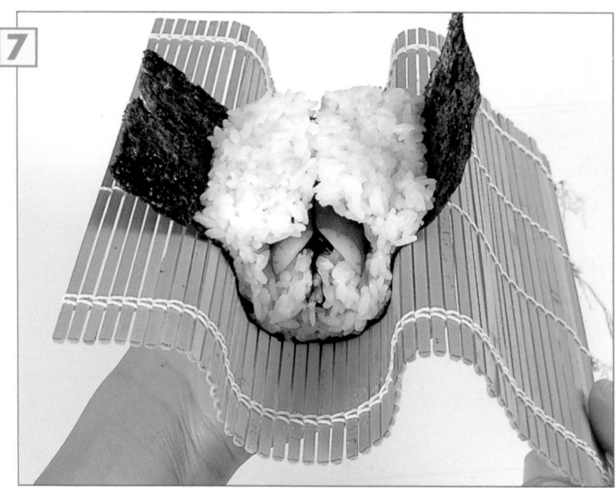

Place the mat in your palm. Round your hand, bringing the two outer peaks together. Fold the remaining nori over the rice, one side at a time.

8

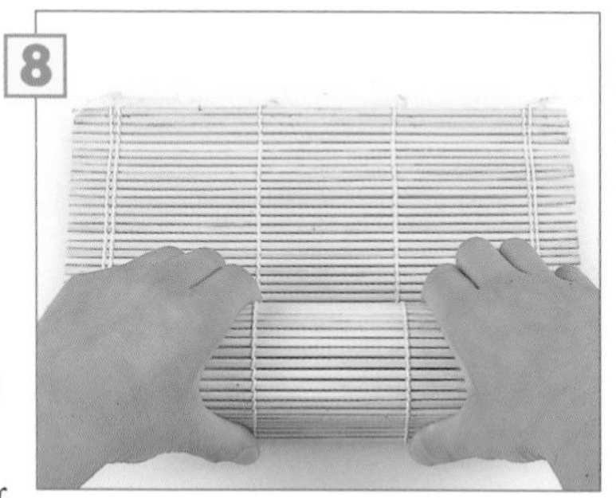

Putting the seam side down, form the roll into a tunnel shape.

9

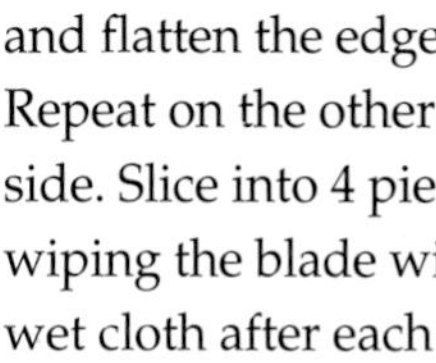

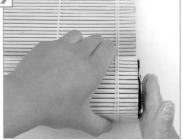

Slide the roll over to the end of the mat and flatten the edge. Repeat on the other side. Slice into 4 pieces, wiping the blade with a wet cloth after each slice.

Dandelion

(for 1 roll)

2 tsp egg sprinkles (p. 80)
$^3/_4$ oz (20 g) nozawana leaves
9 oz (250 g) sushi rice (p. 9)
Roasted nori

Setup: Squeeze out the nozawana leaves and cut into 4 $^1/_3$" (11 cm) lengths. (Blanched spinach may be substituted for the nozawana.)

1

Using 3 grains of rice, attach $^1/_3$ halfsheet to 1 halfsheet of nori (see p. 85, Fig. 4). Leaving 1" (3 cm) at both ends, evenly spread 3 1/2 oz (100 g) of the rice on the strip. Place two $^7/_5$ oz (25 g) ridges in the center of the rice, and then place two $^3/_4$ oz (20 g) ridges on each side. (There will be some rice left.) Note that the center ridges are taller than the others.

2

Spoon the egg sprinkles between the two center ridges and press into place with a chopstick. Cut two $^3/_4$" (2 cm)-wide strips from a halfsheet and press them on the insides of the center ridges *(top)*. Press the center ridges together *(above)*.

3

Cover all ridges (except the outside ridges at the edges) with the nozawana leaves.

4

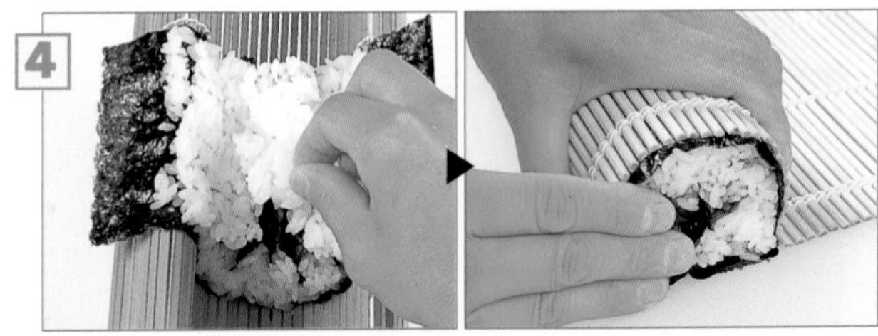

Place the mat in your palm and round your hand so that the outside ridges come together. Put the remaining rice into the center *(above left)*. Fold the nori ends over the rice and place seam side down. Form a tunnel shape and flatten the ends *(above right)*. Slice into 4 pieces.

Rose

(for 1 roll)

1 $^1/_2$ oz (40 g) cod roe
$^1/_2$ oz (15 g) red pickled ginger
2 Tbsp oboro sprinkles (p. 18)
13" (33 cm) nozawana stalks
2 thin omelets (4 x 7", 10.5 x 18 cm)
7 oz (200 g) sushi rice (p. 9)
Roasted nori

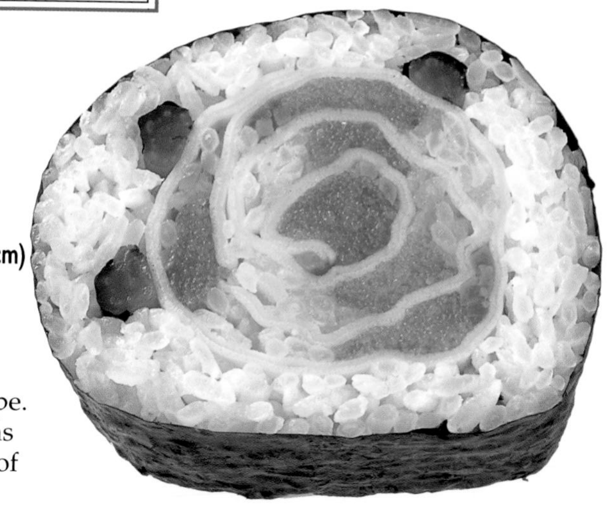

Setup: Use only the stalks of the nozawana pickles in this recipe. Cut them into 4 $^1/_3$" (11 cm) lengths. Prepare the thin omelets as for Ham and Egg, p. 74, and trim them to match the halfsheet of nori. Mix the oboro thoroughly into 3 oz (80 g) of the rice.

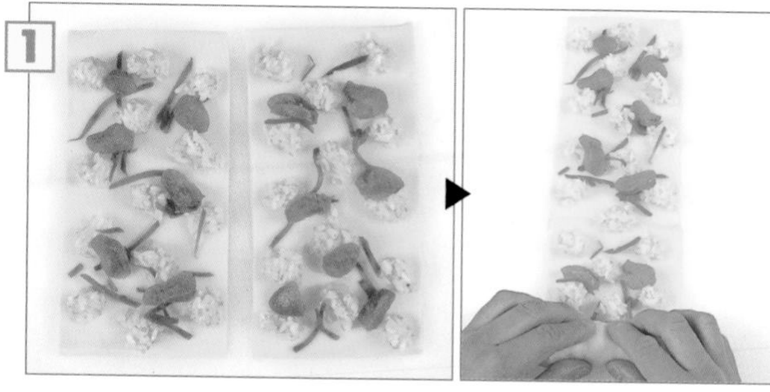

1 Place the pink rice in clumps on the omelets, then randomly scatter the roe and red ginger on top *(above left)*. Line them up together and roll tightly, as though to crush the rice *(above right)*. Squeeze the finished roll in a rolling mat and let stand in the mat.

2 With 3 grains of rice, attach $^1/_3$ halfsheet to 1 halfsheet. Spread 4 $^1/_4$ oz (120 g) of the rice on the nori, leaving 1" (3 cm) at the top. Place three $^3/_8$" (1 cm)-wide strips of nori on the rice, pressing them in with a chopstick *(above left)*. Place the nozawana stalks into the grooves *(above right)*. These will be the leaves.

3 Place the omelet roll between the second and third stalks, counting from the front.

4 Lifting the mat, roll so that the front edge meets the rice at the far edge. Finish with the seam side down and form into a tunnel shape.

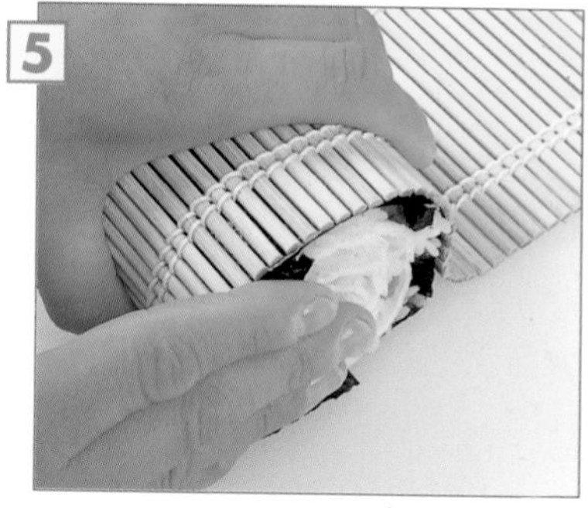

5 Slide the sushi to the ends of the mat to flatten the ends. Slice into 4 pieces, wiping the blade with a wet towel after each slice.

Plum Blossom

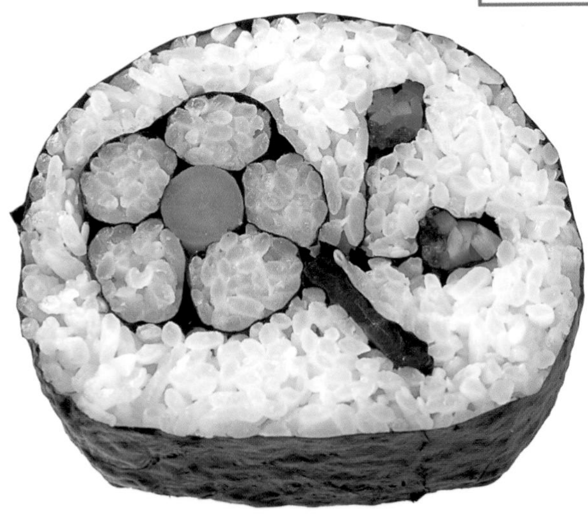

(for 1 roll)

4 $^1/_3$" (11 cm) misozuke yamagobo (miso-pickled wild burdock root)
$^1/_3$ oz (10 g) mibuna pickles
8 $^2/_3$" (22 cm) simmered gourd
$^1/_3$ oz (10 g) red pickled ginger
2 Tbsp oboro sprinkles (p. 18)
1 tsp roasted sesame seeds
10 oz (290 g) sushi rice (p. 9)
Roasted nori

Setup: Cut the mibuna pickles into 4 $^1/_3$" (11 cm) lengths. Cut the gourd strips in half crosswise. Mix the oboro thoroughly into 2 $^1/_3$ oz (65 g) of the rice. If the yamagobo is unavailable, try cutting a carrot into a long cylinder, then blanch.

1

To make the 5 petals, cut halfsheets of nori into five 2" (5 cm) -wide strips. Place $^1/_2$ oz (15 g) of the pink rice along the center of each strip.

Roll each strip as usual, then form a cylinder by folding the mat around the roll and rubbing the sides of the mat together *(left)*.

2

Place $^2/_3$ of a halfsheet of nori in the mat. Arrange the 5 cylinders of pink rice in the mat with the yamagobo in the center. Slide the roll to the edge of the mat for easier viewing during assembly *(below)*.

3

Stack the two gourd strips in the center of a $^1/_3$ halfsheet of nori. Fold the nori over as if to wrap the gourd. This package will become the branch.

Using 3 grains of rice, attach $^{1}/_{2}$ halfsheet to 1 halfsheet of nori. Spread 4 $^{1}/_{4}$ oz (120 g) of the rice on the nori, leaving 1" (3 cm) at the top. Place the rice on the nori in 3 batches *(left)* for even spreading.

Make three $^{3}/_{4}$ oz (25 g) ridges and place them below the center line. There will be 1 oz (30 g) of the rice left. Sprinkle the sesame seeds on the rice.

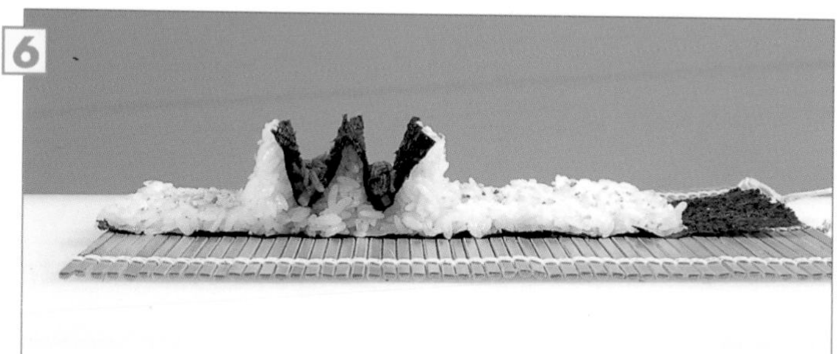

Fold two $^{1}/_{3}$ halfsheets of nori in half lengthwise. Place them in the valleys between the ridges. Put the red ginger in the folds and then the mibuna pickles. Press into place with a chopstick. These will be the buds. The chopstick pressure keeps the buds tightly formed.

Place the branch package from step 3 on the outside face of the bottom (nearest) ridge. Place the flower roll against the top (farthest) ridge.

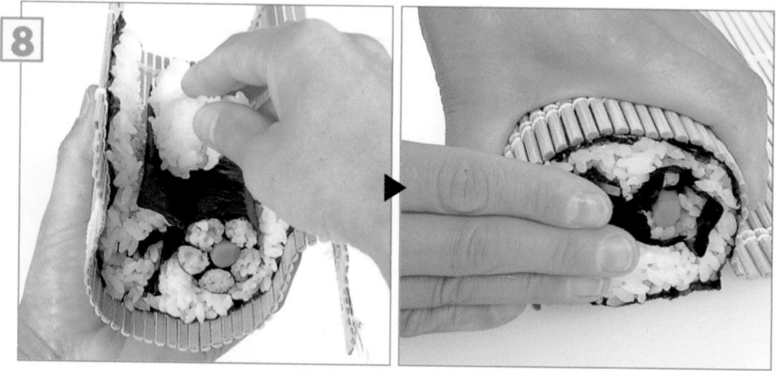

Place the mat in your hand. Curve your hand so that the branch package touches the flower roll. Cover the two exposed sides of nori with the remaining rice *(far left)* and close the roll. Place the roll seam side down and form into a tunnel shape. Slide the sushi to the ends of the mat to flatten the edges *(left)*. Slice into 4 pieces, wiping the blade with a wet towel after each slice.

Cherry Tree

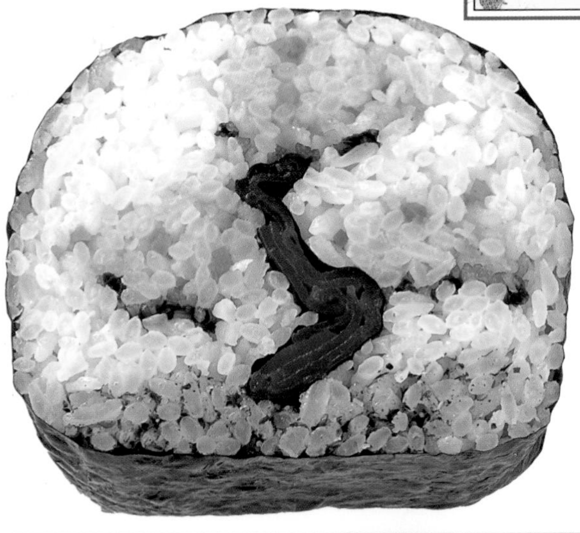

(for 1 roll)

43 1/3" (110 cm) simmered gourd (p. 17)
1/3 oz (10 g) mibuna pickles
2 Tbsp oboro sprinkles (p. 18)
Red pickled ginger
1/2 Tbsp black sesame seeds
13 oz (370 g) sushi rice (p. 9)
Roasted nori

Setup: Cut the gourd and mibuna into 4 1/3" (11 cm) lengths. Mince the red pickled ginger. Mix the oboro and ginger thoroughly into 3 oz (90 g) of the rice. Mix the grounded sesame seeds into 1 1/2 oz (40 g) of the rice.

Trunk

1

2

1. Place the gourd strips on the bottom third of a halfsheet of nori, piling up more strips at the bottom (base of the trunk) and fewer toward the top (upper branches).

2. Fold the nori over the gourd as if wrapping a package.

1

Using 3 grains of rice, attach 2/3 of a halfsheet onto 1 halfsheet of nori. Leaving 2" (5 cm) of nori at both ends, spread 3 1/4 oz (100 g) in the center of the nori. Form a cylinder with 1 1/2 oz (40 g) of the pink rice and place it in the center. Place 1/3 of the mibuna pickles on top.

2

Make a cylinder with 1 1/2 oz (40 g) of white rice and place it next to the pink cylinder. The top of the white rice should be slightly higher than the top of the pink rice. This white rice will form the space between the upper and lower branches.

Place the edge of the trunk package against the center of the pink cylinder. Spread 1 $^1/_2$ oz (40 g) of white rice to cover the pink cylinder on top and on the right side.

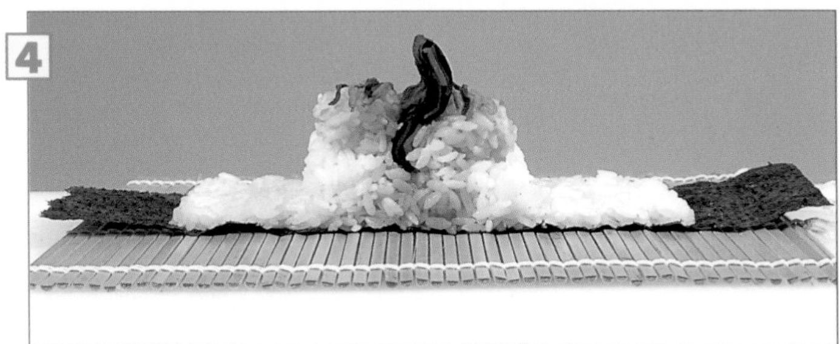

Bending the trunk slightly, spread half of the remaining pink rice on each side of the trunk. Divide the remaining mibuna pickles and place on both pink cylinders.

Place 1 $^1/_2$ oz (40 g) of white rice to the left of the trunk, bending the trunk back over the rice to make a backwards S. Place $^3/_4$ oz (20 g) of white rice to the right of the trunk. Shape the white rice to match the width of the pink rice and the height of the bent trunk.

Place the mat in your hand and bring the sides up. Cover the bottom with the black-sesame rice *(far left)*. Fold the remaining nori over the rice *(left)*. Place the roll seam side down and form into a tunnel shape. Slide the sushi to the ends of the mat to flatten the edges. Slice into 4 pieces.

Japanese Pine

1. Make green rice by mixing 1 Tbsp of aonori (green seaweed sprinkles) into 3 $^1/_2$ oz (100 g) of the rice. The mibuna pickles are not used in this recipe.
2. Assemble as for the cherry blossom tree, using the green rice in place of the pink.

Peach

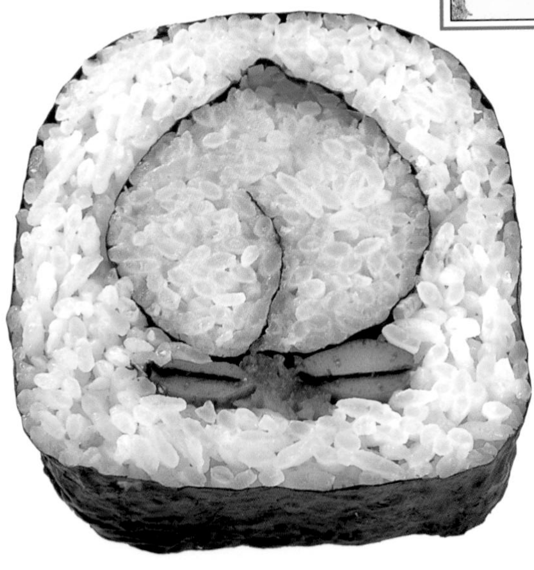

(for 1 roll)

4 1/3" (11 cm) cucumber
1/3 oz (10 g) mibuna pickles
1/2 oz (15 g) red pickled ginger
2 Tbsp oboro sprinkles (p. 18)
1 tsp roasted sesame seeds
11 1/4 oz (320 g) sushi rice (p. 9)
Roasted nori

Setup: Use a relatively straight portion of the cucumber. Squeeze the liquid from the mibuna stalks and cut to 4 1/3" (11 cm). Stir the oboro into 4 1/4 oz (120 g) of the rice.

Leaves

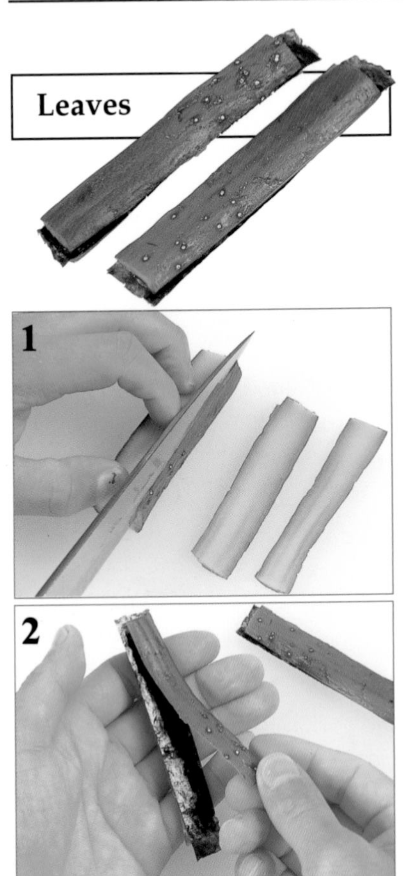

Make 4 strips of slightly rounded cucumber peel by slicing the cucumber as if to square it off (Fig. 1). Cut two nori strips and place each strip between two cucumber slices (Fig. 2).

Fruit

1. Spread the ginger in the center of one halfsheet of nori. Form a firm cylinder with the pink rice and place it on top of the ginger (Fig. 1).
2. Roll up the cylinder in the nori (Fig. 2) with the rolling mat. Seal the edge with 2–3 grains of sushi rice.
3. Following the dotted line in Fig. 3, slice about 2/3 of the way into the roll (Fig. 4). To make the curved slice, hold the knife steady and turn the roll up into the blade.
4. Insert a 1" (3 cm)-wide strip of nori into the opening. Reclose the roll in the mat, pinching the red ginger end into a point (Fig. 5).

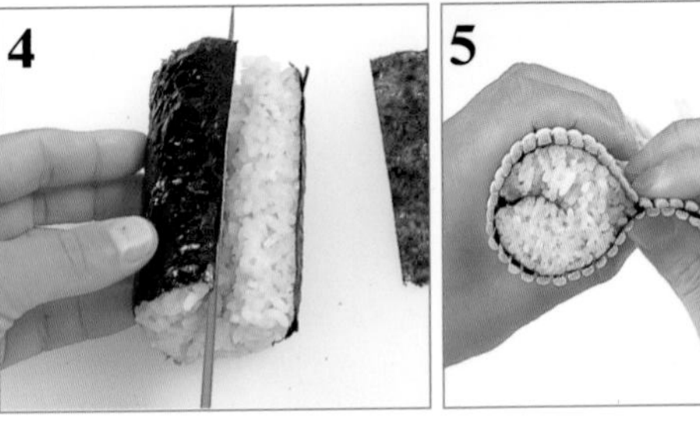

Using 3 grains of rice, attach $^1/_2$ of a halfsheet onto 1 halfsheet of nori (see p. 85, Fig. 4). Leaving 1" (3 cm) at each end, spread 3 $^1/_2$ oz (100 g) of the rice evenly on the nori. Place two $^3/_4$ oz (20 g) ridges in the center and sprinkle the sesame seeds over the whole surface. There will be 2 oz (60 g) of rice left.

Place the peach roll between the ridges, pointed end down.

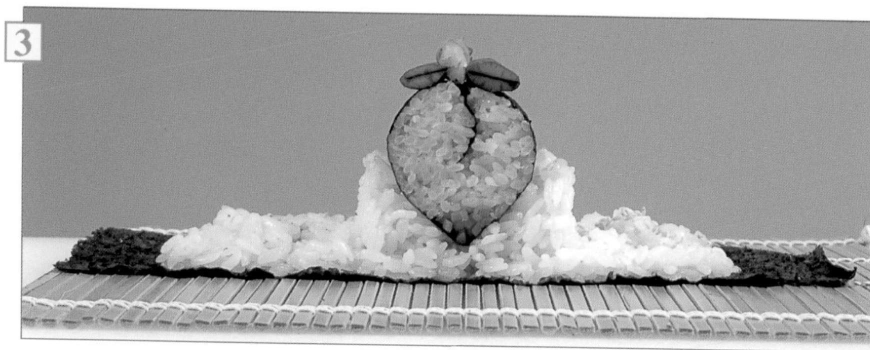

Make a line of mibuna pickles on top of the peach roll. Lay the cucumber-nori packages on either side of the mibuna.

Place the mat in the palm of your hand and bring the edges up. Tuck $^1/_4$ oz (10 g) of the rice between each cucumber package and the fruit.

Place the remaining 1 $^1/_2$ oz (40 g) of the rice over the cucumber and mibuna. Fold over the remaining nori and close.

Place the roll seam side down and form into a tunnel shape. Slide the sushi to the ends of the mat to flatten the edges. Slice into 4 pieces.

Orange

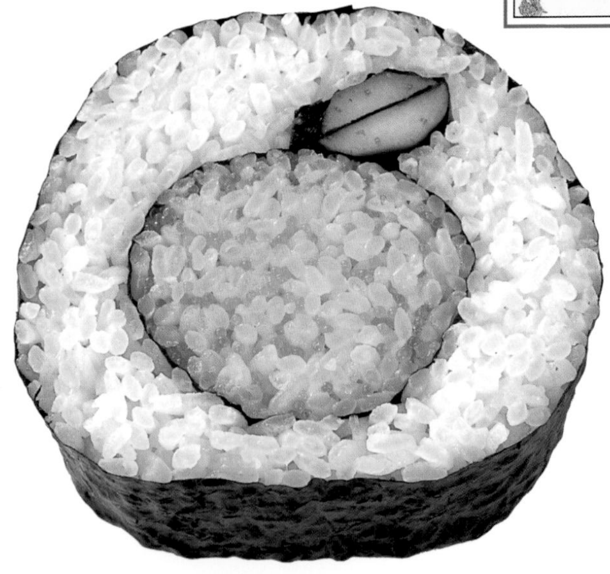

(for 1 roll)
4 1/3" (11 cm) cucumber
4 1/3" (11 cm) nozawana leaves
3 Tbsp flying-fish roe (tobiko)
10 3/4 oz (305 g) sushi rice (p. 9)
Roasted nori

Setup: Cut the 4 1/3" (11 cm) length from the straightest part of the cucumber. Stir the tobiko thoroughly into 4 1/4oz (120 g) of the rice. If flying-fish roe (tobiko) is unavailable, substitute salmon roe, or use egg sprinkles to make lemon-colored rice. If nozawana pickles are unavailable, substitute blanched spinach.

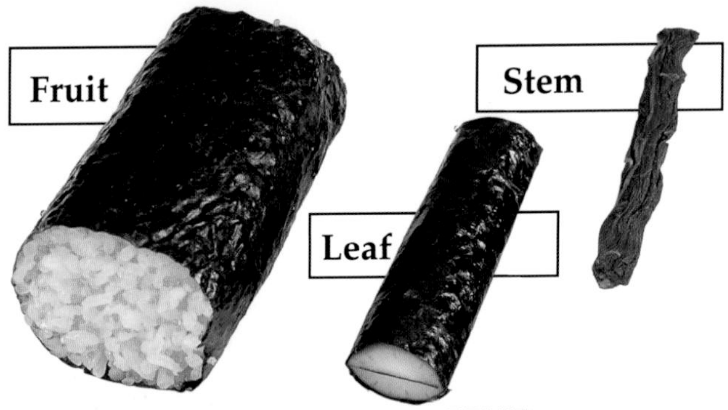

FRUIT
Place a cylinder of orange rice on a halfsheet of nori. Roll with a rolling mat and seal the end with 2–3 grains of rice.

LEAF
Cut two rounded slices of peel from the cucumber. Place a strip of nori between the slices and wrap them in 1/3 of a halfsheet of nori.

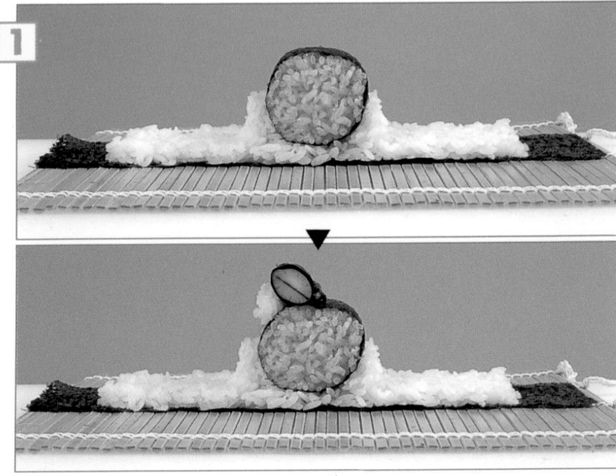

Using 3 grains of rice, attach 1/2 halfsheet onto 1 halfsheet of nori and spread with 3 1/2 oz (100 g) of the rice, leaving 1" (3 cm) at each end. Place the fruit cylinder, packing 1/2 oz (15 g) more rice on each side *(top)*. Place the nozawana (stem) and the leaf package on top, with 1/4 oz (5 g) of the rice under-neath *(above)*.

Placing the mat in your hand, bring the sides together and place 1 3/4 oz (50 g) of the rice on top. Fold the nori over the top. Place the roll seam side down and form into a tunnel shape, flatten the ends, and slice into 4 pieces.

Cherries

(for 1 roll)
1 bunch mitsuba (honewort)
1 Tbsp oboro sprinkles (p.18)
11 oz (310 g) sushi rice (p. 9)
Roasted nori

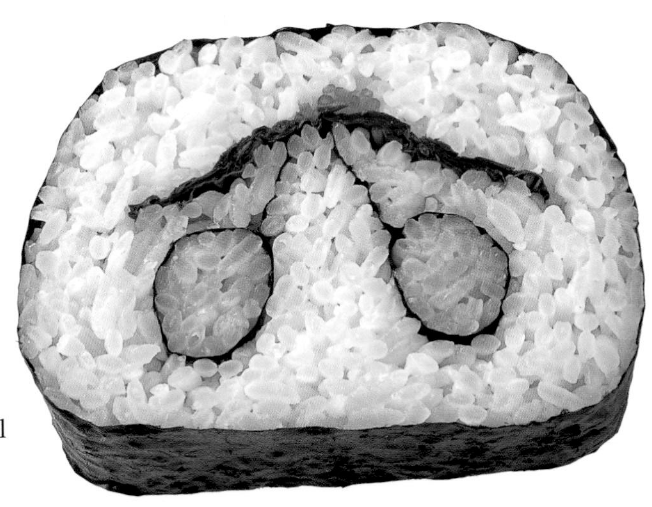

Setup: Blanch the mitsuba, plunge in cold water, squeeze well, and cut into 4 1/3" (11 cm) lengths. Mix the oboro thoroughly into 1 3/4 oz (50 g) of the rice. This pink rice will become the cherries; thin sausages may be used instead.

Cut a 3 x 7" (8 x 18 cm) rectangle from a full sheet of nori. Form the pink rice into a cylinder and place in the middle of the strip. Roll, finishing by rubbing the mat together *(p. 84, bottom left)*. Cut into two equal lengths.

Using 3 grains of rice, attach 1/3 halfsheet onto 1 halfsheet of nori *(p. 85, Fig. 4)*. Leaving 1" (3 cm) of nori at both ends, spread 3 1/2 oz (100 g) of the rice on the nori. Place a 1 3/4 oz (50 g) ridge in the center. Then place two 7/8 oz (25 g) ridges 3/4" (2 cm) above and below the first one. Fold 1/2 of a halfsheet of nori into each valley and press into shape with a chopstick. Place the pink cylinders in the valleys.

Press the ridges together *(top)* and arrange the mitsuba over the top *(above)*.

Place the mat in your hand and bring the sides together. Put 3/4 oz (20 g) of the rice on each side (*left*) and an additional 3/4 oz (20 g) in the middle. Fold the nori over the rice. Place the roll seam side down, form into a tunnel shape, flatten the ends, and slice into 4 pieces.

Panda

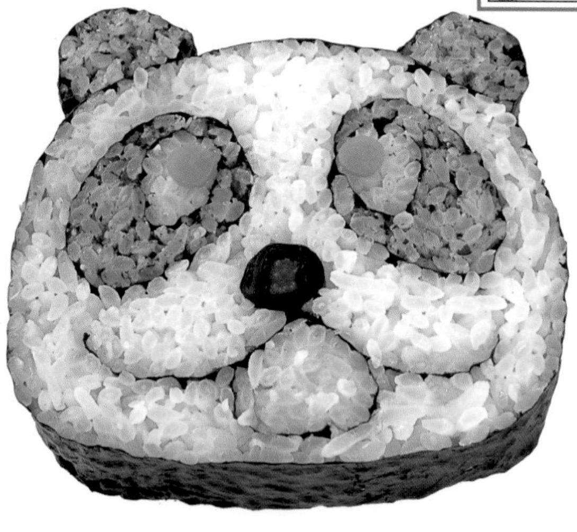

(for 1 roll)
13 in (33 cm) simmered gourd (p. 17)
4 $^1/_3$" (11 cm) nozawana stalks
Small piece misozuke yamagobo
$^1/_2$ Tbsp oboro sprinkles (p.18)
1 tsp yukari sprinkles
1 $^1/_2$ Tbsp black sesame seeds
17 oz (480 g) sushi rice (p. 9)
Roasted nori

Setup: Prepare the gourd as on p.17 and cut into 4 $^1/_3$" (11 cm) lengths. For the pink rice, mix the oboro thoroughly into 1 oz (30 g) of the rice. For the black rice, grind the black sesame seeds and mix with the yukari into 4 $^1/_2$ oz (130 g) of the rice.

Eyes

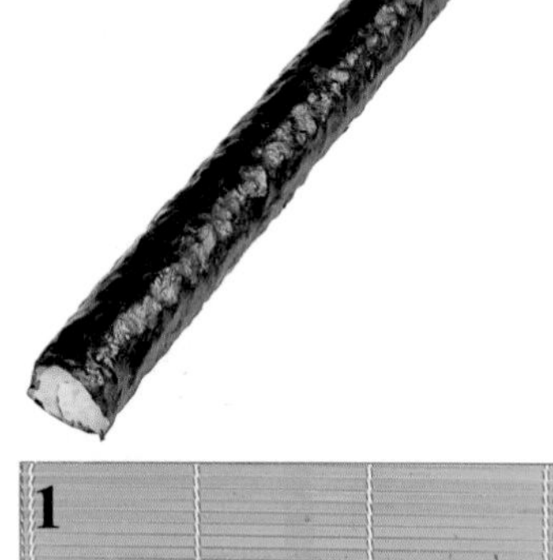

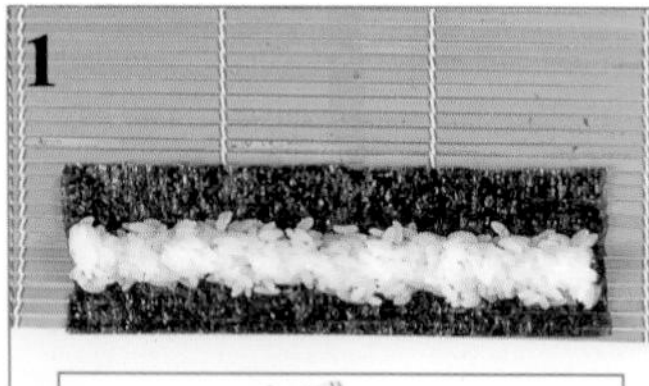

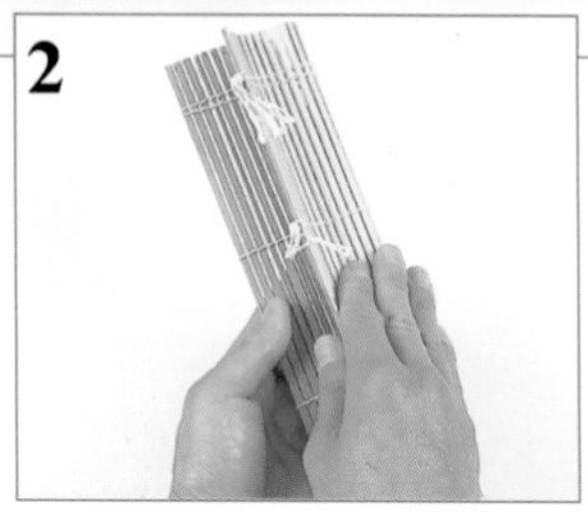

Cut $^1/_4$ of a full sheet of nori horizontally. Place 1 $^1/_2$ oz (40 g) rice in a line in the center (Fig. 1). Roll, then finish the cylinder by folding the mat around the roll and rubbing the sides of the mat together (Fig. 2).

Nose

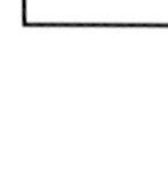

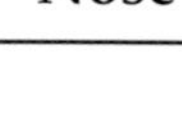

Spread the gourd on $^1/_2$ of a halfsheet. Place the nozawana stalk at the bottom (Fig. 1). Roll by hand (Fig. 2).

Cheeks

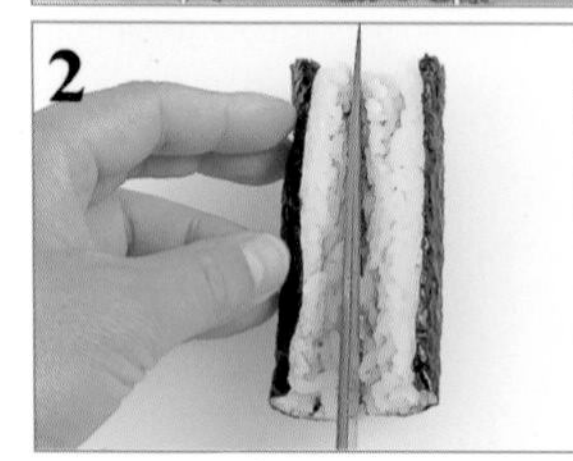

Place a 1 $^4/_3$ oz (50 g) cylinder of the rice on $^1/_2$ of a halfsheet (Fig. 1). Roll with a mat, then cut in half lengthwise (Fig. 2).

Mouth

Form the pink rice into a cylinder and place on $^1/_3$ of a halfsheet (Fig. 1). Using the rolling mat, press into a round teardrop (Fig. 2).

1

Spread 2 $^1/_2$ oz (70 g) of the black rice on $^2/_3$ of a full sheet of nori, leaving 1" (3 cm) at the top. With $^1/_3$ oz (10 g) of the black rice, make a low hill in the center. Place the eye cylinder on top *(above)*. Roll into an oval with the mat *(left)*. Cut into two equal lengths.

2

Using 3 grains of rice, attach $^2/_3$ halfsheet onto 1 halfsheet of nori *(p. 85, Fig. 4)*. Leaving 1" (3 cm) at both ends, spread 4 $^1/_4$ oz (120 g) of the rice on the nori. Place a $^3/_4$ oz (20 g) ridge in the center. Place one eye cylinder on each side of the ridge, white circles inward *(Fig. 2, top)*. Place another $^3/_4$ oz (20 g) of the rice between the eyes and put the nose on top *(Fig. 2, middle)*. Place $^1/_2$ oz (15 g) on top of each eye to match the height of the nose *(Fig. 2, bottom)*.

3

Place the cheeks on top, rice side down. Put the pink mouth between them, pointed side down.

4

Use 1 $^1/_2$ oz (40 g) rice to cover the nose and cheeks. Place the mat in your hand and bring the sides together, folding the nori over the rice. Place the roll seam side down, form into a tunnel shape, flatten the ends, and slice into 4 pieces.

5

To make the ears, place a cylinder of the remaining black rice on $^1/_2$ of a halfsheet of nori *(above left)*. Roll into an oval shape, slice in half lengthwise, then cut into 4 lengths *(above right)*.

6

Place the ears on the panda's head. Slice the yamagobo into thin rounds and place on the eye circles.

Dragonfly

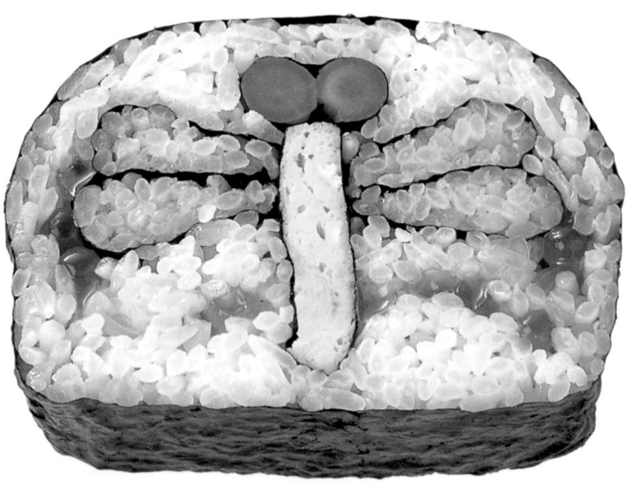

(for 1 roll)
8 2/3" (22 cm) misozuke yamagobo
1 omelet, 3/8" (1 cm) thick
1 1/2 oz (40 g) salmon roe
1 1/2 Tbsp oboro sprinkles (p. 18)
10 1/2 oz (300 g) sushi rice (p. 9)
Roasted nori

Setup: Cut the yamagobo into two equal lengths. (If yamagobo is not available, peel carrots down to size and boil with sugar and soy sauce.) Make the omelet as on p. 19. Mix the oboro thoroughly into 3 oz (80 g) of the rice.

Wings

1. Slice a full sheet of nori into thirds horizontally. Spread half of the pink rice on the top half of the nori, leaving 1/5" (5 mm) from the top (Fig. 1).
2. Folding the bottom half over the top half, make a thin teardrop shape (Fig. 2).
3. Make a second teardrop and press it to the first (Fig. 2). Cut into two equal lengths.

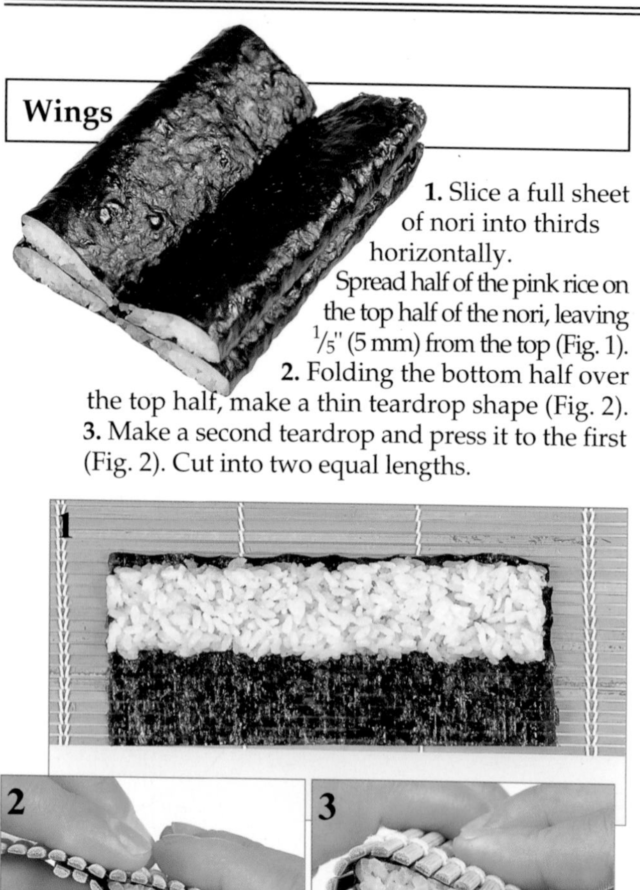

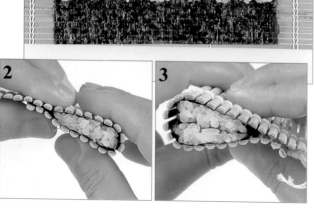

Body

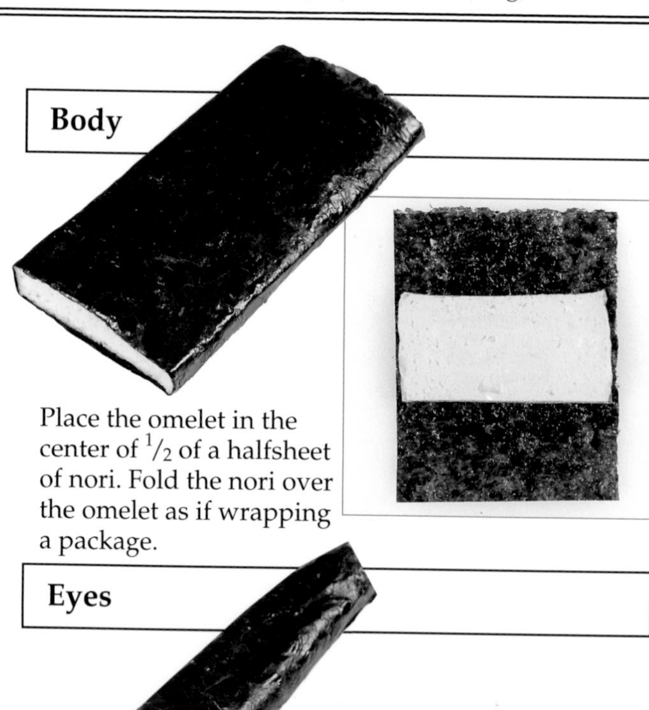

Place the omelet in the center of 1/2 of a halfsheet of nori. Fold the nori over the omelet as if wrapping a package.

Eyes

Place 1 length of yamagobo just below the center of 1/2 of a halfsheet and begin rolling. Incorporate the other length of yamagobo into the roll *(right)*. Seal with 2–3 grains of rice.

Using 3 grains of rice, attach a $^1/_2$ half-sheet onto 1 halfsheet of nori (see p. 85, Fig. 4). Spread 3 $^1/_2$ oz (100 g) of the rice on the nori, leaving 1" (3 cm) at both ends. Place the eyes in the center and add two $^1/_4$ oz (10 g) cylinders of the rice on either side.

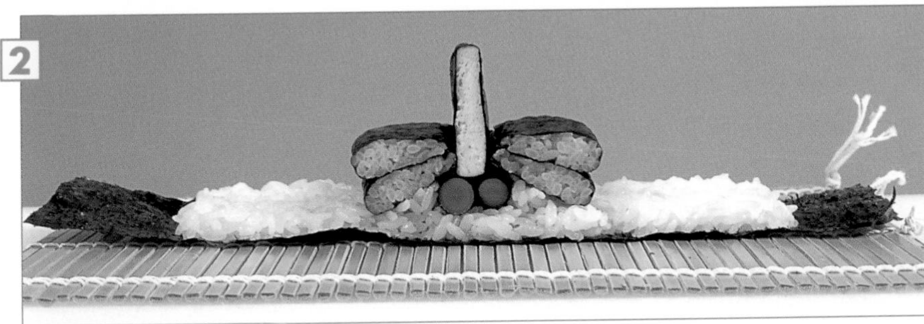

Center the body on top of the eyes. Place the wings on either side of the body to hold it in place, pointing the lower wing down so that the upper wing is parallel to the board.

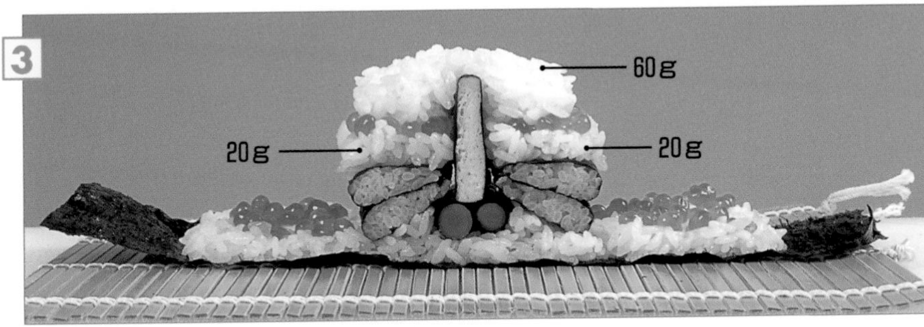

Spread $^3/_4$ oz (20 g) of the rice on top of each wing. Spread the salmon roe on top and on the surface of the original layer of rice. Place 2 oz (60 g) of the rice to cover the roe and the body. (The salmon roe forms a sunset behind the dragonfly.)

Lifting the mat with both hands, fold the sides together so that the original layer of rice meets the top layer of rice.

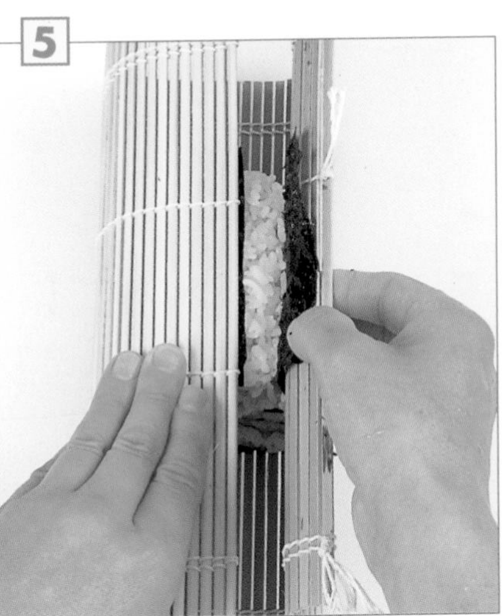

Fold the nori over, one side at a time. Place the roll seam side down and form into a tunnel shape.

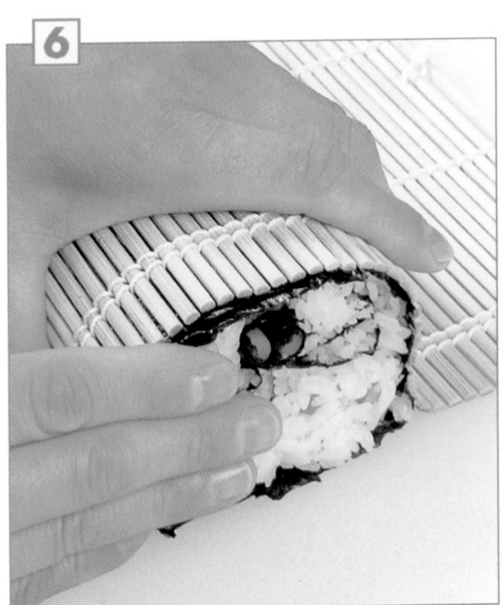

Slide the sushi to the ends of the mat to flatten the ends. Slice into 4 pieces, wiping the blade with a wet towel after each slice.

Butterfly

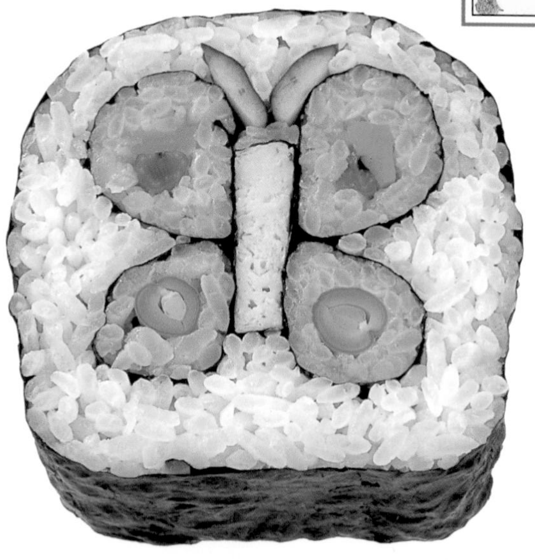

(for 1 roll)

1 omelet, $^{3}/_{8}$" (1 cm)-thick
4 $^{1}/_{3}$" (11 cm) cucumber
8 $^{2}/_{3}$" (22 cm) nozawana stalks
4 $^{1}/_{3}$" (11 cm) takuan
2 string beans
1 $^{1}/_{2}$ oz (40 g) cod roe
1 $^{1}/_{2}$ Tbsp oboro sprinkles (p. 18)
9 $^{1}/_{2}$ oz (270 g) sushi rice (p. 9)
Roasted nori

Setup: Prepare the omelet as on p. 19. Cut the takuan into two thin sticks. Blanch the string beans and cut to match the takuan. Remove the roe from its sac and mix thoroughly, together with the oboro, into 2 $^{1}/_{2}$ oz (70 g) of the rice.

Wings

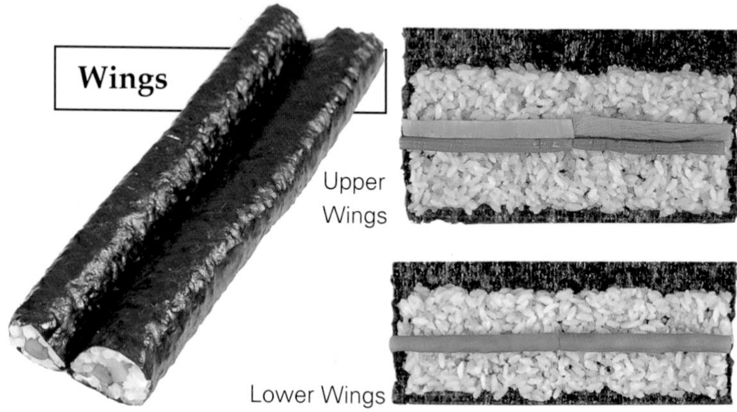

Upper Wings Cut a 4 $^{1}/_{3}$" (11 cm)-wide horizontal strip from a full sheet of nori. Spread 3 oz (80 g) of the pink rice on the nori, leaving $^{3}/_{8}$" (1 cm) at the top. Place the nozawana and takuan in the center and lift the edge of the mat (Fig. 1) over the rice, pressing into a teardrop shape (Fig. 2).
Lower Wings Cut a 3 $^{1}/_{2}$" (9 cm)-wide strip from a full sheet of nori, spread with the remaining pink rice, and fold into a teardrop with the green beans.

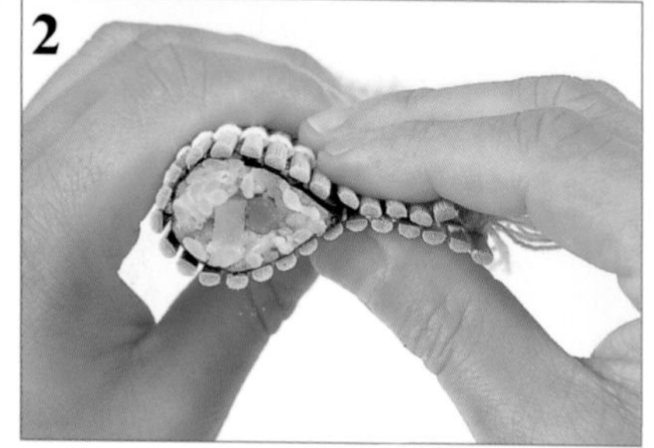

Body

Place the omelet on $^{1}/_{2}$ of a halfsheet. Wrap.

Antennae

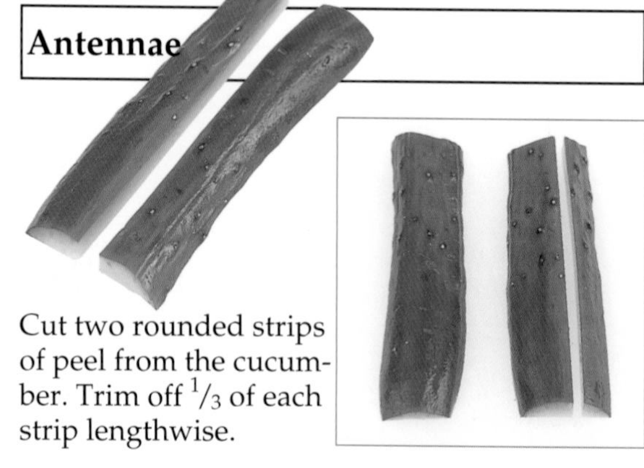

Cut two rounded strips of peel from the cucumber. Trim off $^{1}/_{3}$ of each strip lengthwise.

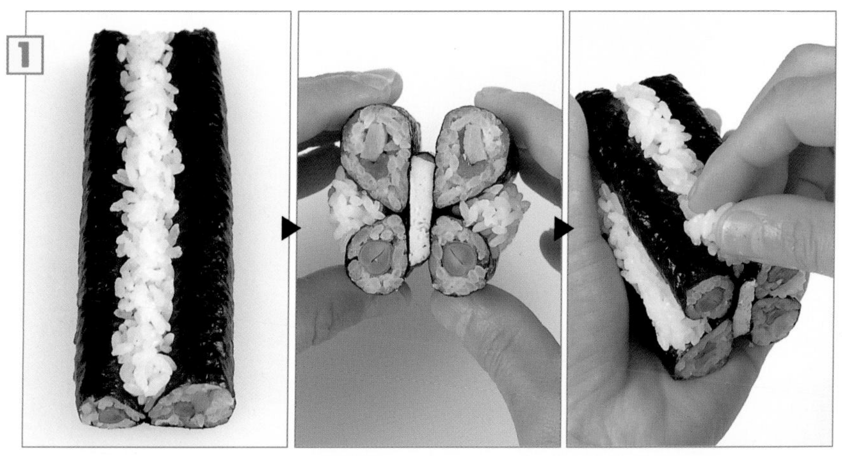

1 Lay the upper and lower wing pieces next to each other, pointed edges touching. Place $1\frac{1}{2}$ oz (40 g) of the rice along the seam *(far left)*. Cut into two equal lengths. Put the two lengths together, with the body package between them *(middle)*. Pack $\frac{1}{4}$ oz (10 g) of the rice between the lower wings *(left)*. This will keep the wings from separating from the body.

2 Using 3 grains of rice, attach $\frac{1}{2}$ halfsheet onto 1 halfsheet of nori (see p. 85, Fig. 4). Leaving 1" (3 cm) at the top and bottom, spread $4\frac{1}{4}$ oz (120 g) of the rice evenly on the nori. Pinch the rice along the center to form a ridge *(left, upper photo)*. Place the cucumber slices on the ridge, peel side down, with the trimmed edges at the top *(left, lower photo)*.

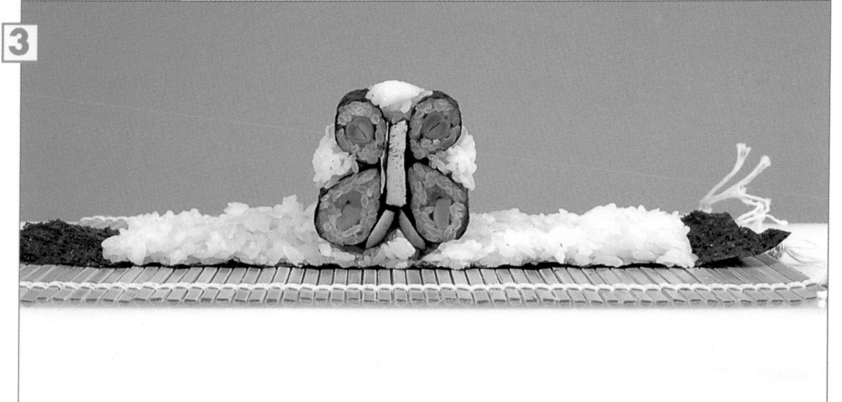

3 Place the butterfly upside down on the ridge, so that the cucumbers touch the body.

4 Place the mat in your hand, bringing the sides together, and spread the remaining 1 oz (30 g) of the rice to cover the lower wings. Fold the nori over the rice. Place the roll seam side down and form into a tunnel shape.

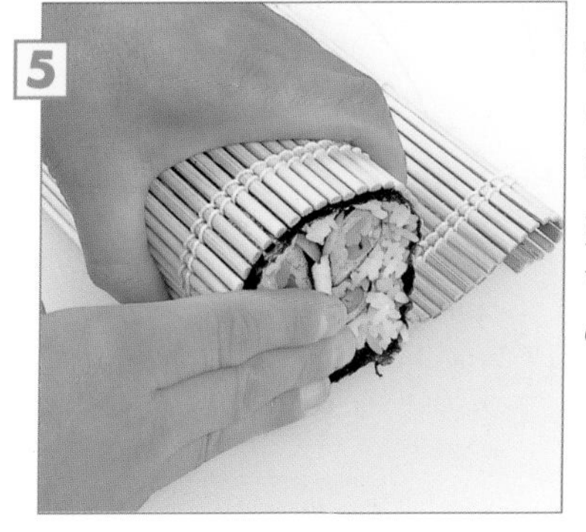

5 Slide the sushi to the ends of the mat to flatten the edges. Slice into 4 pieces, wiping the blade with a wet towel after each slice.

Crab

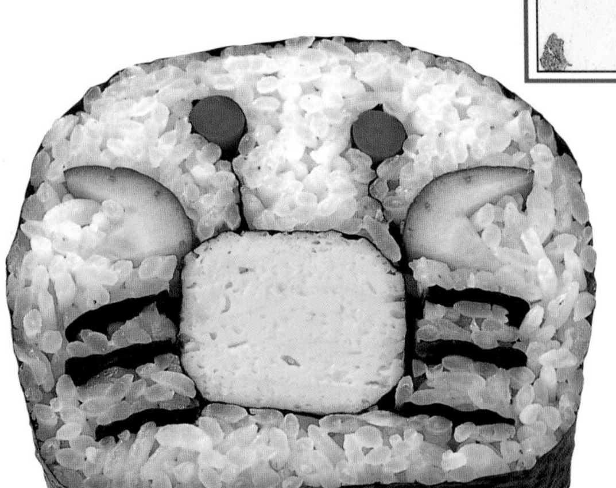

(for 1 roll)
4 1/3" (11 cm) cucumber
8 2/3" (22 cm) misozuke yamagobo
1 omelet, 1 1/3" (3.5 cm) square
26" (66 cm) simmered gourd (p. 17)
9 oz (255 g) sushi rice (p. 9)
Roasted nori

Setup: Prepare the omelet as on p. 19. Choose a relatively thick, straight Japanese cucumber. Cut the yamagobo and gourd into 4 1/3" (11 cm) lengths.

Pincers

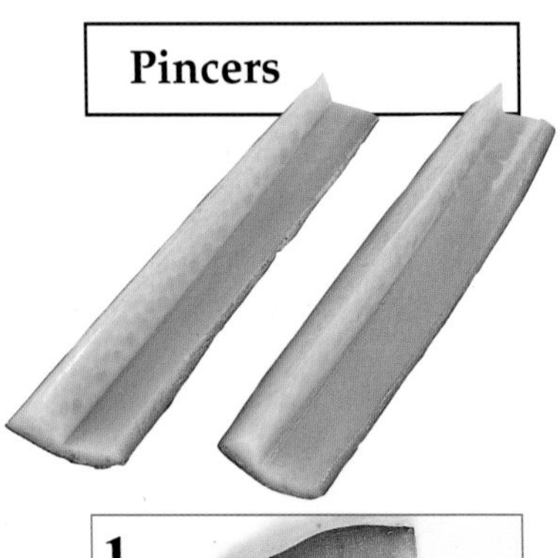

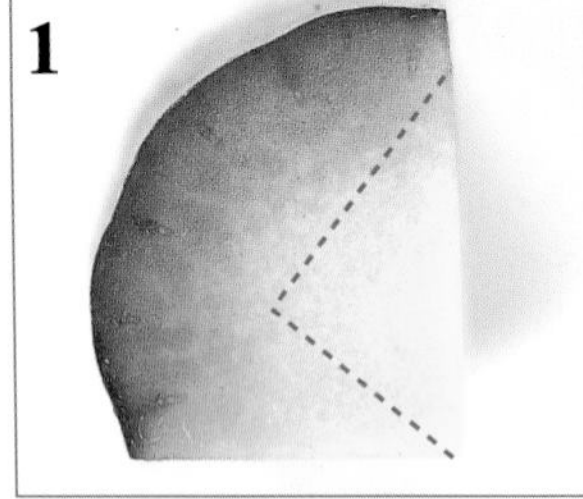

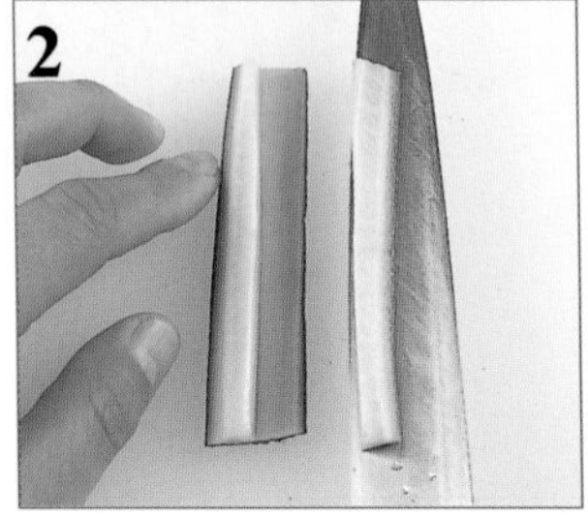

Quarter the cucumber lengthwise. Cut a V shape from one quarter as shown above. Repeat with another quarter.

Body

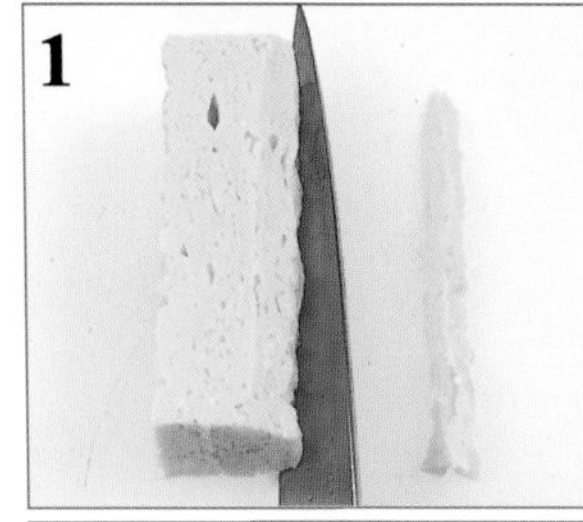

Trim off the four corners of the omelet (Fig. 1) and wrap in 2/3 of a halfsheet of nori (Fig. 2).

Legs

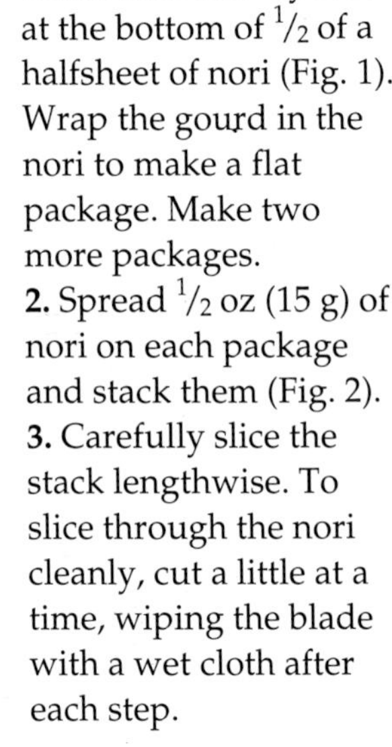

1. Place two gourd strips in 1" (3 cm) widthwide side by side at the bottom of 1/2 of a halfsheet of nori (Fig. 1). Wrap the gourd in the nori to make a flat package. Make two more packages.
2. Spread 1/2 oz (15 g) of nori on each package and stack them (Fig. 2).
3. Carefully slice the stack lengthwise. To slice through the nori cleanly, cut a little at a time, wiping the blade with a wet cloth after each step.

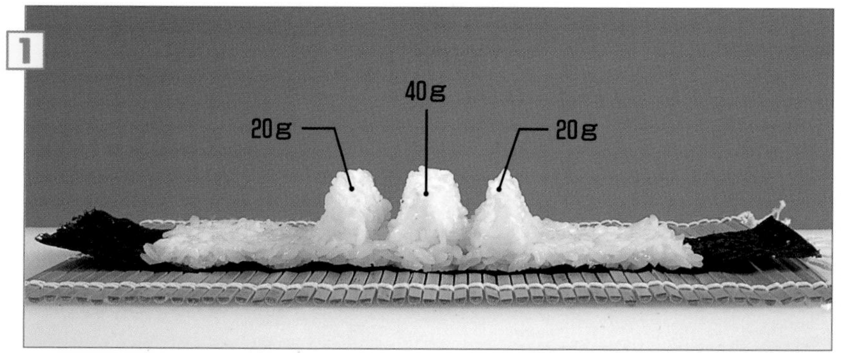

Using 3 grains of rice, attach $^1/_2$ halfsheet onto 1 halfsheet of nori (see p. 85, Fig. 4). Leaving 1 $^1/_2$" (4 cm) at both ends, spread 3 $^1/_2$ oz (100g) of the rice evenly on the nori. Make a ridge with 1 $^1/_2$ oz (40 g) of the rice and place it in the center. Place one $^3/_4$ oz (20 g) ridge on each side. Flatten the center ridge so that all three are the same height.

Cut two 2" (5 cm) strips from a halfsheet of nori. Fold in half and place in the valleys between the ridges. Press into place with a chopstick and insert the yamagobo. These will be the eyes.

Assemble the legs and body by placing the cut edge of the legs next to the body *(far left).* Place the rolling mat in your hand and bring the sides together so that the ridges meet. Place the cucumbers next to the ridges, Vs pointing outward *(left).*

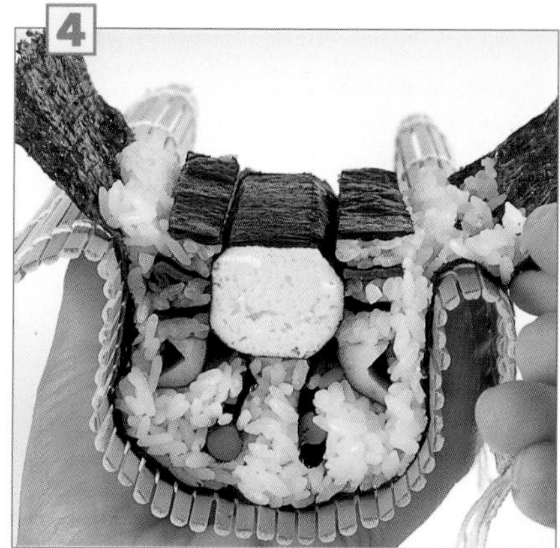

Place the body-and-legs assembly upside down in the mat.

Spread the remaining 1 oz (30 g) of the rice over the body and legs. Fold the nori over the rice. Place the roll seam side down and form into a tunnel shape.

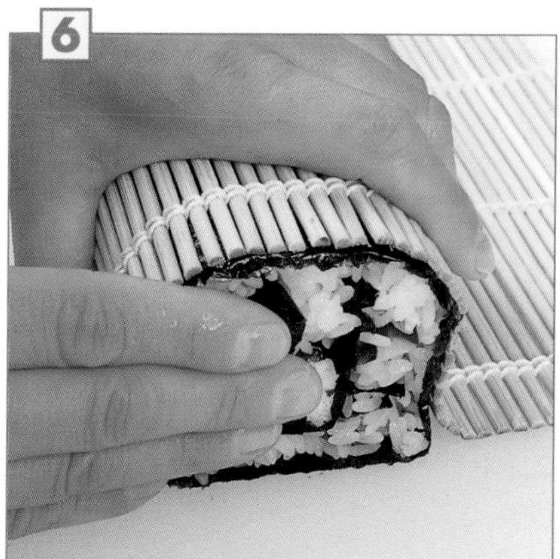

Slide the sushi to the ends of the mat to flatten the edges. Slice into 4 pieces, wiping the blade with a wet towel after each slice.

Snail

(for 1 roll)

1 omelet, $^1/_5$" (5 mm) thick
30 $^1/_3$" (77 cm) simmered gourd (p. 17)
8 $^2/_3$" (22 cm) misozuke yamagobo
1 $^1/_2$ Tbsp oboro sprinkles (p. 18)
11 oz (315 g) sushi rice (p. 9)
Roasted nori

Setup: Cut the gourd into 7 equal lengths. Prepare the omelet as shown on p. 19. Mix the oboro thoroughly into 2 $^1/_2$ oz (70 g) of the rice.

Body

Place the omelet on $^1/_2$ halfsheet of nori (Fig. 1) and wrap (Fig. 2).

Shell

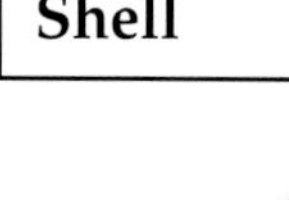

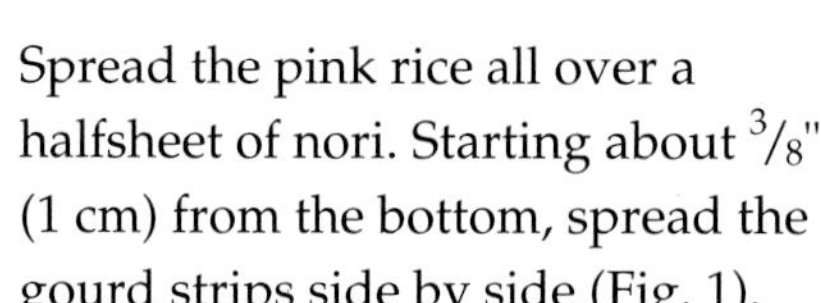

Spread the pink rice all over a halfsheet of nori. Starting about $^3/_8$" (1 cm) from the bottom, spread the gourd strips side by side (Fig. 1).

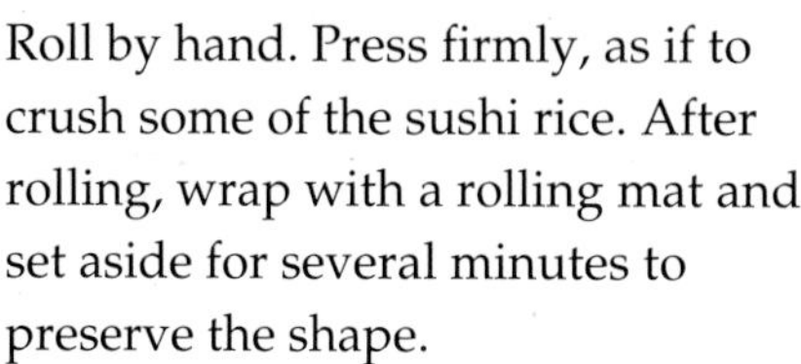

Roll by hand. Press firmly, as if to crush some of the sushi rice. After rolling, wrap with a rolling mat and set aside for several minutes to preserve the shape.

1

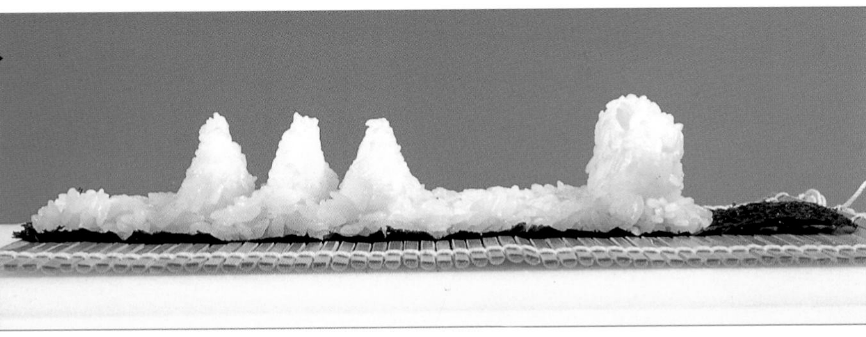

Using 3 grains of rice, attach $^1/_2$ halfsheet onto 1 halfsheet of nori (see p. 85, Fig. 4). Leaving 1" (3 cm) at the top, spread 4 $^1/_4$ oz (120 g) of the rice on the nori. Place one $^3/_4$ oz (25 g) ridge in the center, then place two more ridges below the first. Place the remaining 2 oz (50 g) in a cylinder on the top edge of the rice.

2

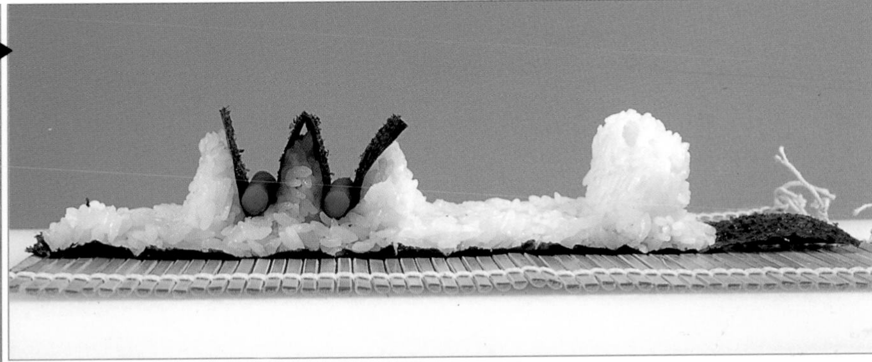

Cut two 2 $^3/_4$" (7 cm) strips from a halfsheet of nori. Fold them in half and place in the valleys. Insert the yamagobo in the folds. These will be the eyes.

3

Holding the shell roll seam side up, place it next to the first ridge you placed on the rice. Place the body package on top.

4

Lift the edge of the mat and begin rolling so that the front edge of rice meets the top of the cylinder that was in back. Continue rolling, ending with the seam side down, and form into a tunnel shape.

5

Slide the sushi to the ends of the mat to flatten the edges. Slice into 4 pieces, wiping the blade with a wet towel after each slice.

Frog

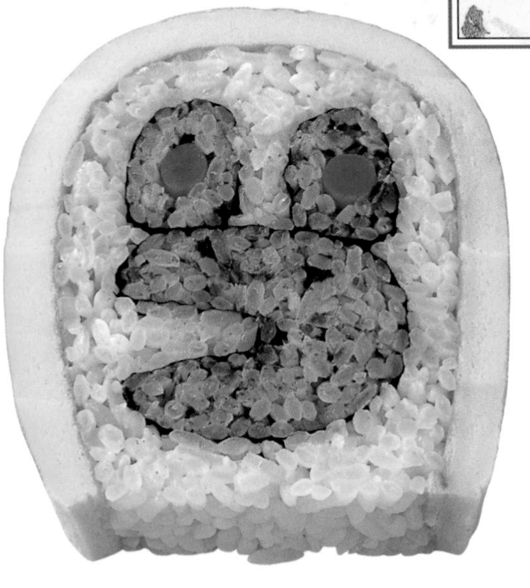

(for 1 roll)

8 2/3" (22 cm) misozuke yamagobo
1/3 oz (10 g) mibuna pickles
1 1/2 Tbsp aonori sprinkles
1 omelet sheet (p. 23)
11 3/4 oz (330 g) sushi rice (p. 9)
Roasted nori

Setup: Trim the omelet sheet to 4 x 8" (10.5 x 20 cm). Cut the yamagobo into two equal lengths. Mince the mibuna pickles. Stir the mibuna and aonori (green seaweed sprinkles) thoroughly into 5 1/4 oz (150 g) of the sushi rice. (Boiled pared carrot and steamed spinach may be substituted for the misozuke and mibuna pickles.)

Eyes

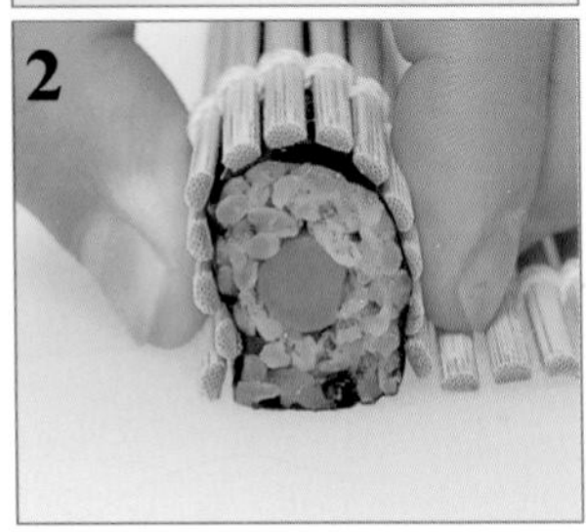

Cut a 3" (8 cm) strip horizontally from a full sheet of nori. Spread with 1 3/4 oz (50 g) of the green rice, leaving 3/8" (1 cm) at the top. Place the yamagobo in the center (Fig. 1). Roll as for hosomaki, finishing with the seam side down and shaping into a narrow tunnel (Fig. 2).

Mouth

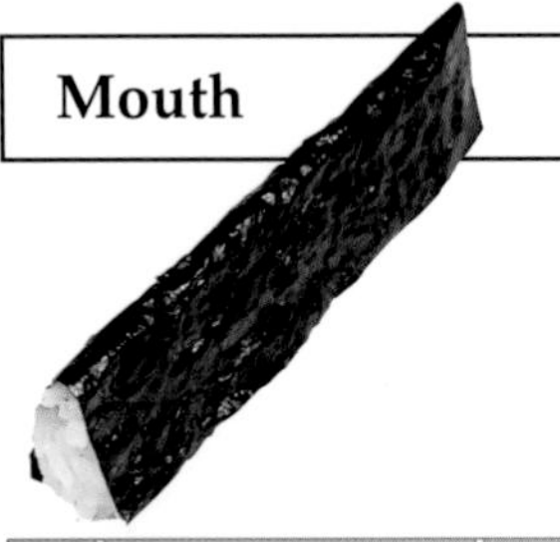

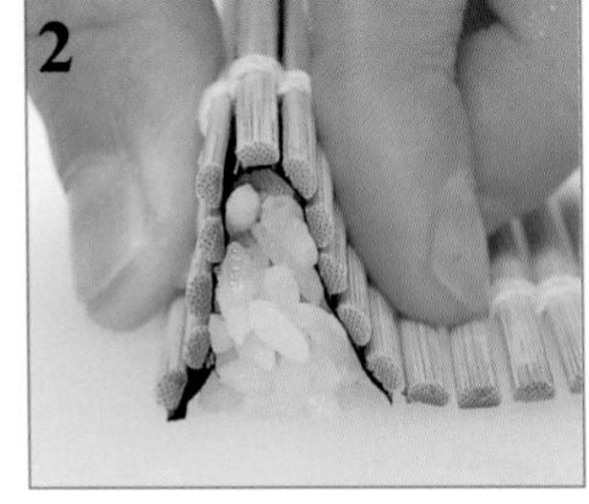

Cut a 2" (5 cm) strip horizontally from a halfsheet of nori. Spread 3/4 oz (20 g) of the white rice in a wedge on the back half of the strip (Fig. 1). Fold the nori up to meet the rice and press into a triangle with the mat (Fig. 2).

Face

1. Gather the remaining green rice into a cylinder and place it at the bottom of 2/3 of nori (Fig. 1).
2. Lift the bottom edge of the mat (Fig. 2) and roll into a round shape.
3. Use your fingertips to flatten the sides of the circle (Fig. 3).

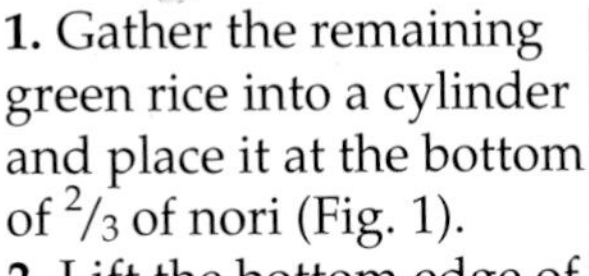

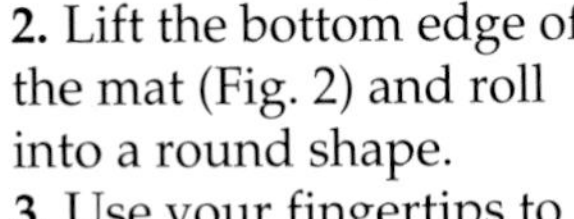

Make a 1" (3 cm)-deep cut into one short side of the flattened circle *(far left)*. Insert the mouth triangle into the opening *(middle left)*. Using a mat, restore the roll to its flattened-circle shape.

Place the omelet sheet vertically on the mat. Spread 3 oz (80 g) of the rice on the omelet, leaving 1" (3 cm) at the top and bottom. Place a $^{3}/_{4}$ oz (20 g) ridge in the center.

Cut the eye roll into two equal lengths. Place the lengths on both sides of the ridge, seam side down. Place the face roll on top.

Place the mat in your hand and bring the sides together. Spread the remaining 2 oz (60 g) of the rice on top of the face roll.

Place the roll and mat on a board, rice side down, and form into a tunnel shape. Slide the sushi to the ends of the mat to flatten the edges.

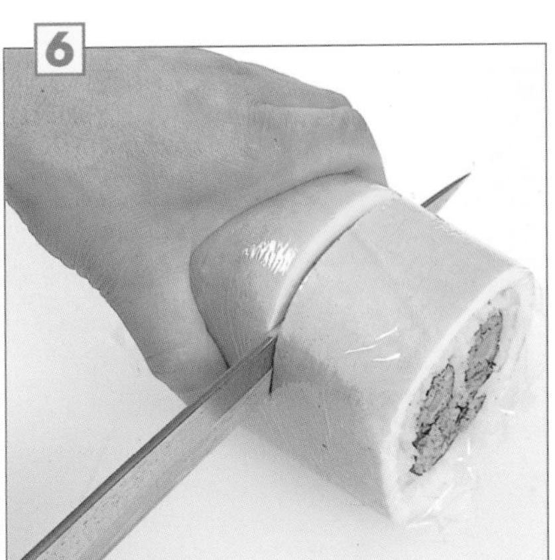

Drape the roll with plastic wrap and slice into 4 pieces, wiping the blade with a wet towel after each slice.

Ladybug

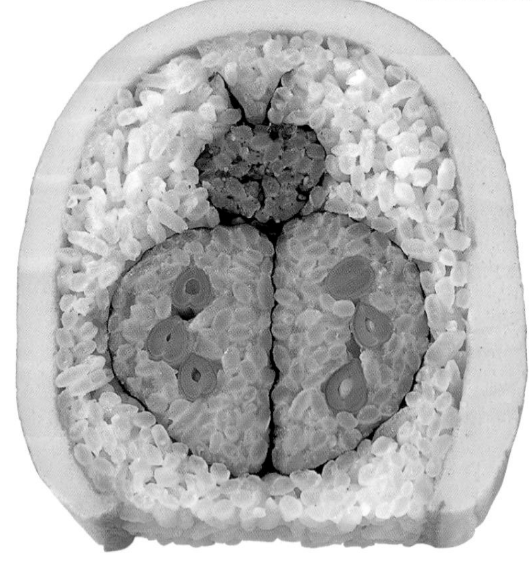

(for 1 roll)
6 string beans
1 $^{1}/_{2}$ oz (40 g) cod roe
1 tsp black sesame seeds
1 omelet sheet (p. 23)
11 oz (310 g) sushi rice (p. 9)
Roasted nori

Setup: Blanch the green beans and cut into 4 $^{1}/_{3}$" (11 cm) lengths. Trim the omelet sheet to 4 x 8" (10.5 x 20 cm). For red rice, mix the cod roe thoroughly into 3 oz (80 g) of the sushi rice. For black rice, grind the black sesame seeds and mix them into $^{3}/_{4}$ oz (20 g) of the sushi rice.

Wings

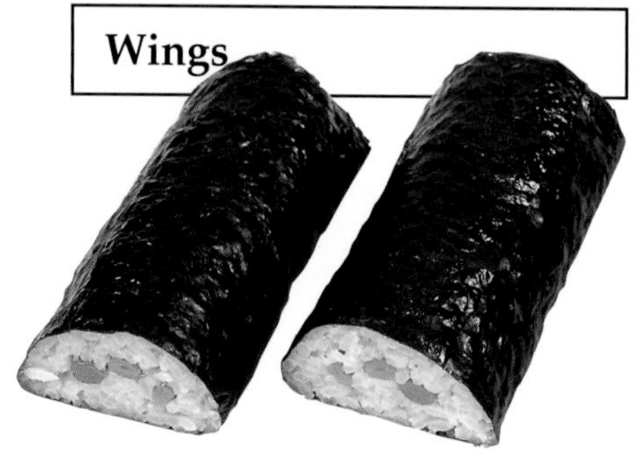

1. Place $^{2}/_{3}$ of a full sheet of nori horizontally on the mat. Spread 3 oz (80 g) of the red rice on the bottom third. Make 3 grooves in the rice with a chopstick (Fig. 1).
2. Place the beans in the grooves (Fig. 2) and place the remaining red rice on top (Fig. 3).
3. Roll (Fig. 4), ending with the seam side down. Form into a half moon (Fig. 5) and slice into two equal lengths.

1

2

3

4

5
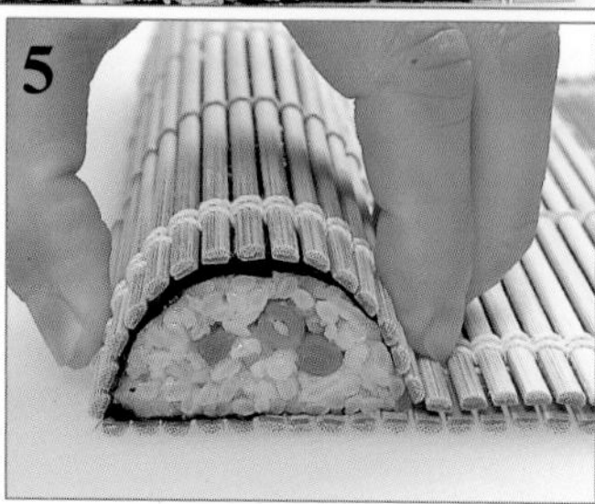

Head

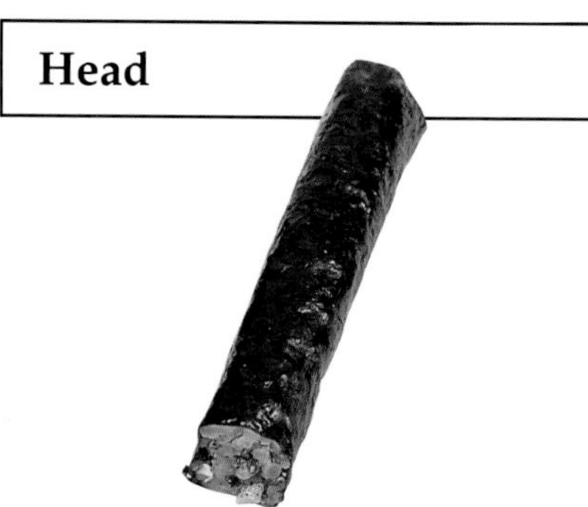

Form the black rice into a cylinder and place on $^{1}/_{3}$ of a halfsheet of nori (Fig. 1). Roll, ending with the seam side down. Form into a tunnel shape (Fig. 2).

1

2

Place the omelet sheet lengthwise on the mat. Leaving 1" (3 cm) at the top and bottom, spread 3 $^{1}/_{2}$ oz (100 g) of the white rice evenly on the omelet. Place a small $^{1}/_{4}$ oz (10 g) ridge in the center. Cut a $^{3}/_{4}$" (2 cm)-wide strip from a halfsheet of nori, fold it in half, and place it on top of the ridge. This nori will become the antennae.

Place the head on the ridge, seam side down. Pack 1 oz (30 g) of the rice on each side of the head.

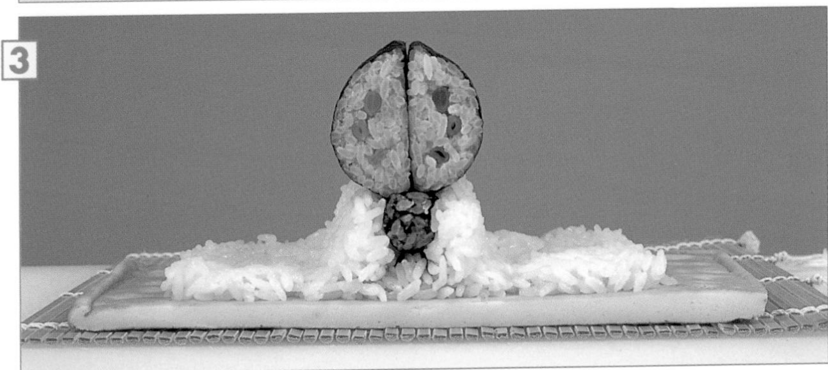

Place the wings, flat sides together, on top of the head.

Holding the mat in your hand, bring the two sides together. Place the remaining 1 $^{1}/_{2}$ oz (40 g) of rice on top, starting with the space above each wing and finishing with the center.

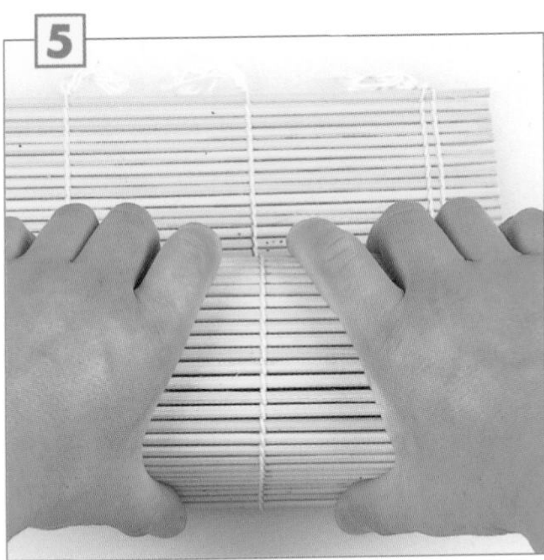

Place the roll and mat on a board, rice side down, and form into a tunnel shape.

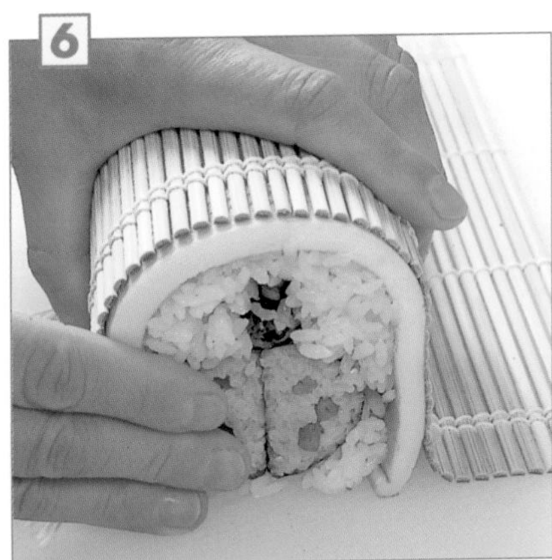

Slide the sushi to the ends of the mat to flatten the edges. Drape the roll with plastic wrap and slice into 4 pieces, wiping the blade with a wet towel after each slice.

Fish

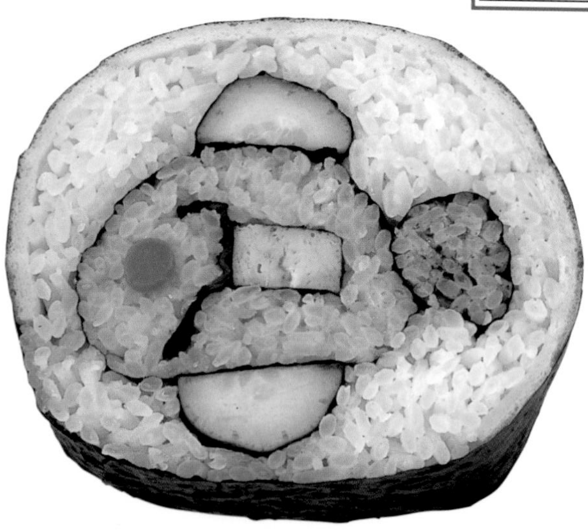

(for 1 roll)

4 $^{1}/_{3}$" (11 cm) cucumber
8 $^{2}/_{3}$" (22 cm) simmered gourd (p. 17)
1 omelet stick (p. 19)
Small piece misozuke yamagobo
1 tsp aonori sprinkles
3 Tbsp oboro sprinkles (p.18)
$^{1}/_{2}$ thickness of omelet sheet (p. 23)
12 $^{1}/_{2}$ oz (360 g) sushi rice (p. 9)
Roasted nori

Setup: Cut the omelet stick into a stick $^{3}/_{8}$" thick and $^{3}/_{4}$" wide (1 x 2 cm). Trim the omelet sheet to 4 x 7" (10.5 x 18 cm). Mix the oboro into 3 $^{3}/_{4}$ oz (110 g) of the rice. Mix the aonori into 1 oz (30 g) of the rice.

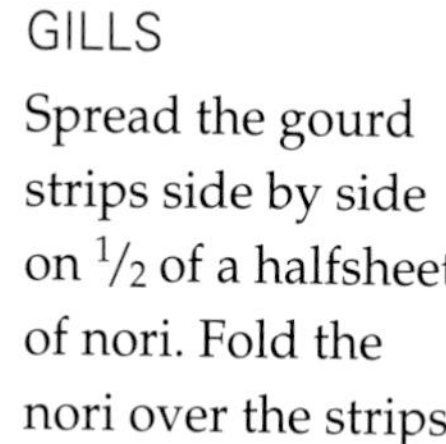

GILLS

Spread the gourd strips side by side on $^{1}/_{2}$ of a halfsheet of nori. Fold the nori over the strips.

FINS

For the top and bottom fins, slice the cucumber in half lengthwise. Wrap each slice in $^{1}/_{2}$ of a halfsheet of nori.

FIN

For the side fin, place the omelet stick on $^{1}/_{3}$ of a halfsheet of nori. Wrap the omelet in the nori.

TAIL

Roll the green rice in $^{1}/_{2}$ of a halfsheet of nori, then form into a triangle.

1. Place a halfsheet of nori vertically on the mat. Form $1\frac{1}{2}$ oz (40 g) of the pink rice into a half moon that is $1\frac{1}{2}$" (4 cm) wide. Place this half moon on the rice *(far left)*. Place the gill package on top, curving it to cover the rice. Place the yellow fin package on top *(left)*.

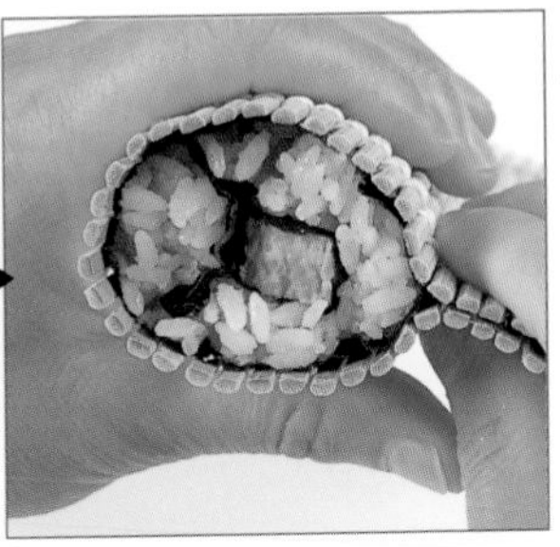

2. Cover the fin with the remaining pink rice, using 1 oz (30 g) on each side and $\frac{3}{4}$ oz (20 g) on top *(far left)*. Holding the mat in your hand, curve each side of the nori to meet the rice. Press into an oval shape *(left)*.

30g
20g
7 cm

3. Using 3 grains of rice, attach $\frac{1}{2}$ halfsheet onto 1 halfsheet of nori. Place the omelet sheet in the middle of the nori. Spread $3\frac{1}{2}$ oz (100 g) of the rice on the omelet sheet. Place one cucumber fin $2\frac{3}{4}$" (7 cm) from the top of the omelet. Place a 1 oz (30 g) ridge of rice below the fin and a $\frac{3}{4}$ oz (20 g) ridge above it. Both ridges should be higher than the fin.

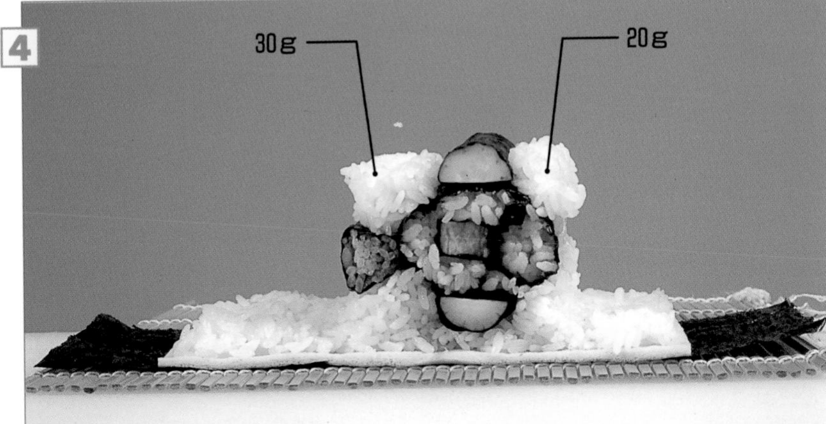

4. Place the body package on the fin so that the C of the gill points away from you. Place the other cucumber fin on top, flat side down. Rest the tail on the ridge closest to you. Place 1 oz (30 g) of the rice on top of the tail and the back of the body. Place another $\frac{3}{4}$ oz (20 g) of the rice on the other side of the fin.

5. Holding the mat in your hand, bring the sides together. Cover the fin with the remaining $\frac{3}{4}$ oz (20 g) of rice. Fold the nori over to close.

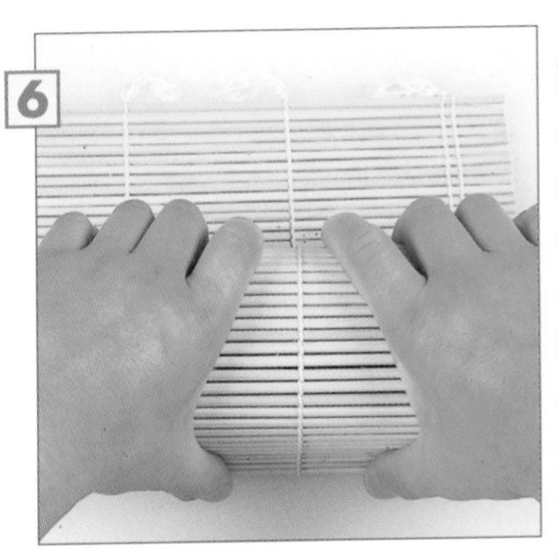

6. Place the roll seam side down, form into a tunnel shape, flatten the ends, and slice into 4 pieces, wiping the blade with a wet towel after each slice. Cut the yamagobo into thin rounds (eyes) and place on the sushi.

Elephant

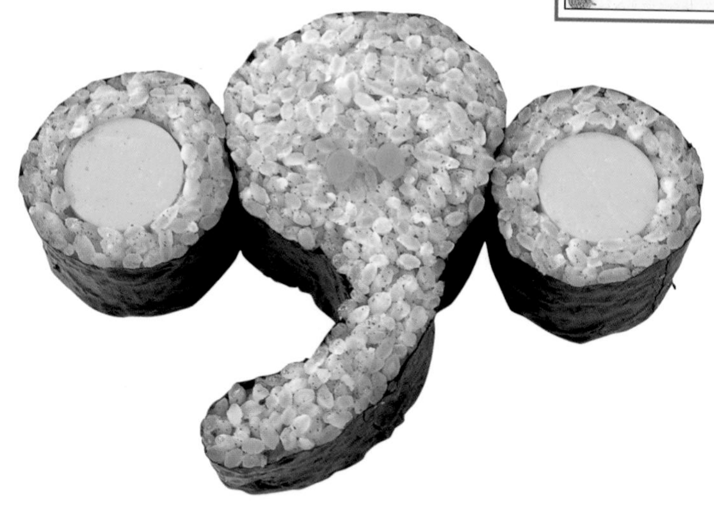

(for 1 roll)

2 hot dogs
Small piece misozuke yamagobo
2 Tbsp yukari sprinkles
12 oz (340 g) sushi rice
Roasted nori

Setup: Cut the hot dogs into 4 $^{1}/_{3}$" (11 cm) lengths. Stir the yukari (dried minced beefsteak leaves) into all of the rice. If misozuke yamagobo (miso-pickled wild burdock root) is unavailable, substitute small rounds of carrot.

Ear

Trunk

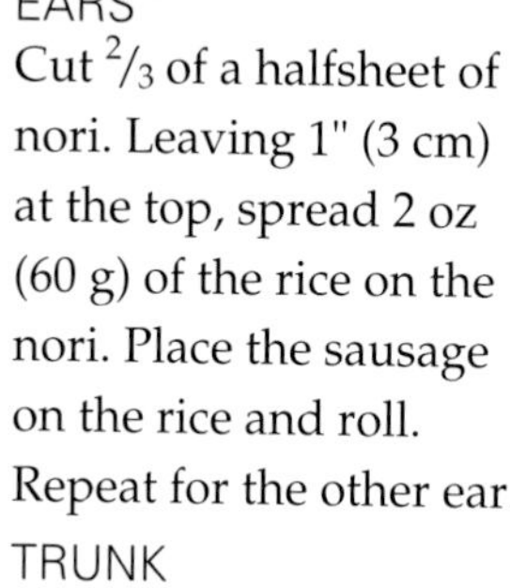

1

2

EARS

Cut $^{2}/_{3}$ of a halfsheet of nori. Leaving 1" (3 cm) at the top, spread 2 oz (60 g) of the rice on the nori. Place the sausage on the rice and roll. Repeat for the other ear.

TRUNK

Spread 1 $^{1}/_{2}$ oz (40 g) of the rice on the lower half of $^{2}/_{3}$ of a halfsheet of nori (Fig. 1). Cover the rice with the remaining nori. Using the mat, curve into shape (Fig. 2). One end of the trunk remains open.

1

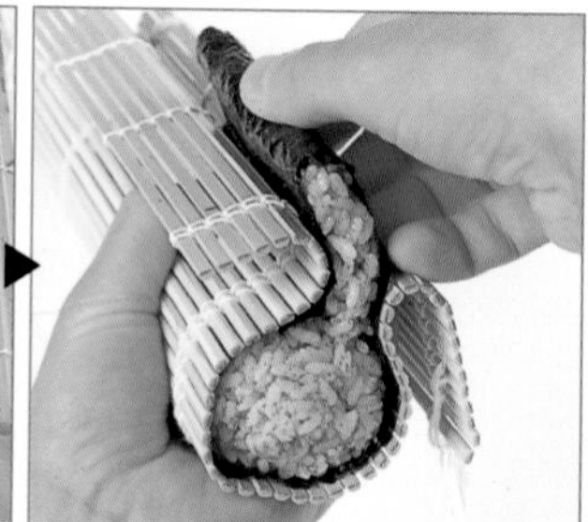

Gather the remaining rice into a cylinder and place in the center of a halfsheet of nori. Press 4–5 grains of rice along each edge *(above left)*. Holding the mat in your hand, bring the nori and rice almost all the way together. Place the trunk in the opening *(above right)*.

2

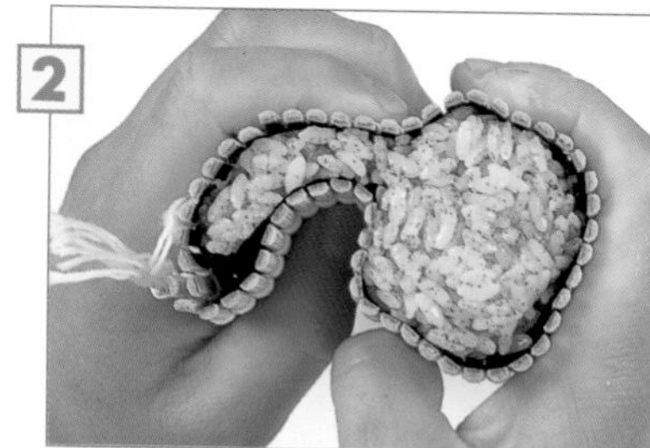

Press the nori and rice layers together at the points where you attached the grains of rice. Slide the roll to the edges of the mat to flatten the ends.

3

Slice the head roll and ear rolls into 4 pieces and arrange on a plate. Slice the yamagobo into thin rounds (eyes) and place them on the elephant faces.

Turtle

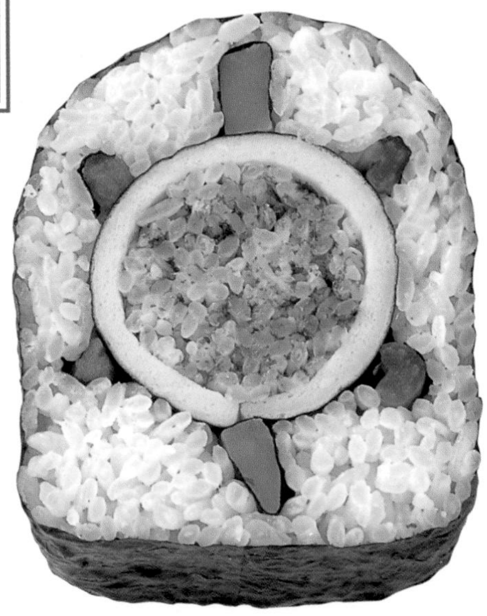

(for 1 roll)

$4\,{}^{1}/_{3}$" (11 cm) takuan pickles
$17\,{}^{1}/_{3}$" (44 cm) nozawana stalks
${}^{1}/_{2}$ Tbsp aonori sprinkles
${}^{1}/_{2}$ thickness of omelet sheet (p. 23)
$8\,{}^{1}/_{2}$ oz (240 g) sushi rice (p. 9)
Roasted nori

Setup: Cut the nozawana stalks (pickled greens) into $4\,{}^{1}/_{3}$" (11 cm) lengths. Trim the omelet sheet to a $4 \times 4\,{}^{1}/_{3}$" (10.5 x 11 cm) rectangle. Mix the aonori (green seaweed sprinkles) into 2 oz (60 g) of the rice.

Shell

Head/ Tail

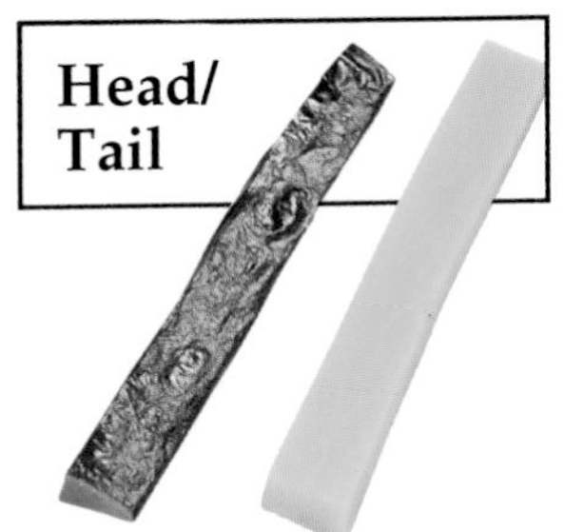

SHELL

Place the omelet sheet at the bottom of ${}^{2}/_{3}$ of a halfsheet of nori and gather the green rice into a cylinder (Fig. 1). And roll as shown (Fig. 2).

HEAD/TAIL

Head: cut one strip of takuan ${}^{1}/_{4}$" (7 mm) thick and ${}^{1}/_{2}$" (1.5 cm) wide.
Tail: cut a wedge of takuan ${}^{1}/_{2}$" (1.5 cm) wide. Wrap the wedge in a 2" (5 cm) strip cut from a halfsheet of nori *(left)*.

1 Using 3 grains of rice, attach ${}^{1}/_{2}$ halfsheet onto 1 halfsheet of nori. Leaving 2" (5 cm) at the top and bottom, spread 5 oz (140 g) of the rice on the nori. Cut five ${}^{3}/_{8}$" (1 cm) strips of nori and press them with a chopstick into the rice at 1" (3 cm) intervals.

2 Place the head takuan piece in the center strip. Place the nozawana stalks in the other strips. Place the shell roll on the takuan.

3 Holding the mat in your hand, bring the sides together. Place the tail package in the center and spread $1\,{}^{1}/_{2}$ oz (40 g) of the rice on top. Close, form into a tunnel shape, flatten the ends, and slice into 4 pieces.

Boat

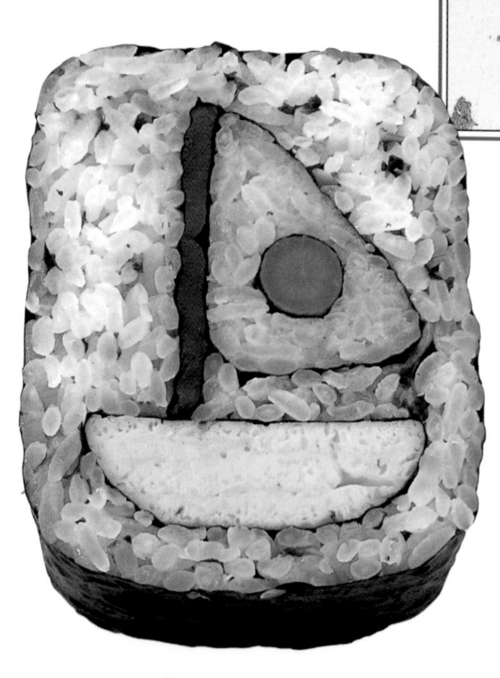

(for 1 roll)

1 omelet (p. 19)
17 $^{1}/_{3}$" (44 cm) simmered gourd (p. 17)
4 $^{1}/_{3}$" (11 cm) misozuke yamagobo
1 Tbsp oboro sprinkles (p. 18)
$^{1}/_{3}$ oz (10 g) mibuna pickles
9 oz (260 g) sushi rice (p. 9)
Roasted nori

Setup: Cut the omelet $^{1}/_{2}$" (1.5 cm) thick and 2" (5 cm) wide. Choose wide gourd strips (1" (2.5 cm)-wide) and cut into 4 equal lengths. Mix the oboro thoroughly into 2 oz (60 g) of the rice. Mince the mibuna (pickled greens) and stir it into the remaining 7 oz (200 g) of the rice.

Hull Slice off the top two corners of the omelet *(upper right)*. Wrap in $^{2}/_{3}$ of a halfsheet of nori.
Mast Place two gourd strips on $^{2}/_{3}$ of a halfsheet. Stack two more strips on top of the first two. Fold them up in the nori *(right)*.
Circle Roll the yamagobo in $^{1}/_{4}$ of a halfsheet *(far right)*.

Spread the pink rice on $^{2}/_{3}$ of a halfsheet, leaving 1 $^{1}/_{2}$" (4 cm) of nori. Place the wrapped yamagobo in the center of the rice *(far left)*. Holding the yamagobo with your fingers, roll *(middle)*. Form into a right triangle *(left)*. This will be the sail.

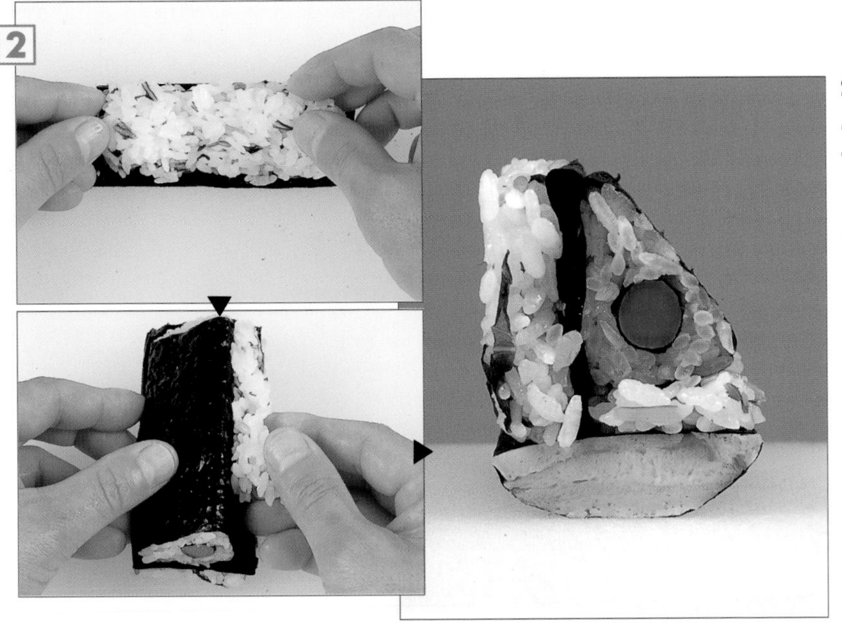

Spread 1 $^1/_2$ oz (40 g) of the green rice on one side of the mast package *(far left, top)*. Turn over and place the sail on the mast (flat side down). Spread $^1/_3$ oz (10 g) of the green rice on the bottom of the sail *(far left, bottom)*. Place this assembly on the flat side of the egg package *(left)*.

Using 3 grains of rice, attach $^1/_2$ halfsheet onto 1 halfsheet of nori. Leaving 1 $^1/_2$" (4 cm) at both ends, spread 3 $^1/_2$ oz (100 g) of the green rice on the nori. Place the boat assembly in the center of the rice.

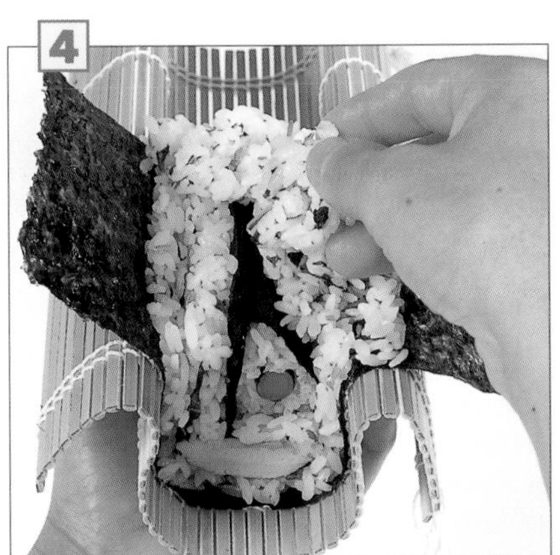

Holding the mat in your hand, bring the sides together. Cover with the remaining green rice, beginning with the side of the sail.

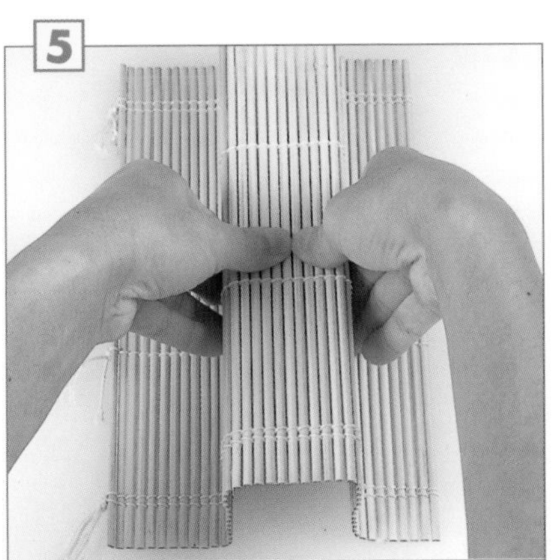

Fold the nori over the rice. Place the roll seam side down and form into a square shape.

Slide the sushi to the ends of the mat to flatten the edges. Slice into 4 pieces, wiping the blade with a wet towel after each slice.

Car

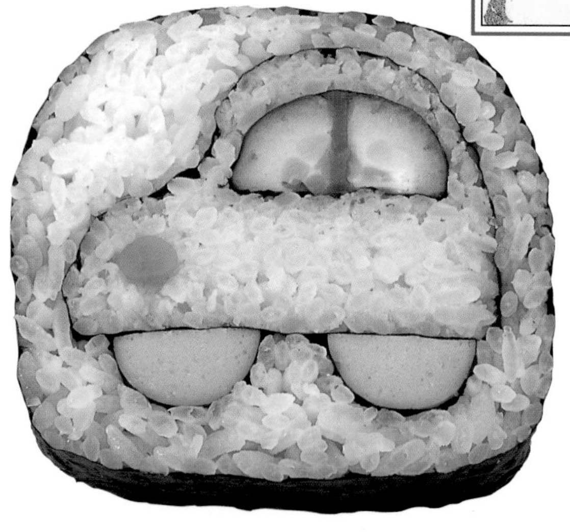

(for 1 roll)

4 1/3" (11 cm) cucumber
4 1/3" (11 cm) simmered gourd (p. 17)
1 hot dog
Small piece misozuke yamagobo
3 Tbsp egg sprinkles (p. 80)
10 oz (280 g) sushi rice (p. 9)
Roasted nori

Setup: Trim the hot dog down to 4 1/3" (11 cm) long. Mix the egg sprinkles thoroughly into 3 1/2 oz (100 g) of the rice. Misozuke can be substituted with cooked carrot.

Windows

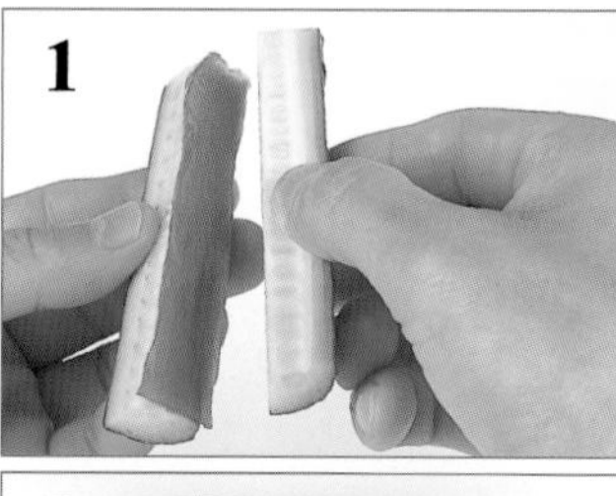

1

2

Slice the cucumber in quarter lengthwise. Place the gourd strip between two of the quarters (Fig. 1) and roll in a 1/2 halfsheet of nori (Fig. 2).

Tires

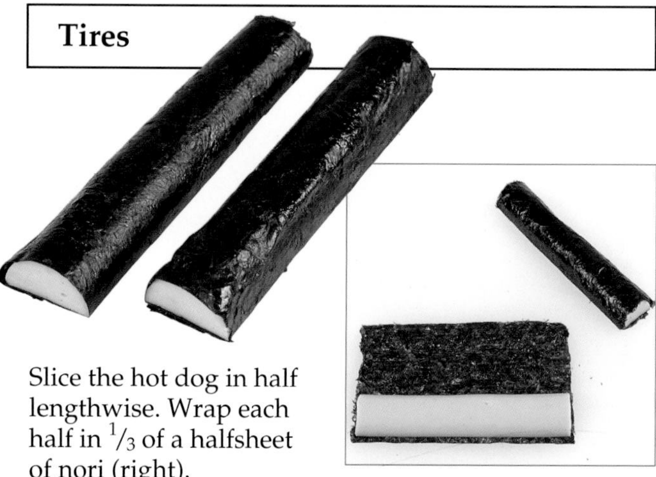

Slice the hot dog in half lengthwise. Wrap each half in 1/3 of a halfsheet of nori (right).

1

Place a halfsheet of nori vertically on the rolling mat. Form 3 1/2 oz (100 g) of the yellow rice into a block 2 1/3" (6 cm) across. Place at the top of the nori. Place the cucumber package 3/8" (1 cm) from the top of the rice.

2

Cover the cucumbers with the remaining yellow rice.

Use the mat to cover the car shape with the nori *(far left, top)*. With the seam side down, press the car into shape with the mat *(far left, bottom)*. Spread 1 oz (30 g) of white rice over the hood *(left)*. Wrap with plastic wrap and press the entire package into a square shape with the rolling mat.

Using 3 grains of rice, attach $^{1}/_{2}$ halfsheet onto 1 halfsheet of nori. Leaving 1 $^{1}/_{2}$" (4 cm) at both ends, spread 3 $^{1}/_{2}$ oz (100 g) of the rice on the nori. Remove the wrap from the car package and place it upside down in the center of the rice. Place the two tire packages on the car, flat side down, and spread $^{1}/_{2}$ oz (10 g) of the rice between the tires.

Holding the mat in your hand, bring the two sides together. Spread the remaining 1 $^{1}/_{2}$ oz (40 g) of rice on top and fold the nori over.

Place the roll seam side down and form into a tunnel shape. Slide the sushi to the ends of the mat to flatten the edges.

Slice into 4 pieces, wiping the blade with a wet towel after each slice. Slice the misozuke into thin rounds and place them on each piece as the headlight.

Heart

(for 1 roll)

2 Tbsp oboro sprinkles (p. 18)
$^1/_2$ thickness of an omelet sheet (p. 23)
6 $^1/_2$ oz (180 g) sushi rice (p. 9)
Roasted nori

Setup: Trim the omelet sheet to 4 x 7" (10.5 x 18 cm). Mix the oboro thoroughly into 3 oz (80 g) of the rice.

1

Cut a 2 $^3/_4$" (7 cm) strip horizontally from a full sheet of nori. Leaving $^3/_4$" (2 cm) at the bottom, spread the pink rice on the strip in a rounded wedge form, with the thick part at the bottom and the thin part at the top.

2

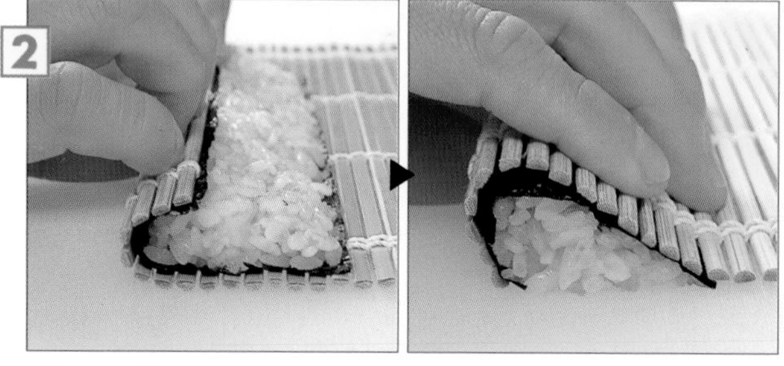

Cover the round part of the wedge with the nori *(above left)*. Turn the roll over and form it into a half-heart shape with the mat *(above right)*.

3

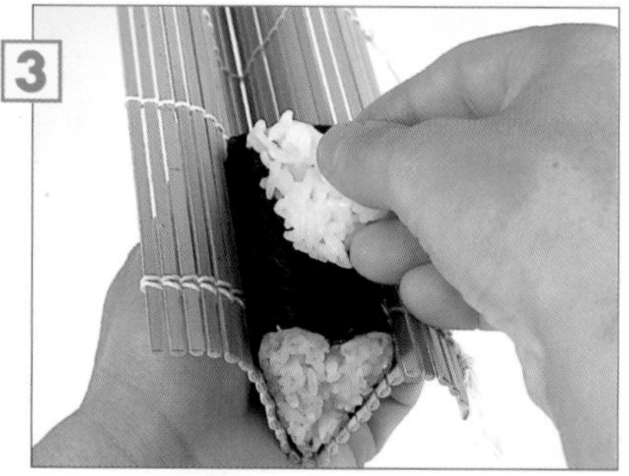

Cut the pink roll into two equal lengths. Place the lengths together to form a heart shape. Place $^1/_2$ oz (20 g) of the rice in the valley.

4

Place the omelet sheet on a mat, cut side up. Place the heart upside down in the center.

5

Holding the mat in your hand, place 3 oz(80 g) of the rice around the heart and close the omelet sheet. Form into a square. Making a 1 $^1/_4$ half-sheet of nori, wrap around the omelet roll, and slice into 4 pieces.

Spade

(for 1 roll)

1 Tbsp black sesame seeds
$^1/_2$ tsp yukari sprinkles
$^1/_2$ thickness of an omelet sheet (p. 23)
6 $^1/_2$ oz (180 g) sushi rice (p. 9)
Roasted nori

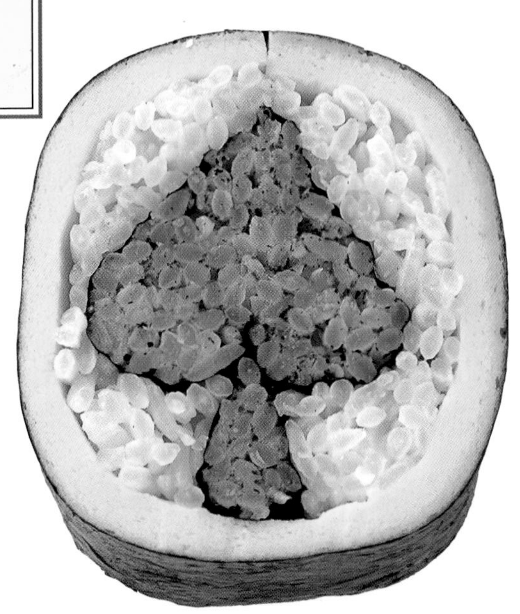

Setup: Trim the omelet sheet to 4 x 7" (10.5 x 18 cm). Grind the black sesame seeds and mix with the yukari (minced dried beefsteak leaves) into 3 oz (80 g) of the rice.

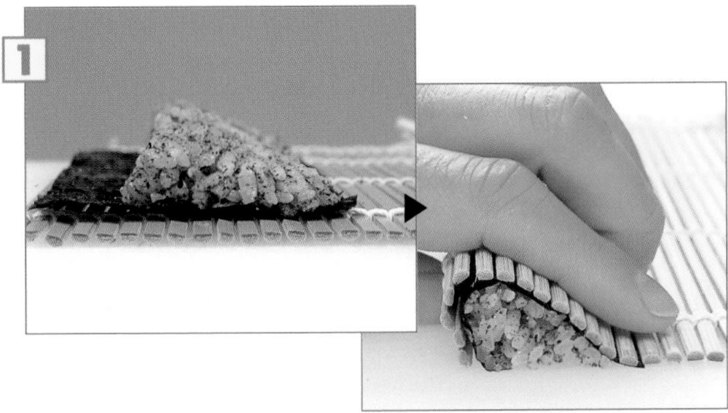

Cut a 2 $^3/_4$" (7 cm) strip horizontally from a full sheet of nori. Place 2 $^1/_2$ oz (70 g) of the black rice in a mound on the nori, leaving $^3/_4$" (2 cm) at the bottom *(above left)*. Cover the round part of the mound with the nori. Turn the roll over and form it into a half-heart shape with the mat *(above right)*. Cut into two equal lengths.

Cut a 2" (5 cm) strip from a halfsheet of nori. Place the remaining black rice in a wedge on the top half of the strip, thick end toward you *(above left)*. Fold the nori over the rice and press into a triangle shape *(above right)*.

Place the triangular stem in the center of the omelet. Place $^3/_4$ oz (20 g) of white rice on each side. Place the two halves of the heart shape together and place them on the rice *(top)*. Cover with 2 oz (60 g) of the rice *(above)*.

Holding the mat in your hand, bring the sides of the omelet together and fold them over the top. Form into a square. Making 1 $^1/_4$ halfsheet of nori, wrap around the omelet roll *(left)*, and slice into 4 pieces.

Diamond

(for 1 roll)
2 Tbsp oboro sprinkles (p. 18)
$^1/_2$ thickness of an omelet sheet (p. 23)
6 $^1/_2$ oz (180 g) sushi rice (p. 9)
Roasted nori

Setup: Trim the omelet sheet to 4 x 7" (10.5 x 18 cm). Mix the oboro thoroughly into 3 oz (80 g) of the rice.

1. Form the pink rice into a block and place it on $^3/_4$ of a halfsheet *(above left)*. Roll as usual and form into a diamond with the mat *(above right)*.

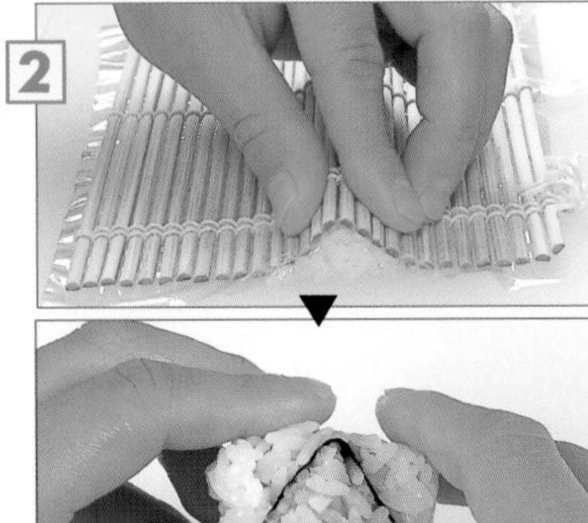

2. Using $^7/_8$ oz (25 g) of the rice, form a line on a board to match the length of the diamond. Drape with plastic wrap and form into a triangle with the mat *(left, top)*. Make 4 of these ridges and place them on the sides of the diamond *(left, bottom)*.

3. Place the omelet sheet on a mat, cut side up. Place the diamond in the center. Holding the mat in your hand, bring the sides together and press into a square shape.

4. Using 3 grains of rice, attach $^1/_4$ halfsheet onto 1 halfsheet of nori. Place the roll seam side down on the nori and wrap.

5. Ending with the seam side down, form into a square once more. Slice into 4 pieces, wiping the blade with a wet towel after each slice.

Club

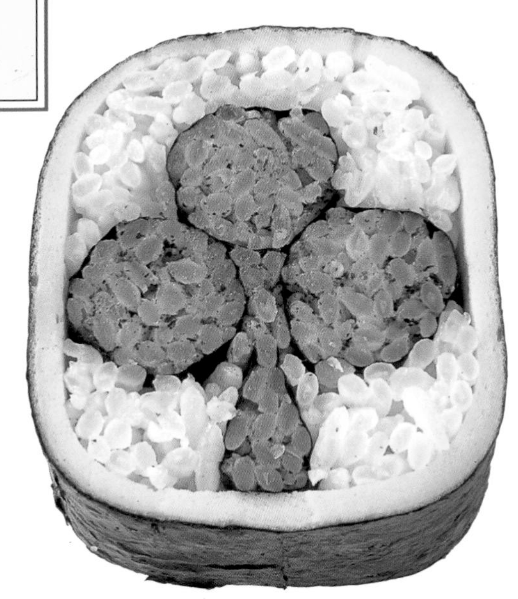

(for 1 roll)

1 Tbsp black sesame seeds
$1/2$ tsp yukari sprinkles
$1/2$ thickness of an omelet sheet (p. 23)
6 $1/3$ oz (180 g) sushi rice (p. 9)
Roasted nori

Setup: Trim the omelet sheet to 4 x 7" (10.5 x 18 cm). Grind the black sesame seeds and mix with the yukari (minced dried beefsteak leaves) into 3 7/8 oz (110 g) of the rice.

1

To make one cloverleaf, place 1 oz (30 g) of the black rice in a cylinder on $2/3$ of a halfsheet of nori *(left, top)*. Roll as usual *(left, bottom)*, then finish by folding the mat around the roll and rubbing the sides of the mat together *(p. 84, bottom left)*. Make two more of these leaves.

2

To make the stem, cut a 2" (5 cm) strip from a halfsheet of nori. Place $1/3$ oz (10 g) of the black rice in a wedge on the top half of the strip, thick end toward you *(left, top)*. Fold the nori over the rice and press into a triangle shape *(left, bottom)*.

3

Place the 3 cloverleaves in the mat. Place the remaining black rice in the center.

4

Place the omelet sheet on a mat and place the stem in the center. Place $1/2$ oz (15 g) of the rice on each side of the stem. Place the 3-leaf assembly on top. Cover with the remaining 1 $1/2$ oz (40 g) of white rice. Holding the mat in your hand, bring the omelet sides together and cover the top. Press into a square, seam side down.

5

Make a 1 $1/4$ halfsheet strip of nori and roll the omelet roll up. Press into a square once more, seam side down. Slice into 4 pieces.

Pine

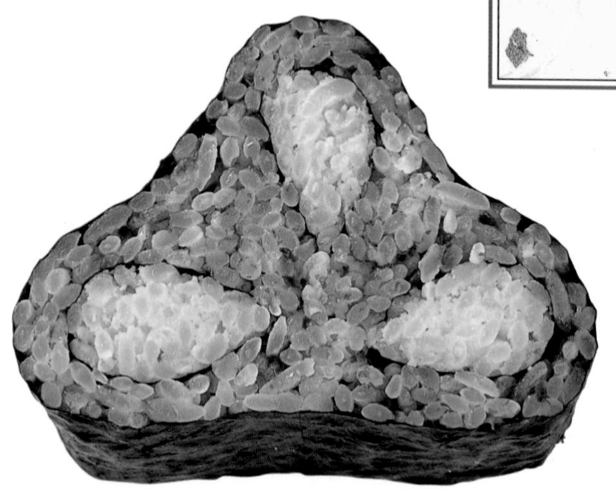

(for 1 roll)

3 Tbsp egg sprinkles (p. 80)
1 $\frac{1}{2}$ Tbsp aonori sprinkles
Roasted sesame seeds
9 oz (250 g) sushi rice (p. 9)
Roasted nori

Setup: Stir the egg sprinkles thoroughly into 2 $\frac{1}{2}$ oz (70 g) of the rice. Stir the aonori (dried seaweed sprinkles) and the sesame seeds into the remaining 6 $\frac{1}{2}$ oz (180 g) of the rice.

Divide the yellow rice into 3 portions. Place one portion in a cylinder in the center of a 2 $\frac{3}{4}$" (7 cm) strip of a halfsheet of nori.

Fold the nori over, pressing the ends together to form a tear shape. Make two more of these teardrops.

Attach $\frac{1}{3}$ of a halfsheet to 1 halfsheet with 3 grains of rice. Leaving 1 $\frac{1}{2}$" (4 cm) at both ends, spread 3 oz (80 g) of green rice on the nori. Holding the mat in your hand, place one teardrop in the center, pointed end up.

Cover the sides and top of the teardrop with 2 oz (60 g) of green rice.

Place the other two teardrops on top, $\frac{3}{4}$" (2 cm) apart, pointed ends toward each other.

Cover the teardrops with the remaining green rice.

Fold the nori over the rice. With the seam side down, press into a triangle and flatten the ends.

Make indentations with your thumb and fingers. Slice into 4 pieces, wiping the blade with a wet cloth.

Bamboo

(for 1 roll)
3 $^{1}/_{2}$" (9 cm) cucumber
2 tsp aonori sprinkles
3 oz (80 g) sushi rice (p. 9)
Roasted nori

Setup: Stir the aonori (green seaweed sprinkles) into the rice.

1 Using a straight cucumber, slice off the peel in 4 straight strips as shown.

2 Cut 2 strips of nori to match the cucumber strips. Place each piece of nori between 2 of the cucumber strips.

3 Place a halfsheet of nori horizontally on the rolling mat. Leaving $^{3}/_{8}$" (1 cm) at the top and bottom, spread all the green rice on the nori. Place the cucumber strips side by side $^{1}/_{2}$" (1.5 cm) from the top of the rice.

4 Holding the mat in your hand, bring the sides together *(above left)*. Press together in a teardrop, lining up the cucumber centers in the middle *(above right)*. Slice into 6 pieces. Serve in groups of 3.

Cloisonné

1. Stir 3 Tbsp of oboro (p. 18) into 5 $^{1}/_{4}$ oz (150 g) of the rice.
2. Make 2 bamboo-leaf rolls but finish in a diamond shape, pinching both ends. Cut into two equal lengths.
3. Press the 4 bamboo rolls around a $^{3}/_{4}$" (2 cm)-square omelet stick. Wrap with nori.

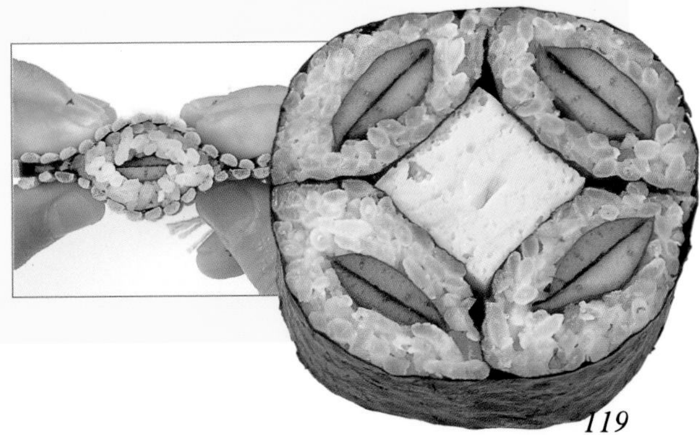

Plum Crest

Note: The following pages present sushi renditions of several traditional Japanese symbols, designs, and family crests.

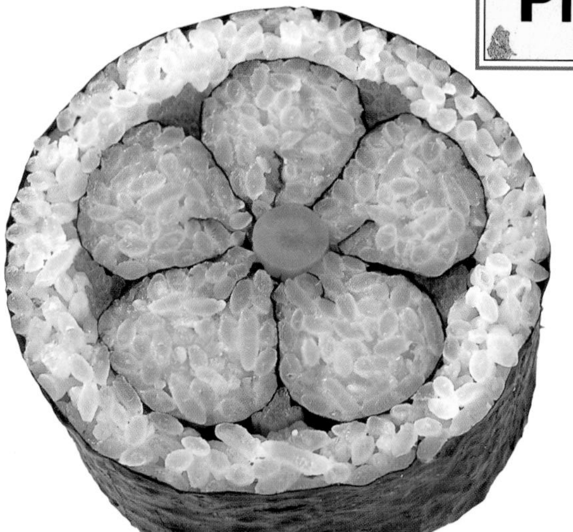

(for 1 roll)

4 1/3" (11 cm) misozuke yamagobo
1 bunch mitsuba (honewort)
1 1/2 oz (40 g) cod roe
4 Tbsp oboro sprinkles (p. 18)
8 1/2 oz (240 g) sushi rice (p. 9)
Roasted nori

Setup: Parboil the mitsuba, plunge in cold water, squeeze well, and trim into 4 1/3" (11 cm) lengths. Remove the roe from its sac and stir well, with the oboro, into 5 oz (140 g) of the rice.

1

Divide the pink rice into 5 portions. Cut five 3" (8 cm) strips and five 1/2" (1.5 cm) strips from halfsheets of nori. Leaving 1/5" (5 mm) at the top and bottom, spread one rice portion on one of the wide strips. Place one of the narrow strips on top.

2

Lift the mat, folding the nori so that the bottom edge meets the top edge of the narrow strip.

3

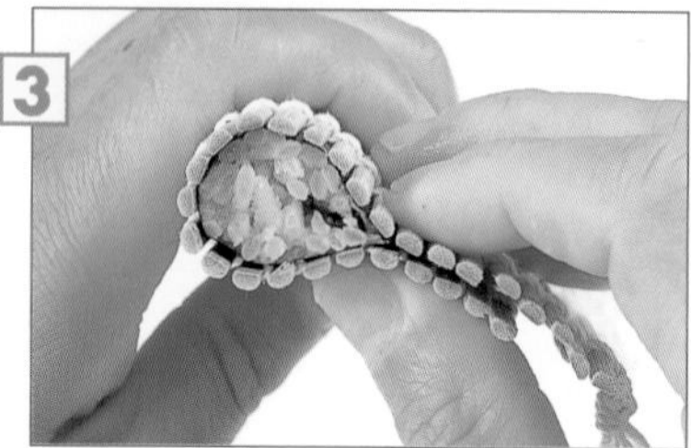

Pressing the ends together, form into a rounded teardrop shape.

4

Slice about 1/5" (5 mm) from the pointed end. This will be one petal. Make 4 more petals like the first.

5

Arrange the 5 petals around the yamagobo in the mat *(above left)*. Twist the mitsuba into 5 ropes and place them between the petals *(above right)*.

6

Using 3 grains of rice, attach 1/3 halfsheet onto 1 halfsheet of nori. Leaving 1" (3 cm) at the top, spread 3 1/2 oz (100 g) of the rice on the nori. Place the assembled flower toward the bottom. With the mat, roll into a cylinder. Flatten the ends and slice into 4 pieces.

Double-Line Crest

(for 1 roll)
1 omelet, 2" (5 cm)-wide (p. 19)
2 Tbsp oboro sprinkles (p. 18)
1 Tbsp aonori sprinkles
7 3/4 oz (220 g) sushi rice (p. 9)
Roasted nori

Setup: Slice the omelet (p. 19) into two 3/8" (1 cm) thicknesses. Mix the oboro thoroughly into 3 1/2 oz (100 g) of the rice. Mix the aonori (green seaweed sprinkles) into 4 1/4 oz (120 g) of the rice.

1 

Slice off the top corners of the omelets on a diagonal, making a trapezoid shape.

2 

Place each omelet on 2/3 of a halfsheet of nori, then wrap.

3 

With plastic wrap and a rolling mat, form 3 oz (80 g) of the green rice into a block twice as long as an omelet package. Round the top of the block.

4 

Spread the remaining green rice on the broader side of one of the omelet packages. Place the other omelet package on top, broad side down.

5 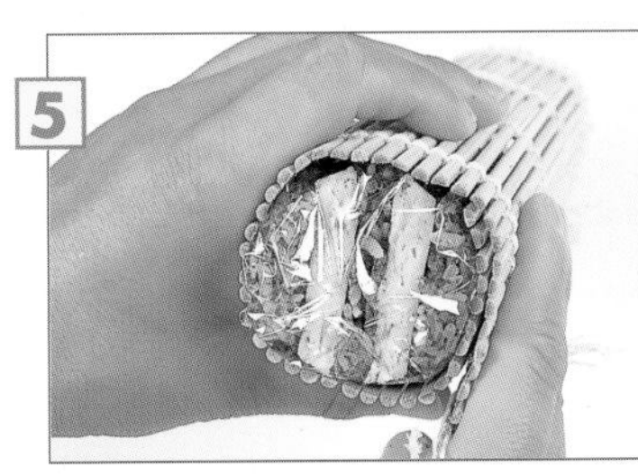

Cut the block from step 3 into two equal lengths and place on the outside of the omelet assembly. Cover with plastic wrap and form into a cylinder with the mat. Roll with 1 halfsheet of nori.

6 

Using 3 grains of rice, attach 1/3 halfsheet onto 1 halfsheet of nori. Leaving 1" (3 cm) at the top, spread the pink rice on the nori. Place the omelet roll at the bottom.

7 

Roll with the mat. Finish the shape by lifting the mat and rolling the cylinder up and down in the mat (see p. 79). Flatten the ends and slice into 4 pieces.

Colored Wheel
(Rokusha)

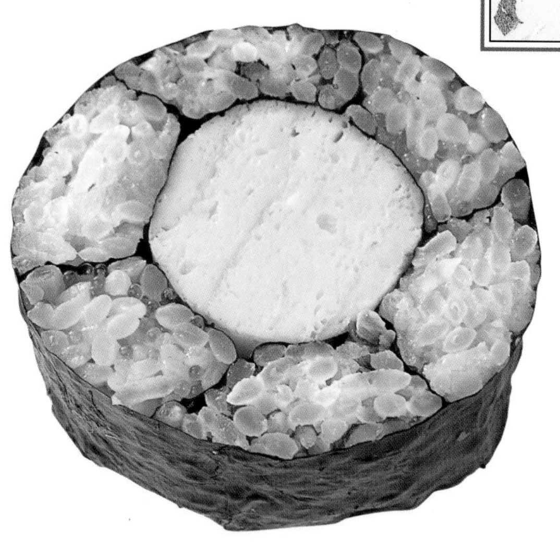

(for 1 roll)

1 omelet (p. 19)
1 Tbsp oboro sprinkles (p. 18)
1 Tbsp flying-fish roe
$^3/_4$ oz (20 g) mibuna pickles
5 $^1/_4$ oz (150 g) sushi rice (p. 9)
Roasted nori

Setup: Slice the omelet into a 1 x 1" (3 x 3 cm) stick. Squeeze the mibunazuke well and mince. (Substitute steamed minced spinach if mibunazuke is unavailable.) Stir each of the colorings oboro, roe, and mibunazuke into 1/3 of the rice.

1

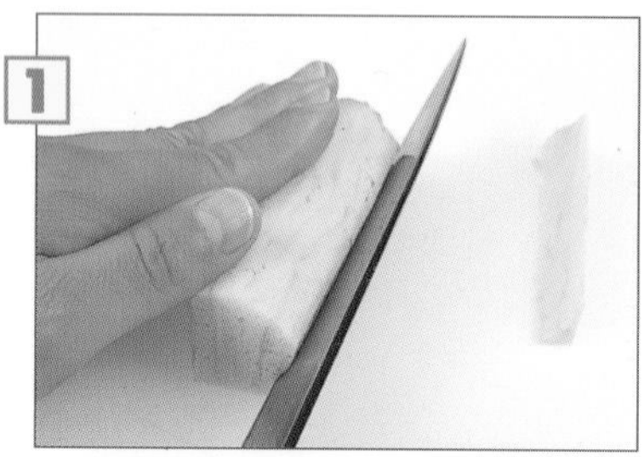

Cut the omelet into a cylinder by trimming off the corners.

2

Form each color of rice into a cylinder and place on $^1/_2$ of a halfsheet, then roll.

3

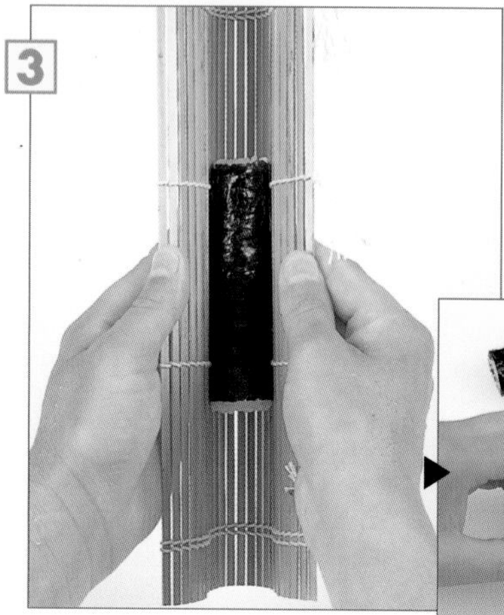

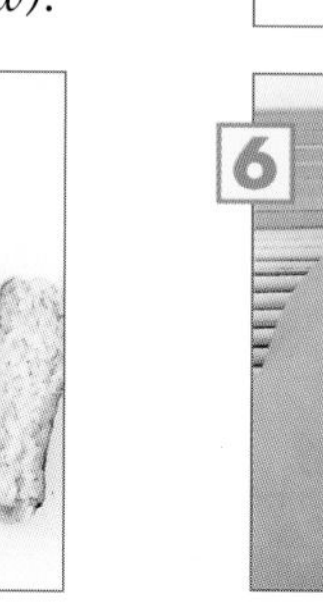

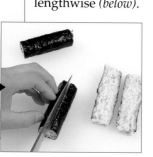

Finish the cylinder shape by rubbing the edges of the mat together *(left)*. Slice each roll in half lengthwise *(below)*.

4

Place 1 halfsheet of nori vertically on the mat and arrange the cut rolls and the omelet as shown.

5

Roll, using your fingers to hold the fillings in place. Finish the shape by lifting the mat and rolling the cylinder up and down in the mat (see p. 79).

6

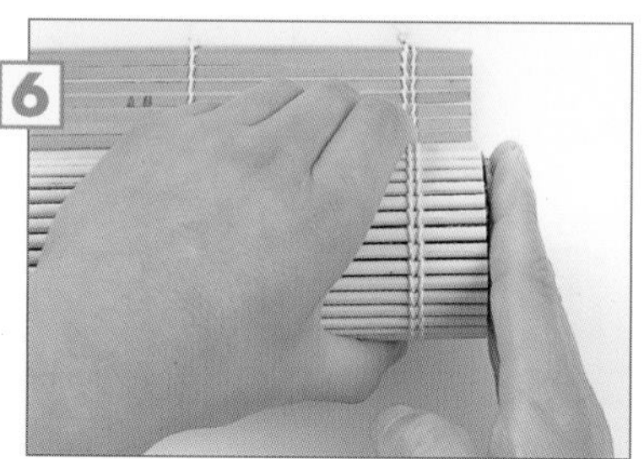

Slide the sushi to the ends of the mat to flatten the edges. Slice into 4 pieces, wiping the blade with a wet towel after each slice.

Tricolor Swirl
(Mitsudomoe)

(for 1 roll)

1/3 oz (10 g) pink pickled daikon	8 2/3" (22 cm) nozawana stalks
8 2/3" (22 cm) misozuke yamagobo	9 oz (240 g) sushi rice
	Roasted nori

Setup: Cut the yamagobo and nozawana into two equal lengths each. Substitute steamed spinach stalks or baby asparagus for the nozawana.

Place a halfsheet of nori horizontally on the mat. Leaving 3/8" (1 cm) at the top and bottom, spread 3 oz (80 g) of the rice on the nori. Place one of the fillings in the center.

Lifting the mat, fold the bottom edge of the nori over to meet the top edge.

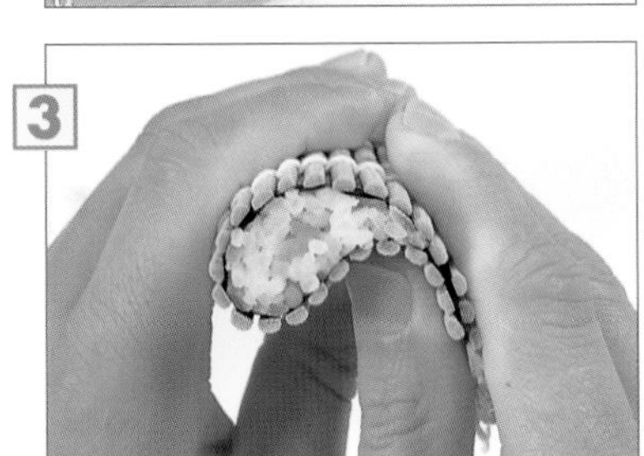

Using the mat, press into a comma shape. Repeat with the two remaining fillings.

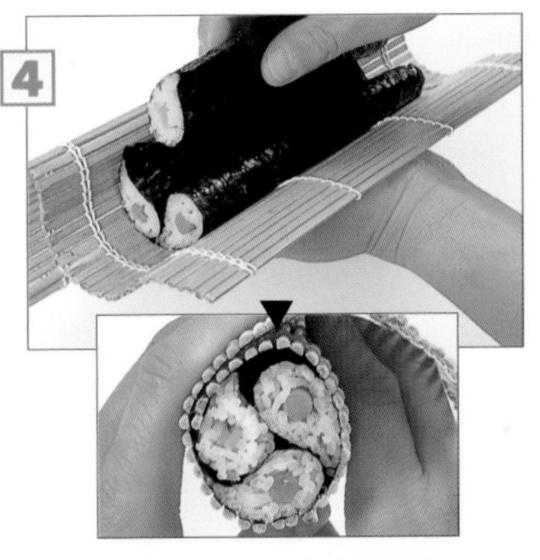

Holding the mat in your hand, arrange the commas so that the points go under the rounded ends *(left, top)*. Press into shape *(left, bottom)*.

Place a full sheet of nori and roll, sealing the end with 4-5 grains of rice.

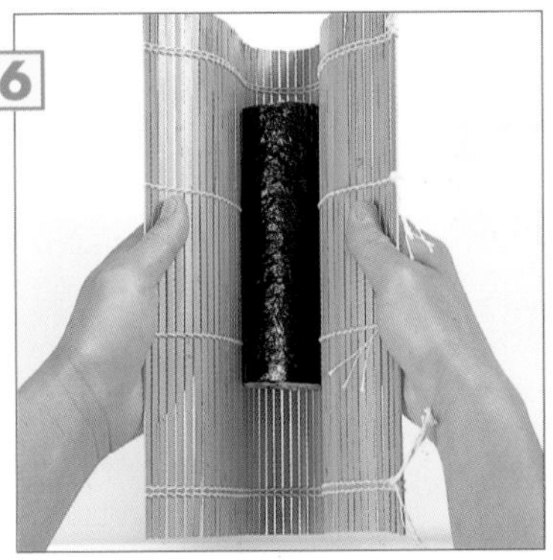

Lifting the mat with both hands, roll the cylinder up and down to finish the shape. Flatten the ends and slice into 8 pieces, wiping the blade with a wet towel after each slice.

Old-Style Coin
(Monsen)

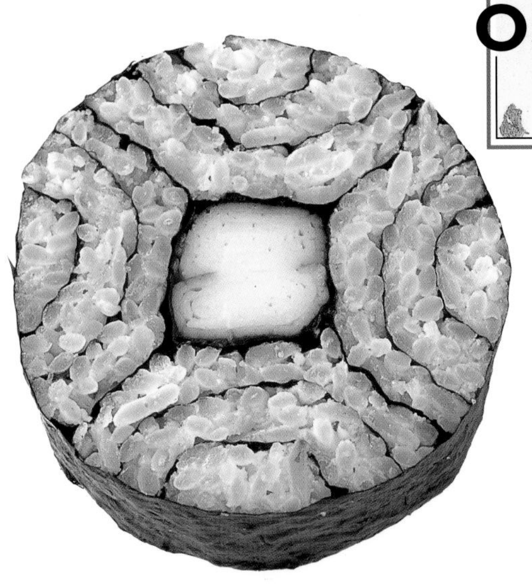

(for 1 roll)

3 artificial crab sticks
4 1/3" (11 cm) nozawana leaves
5 Tbsp egg sprinkles (p. 80)
7 oz (200 g) sushi rice (p. 9)
Roasted nori

Setup: Mix the egg sprinkles thoroughly into all of the rice.

1

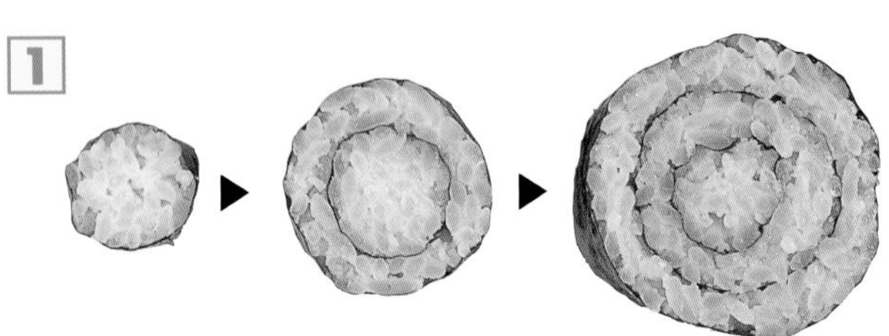

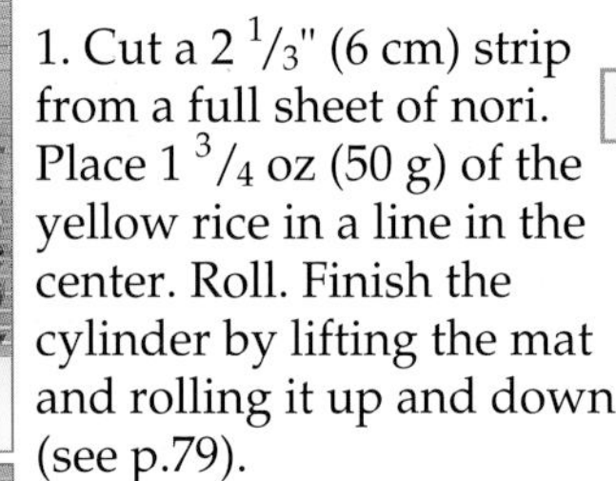

1. Cut a 2 1/3" (6 cm) strip from a full sheet of nori. Place 1 3/4 oz (50 g) of the yellow rice in a line in the center. Roll. Finish the cylinder by lifting the mat and rolling it up and down (see p.79).

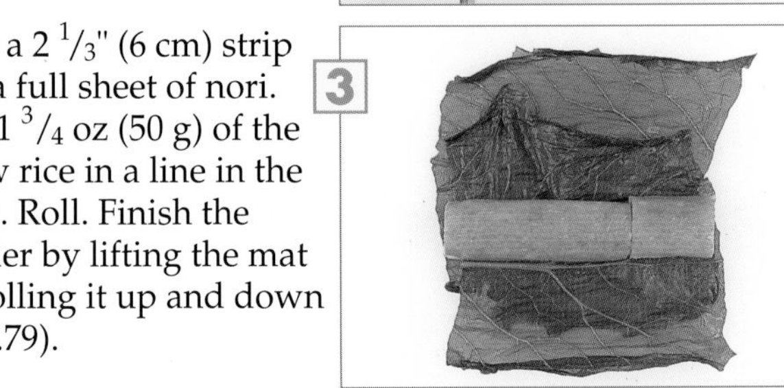

2. Cut a 3 1/2" (9 cm) strip from a full sheet of nori. Leaving 3/8" (1 cm) at the top, spread 3 oz (80 g) of the yellow rice on the nori. Place the cylinder from step 1 in the center. Roll and finish.

3. Cut a 4 3/4" (12 cm) piece of a full sheet of nori. Leaving 3/4" (2 cm) at the top, spread the remaining yellow rice on the nori. Place the cylinder from step 2 in the center. Roll and finish.

2

Cut the roll into 2 equal lengths. Cut each length into 2 lengthwise half-rolls. Slice a fraction at a time, wiping the blade with a wet cloth.

3

Cut one of the crab pieces in half crosswise. Spread out the nozawana leaves and stack all four crab pieces in the center, white sides together. Roll as if to wrap the crab.

4

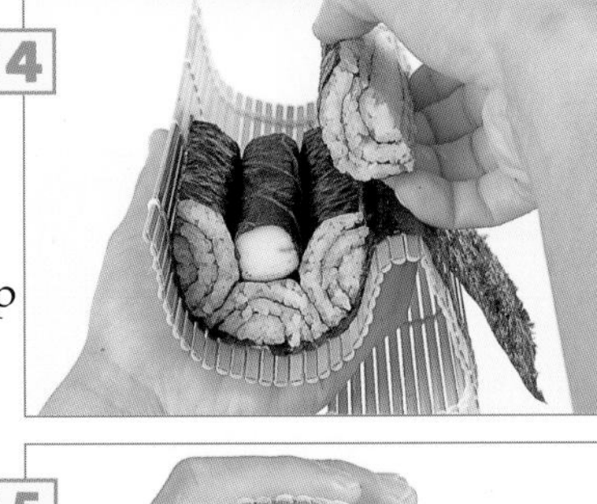

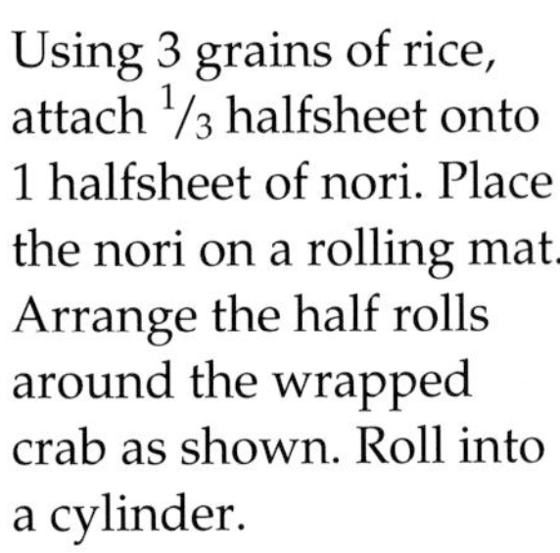

Using 3 grains of rice, attach 1/3 halfsheet onto 1 halfsheet of nori. Place the nori on a rolling mat. Arrange the half rolls around the wrapped crab as shown. Roll into a cylinder.

5

Seal the edge with 2–3 grains of rice. Finish the cylinder shape as on p. 79. Flatten the ends and slice into 4 pieces.

Four Seas

(for 1 roll)

1 omelet (p. 19)
3 Tbsp oboro sprinkles (p. 18)
Roasted sesame seeds
5 $^1/_4$ oz (150 g) sushi rice
Roasted nori

Setup:
Slice the omelet into a 1 x 1" (3 x 3 cm) stick. Stir the oboro and sesame seeds into the rice.

1

Using 3 grains of rice, attach $^1/_2$ halfsheet onto 1 halfsheet of nori. Spread all the pink rice on the nori. Roll as shown *(above left)* and finish by rolling the cylinder up and down in the mat *(above right)*.

2

With the seam side down, slice the cylinder into quarters. Slice a fraction of an inch at a time, wiping the blade with a wet cloth.

3

Place a halfsheet of nori on the mat. Arrange the quarters around the omelet as shown. Roll, then press into a square shape. Slice into 4 pieces.

Four Seas II

Use the Old-Style Coin technique to make three layers and the Four Seas technique to form the square.

1. Mix 1 $^1/_2$ Tbsp oboro sprinkles (p. 18) into 2 $^1/_2$ oz (70 g) of the sushi rice (p. 9).
2. Spread 2 $^1/_2$ oz (70 g) oz white sushi rice onto $^3/_4$ of a halfsheet of nori. Place a 4 $^1/_3$" (11 cm) cucumber in the center and roll. Roll this cylinder in 1 halfsheet of nori that has been spread with the pink rice. Quarter the roll lengthwise.
3. Attach $^1/_4$ halfsheet of nori to 1 halfsheet. Arrange the four quarters around a $^3/_4$" (2 cm)-square omelet (p. 19). Roll into a square.

Four Seas III : Framed Roll

1. Quarter a 4 $^1/_3$" (11 cm) length of cucumber, arrange around a $^1/_2$" (1.5 cm)-thick stick of takuan, and roll in $^2/_3$ of a halfsheet of nori.
2. Mix 3 Tbsp oboro sprinkles (p. 18) into 5 $^1/_4$ oz (150 g) sushi rice (p. 9). Spread evenly on the bottom three-quarters of a halfsheet of nori.
3. Place the cucumber/takuan roll at the bottom of the pink rice and roll into a square.

Four Points

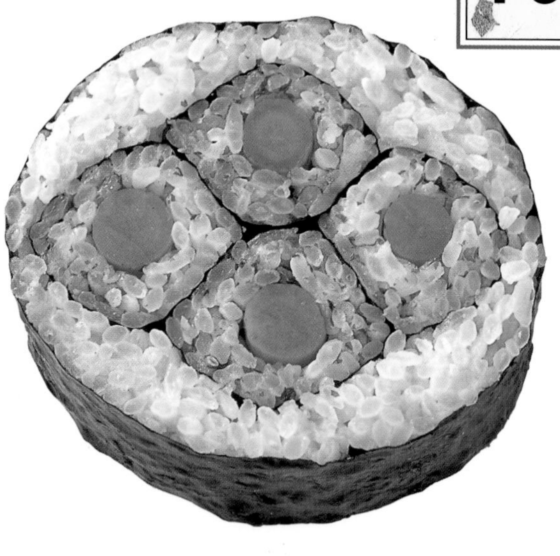

(for 1 roll)

17 $^1/_3$" (44 cm) misozuke yamagobo
1 $^1/_2$ Tbsp aonori sprinkles
3 Tbsp oboro sprinkles (p. 18)
11 oz (310 g) sushi rice (p. 9)
Roasted nori

Setup: Cut the yamagobo (miso-pickled wild burdock root) into four equal lengths. Mix the aonori (green seaweed sprinkles) into 5 $^1/_2$ oz (160 g) of the sushi rice. Mix the oboro into the remaining sushi rice.

1

Cut a full sheet of nori in half horizontally. Leaving $^1/_5$" (5 mm) at the bottom and $^3/_8$" (1 cm) at the top, spread half of the green rice on one of the nori halves. Place 2 lengths of the yamagobo in the center.

2

Pressing the yamagobo in place, lift the sushi mat up and over so that the bottom edge of the nori meets the top edge.

3

Press the roll with your fingertips into a diamond shape. Make a second roll like the first. Cut each into two equal lengths.

4

Place the four folls on a rolling mat and press into a diamond shape.

5

Form the pink rice into two 8 $^2/_3$" (22 cm) lines, pressing each into shape with plastic wrap and a rolling mat.

6

Cut each pink shape into two equal lengths. Place a pink shape on each of the four sides of the diamond. Roll into shape with plastic wrap and the mat.
(continued on p. 127)

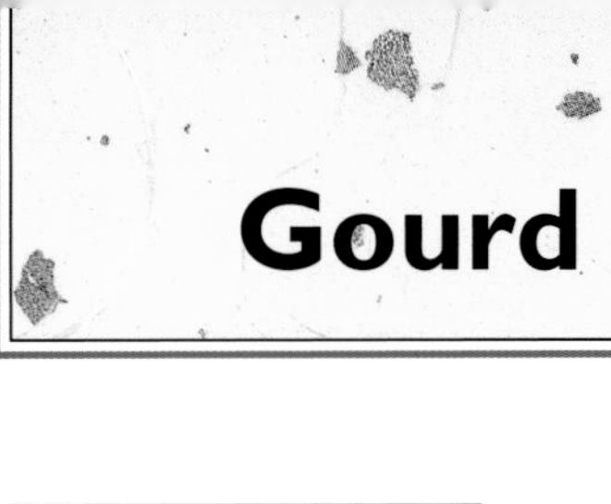

Gourd

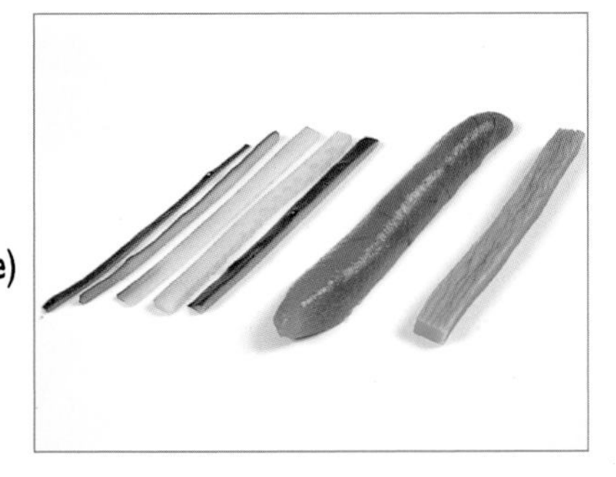

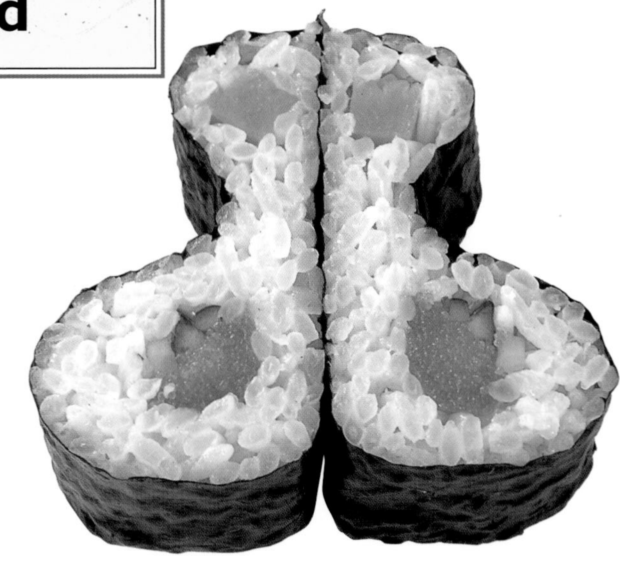

(for 1 roll)
4 $^1/_3$" (11 cm) cucumber
$^1/_4$ sac cod roe (cut lengthwise)
4 $^1/_3$" (11 cm) takuan pickles
3 oz (80 g) sushi rice (p. 9)
Roasted nori

Setup: Julienne the cucumber into 6 lengths. Cut a $^1/_4$" (7 mm)-square stick from the takuan.

Place a halfsheet of nori on the mat. Leaving $^3/_8$" (1 cm) at top and bottom, spread the rice on the nori. Place the cucumber and cod roe slightly above the center. Place the takuan about $^3/_4$" (2 cm) above.

Lift the mat, folding at the halfway point *(above left)* to bring the bottom edge of the nori up to the top edge. Making an indentation between the fillings, press in from the top and bottom *(above right)*. Flatten the edges and cut into four pieces. Assemble the gourds by placing two pieces next to each other.

Using 3 grains of rice, attach $^1/_3$ halfsheet onto 1 halfsheet of nori. Place the roll at the bottom of the sheet.

Roll as usual *(above left)* and finish by rolling the cylinder up and down in the mat *(above right)*. Flatten the ends and cut into 4 pieces.

Chrysanthemum Crest

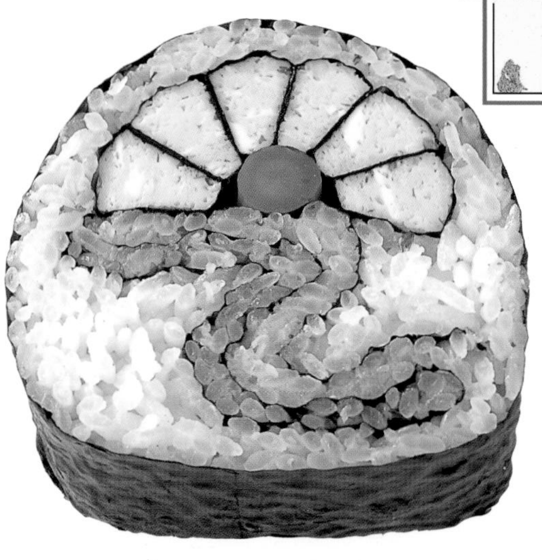

(for 1 roll)

3 omelet, 3/8" (1 cm)-wide
4 1/3" (11 cm) misozuke yamagobo
1/2 Tbsp aonori sprinkles
1 Tbsp oboro sprinkles (p. 18)
7 3/4 oz (220 g) sushi rice (p. 9)
Roasted nori

Setup: Prepare the omelet as on p. 19, then slice. Mix the aonori (green seaweed sprinkles) into 7/8 oz (25 g) of the rice. Mix the oboro into another 7/8 oz (25 g) of the rice.

1

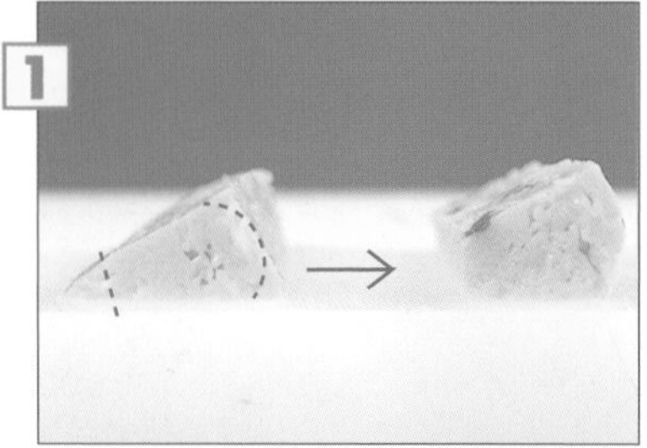

Cut each omelet stick into two wedges. Trim each wedge as shown at left.

2

Place each trimmed wedge onto 1/3 halfsheet of nori and wrap.

3

Arrange the wrapped wedges into a fan shape in a rolling mat. (Use the end of the mat rather than the center, for ease of view.) Place the yamagobo in the center.

4

Spread the green rice on 2/3 of a halfsheet of nori. Place another 2/3 halfsheet on top, then spread the pink rice on it. Cover with another 2/3 halfsheet.

5

Spread 1/2 oz (15 g) of the white rice in a 2" (5 cm)-wide strip on one end of the nori. Turn the stack over and spread 1/2 oz (15 g) on the opposite end.

6

Fold into a Z shape. The width of the river shape should now match that of the fan shape.

7

Place 3/4 oz (20 g) of the rice next to each bend of the river. Drape with plastic wrap and use a rolling mat to press into a rectangular shape.

(continued on p. 129)

Chrysanthemum Variation: **Sunrise**

(for 1 roll)

3 omelet, 3/8" (1 cm)-wide
4 1/3" (11 cm) misozuke yamagobo
1/2 bunch mitsuba (honewort)
2 Tbsp oboro sprinkles (p. 18)
1/2 Tbsp black sesame seeds
4 1/2 oz (130 g) sushi rice (p. 9)
Roasted nori

In this roll, the sun rises over pink clouds and a black mountain range.

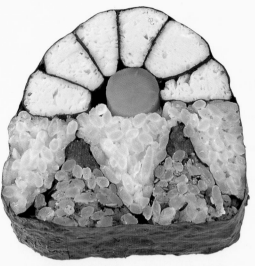

1. Mix the oboro into 3 oz (90 g) of the rice. Spread 1 1/2 oz (40 g) evenly on 2/3 of a halfsheet of nori. Place the remaining pink rice in three ridges on top.

2. Turn the rice and nori over. Form the nori into a W shape.

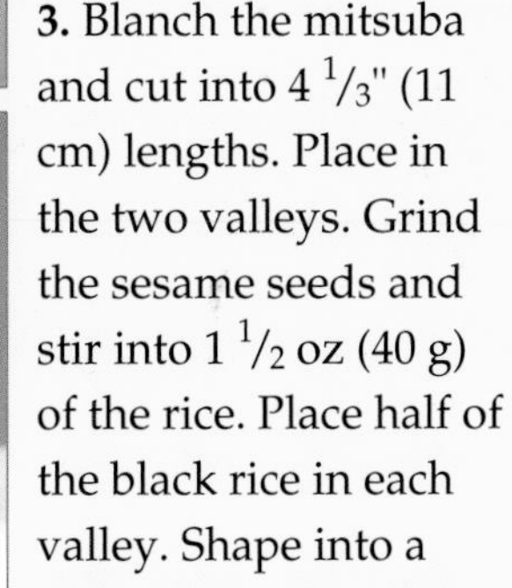

3. Blanch the mitsuba and cut into 4 1/3" (11 cm) lengths. Place in the two valleys. Grind the sesame seeds and stir into 1 1/2 oz (40 g) of the rice. Place half of the black rice in each valley. Shape into a rectangle with plastic wrap and a rolling mat.

4. Make the sun by following steps 1–3 on the facing page. Place the mountain block on the bottom edge of a halfsheet of nori. Place the sun on top and roll. Seal the end with 2–3 grains of rice.

8

Using 3 grains of rice, attach 1/2 halfsheet onto 1 halfsheet of nori. Leaving 1 1/2" (4 cm) at the top, spread the remaining 3 1/2 oz (100 g) of the rice on the nori. Place the river block along the bottom edge. Place the chrysanthemum fan shape on top.

9

Roll carefully into a tunnel shape. Flatten the ends and slice into 4 pieces.

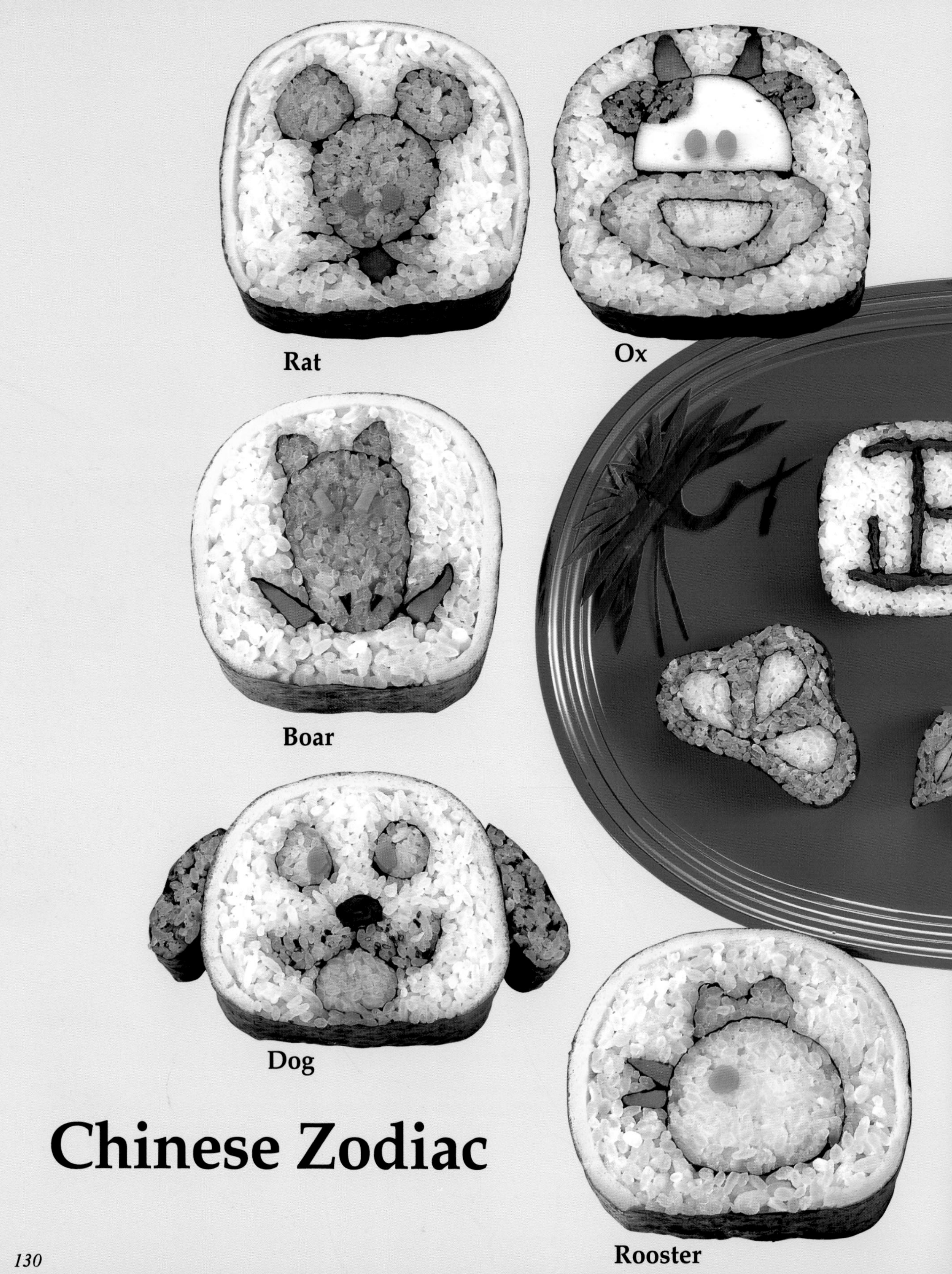

Rat

Ox

Boar

Dog

Rooster

Chinese Zodiac

Tiger
Rabbit
Dragon
Snake
Horse
Monkey
Ram

Rat

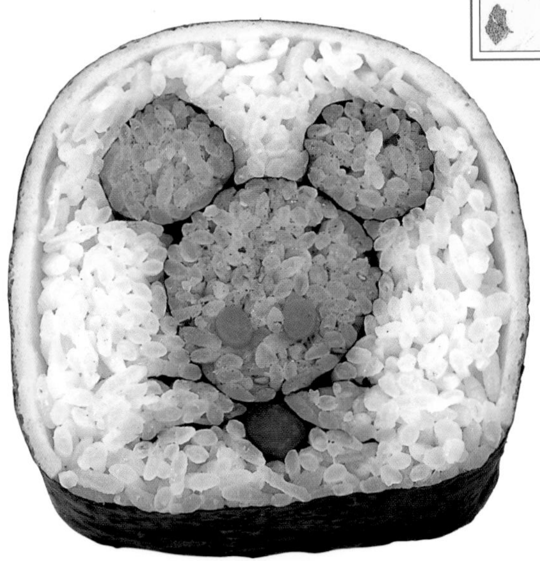

(for 1 roll)

$4\,^1/_3$" (11 cm) nozawana stalk
Small piece misozuke yamagobo
$^1/_2$ tsp yukari sprinkles
1 tsp ground black sesame seeds
$^1/_2$ thickness of an omelet sheet (p. 23)
$13\,^3/_4$ oz (390 g) sushi rice (p. 9)
Roasted nori

Setup: Trim the omelet sheet to 4 x 7" (10.5 x 18 cm). Stir the yukari (dried beefsteak leaves) and sesame seeds into 5 oz (140 g) of the sushi rice. (Use cooked carrot if yamagobo is unavailable.)

Face

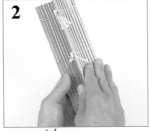

Form 3 oz (80 g) of the grey rice into a cylinder and place it at the bottom of $^2/_3$ of a halfsheet of nori (Fig. 1). Roll with the mat into a teardrop shape (Fig. 2).

Ears

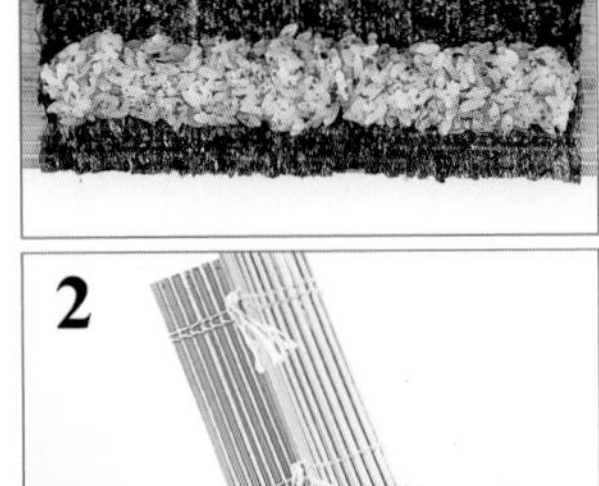

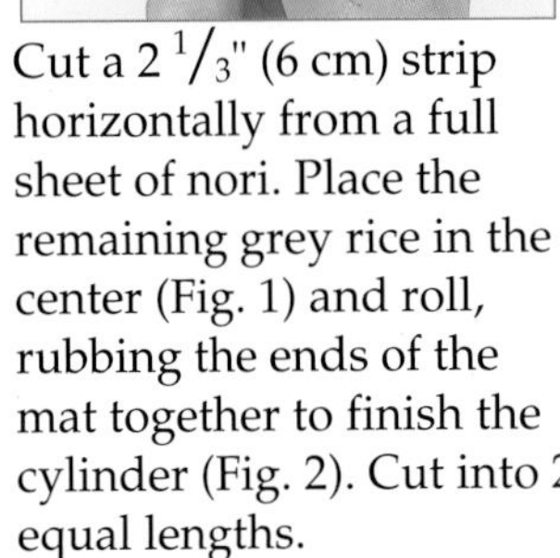

Cut a $2\,^1/_3$" (6 cm) strip horizontally from a full sheet of nori. Place the remaining grey rice in the center (Fig. 1) and roll, rubbing the ends of the mat together to finish the cylinder (Fig. 2). Cut into 2 equal lengths.

Nose

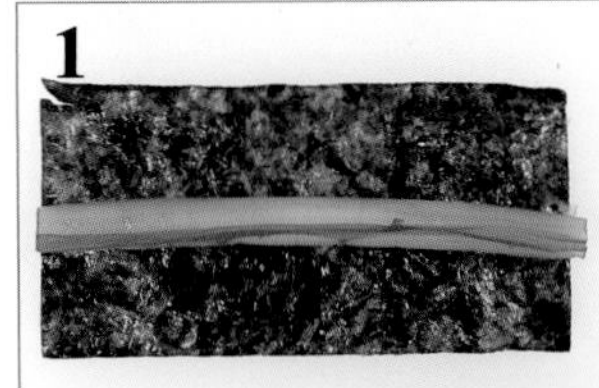

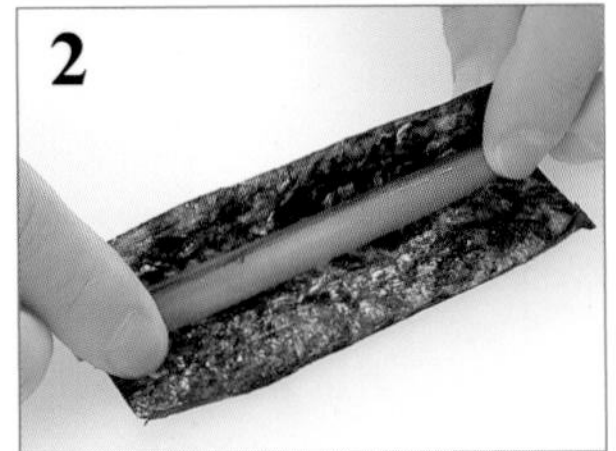

Place the nozawana on $^1/_4$ of a halfsheet of nori (Fig. 1). Roll by hand (Fig. 2).

Whiskers

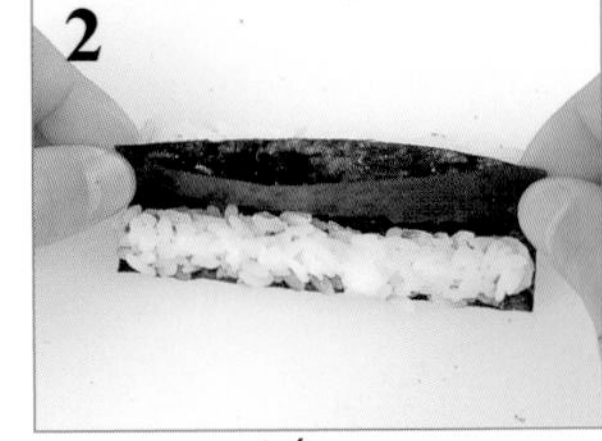

Cut two $1\,^1/_2$" (4 cm) strips from a halfsheet of nori. Spread $^3/_4$ oz (20 g) of the white rice on one of the strips, leaving a space along the center. Fold the other strip in half and tuck it in the space.

Using 3 grains of rice, attach $^1/_2$ halfsheet onto 1 halfsheet of nori (see p. 85, Fig. 4). Place the omelet sheet in the center of the nori. Spread 3 $^1/_2$ oz (100 g) of the rice on the omelet. Place a $^3/_4$ oz (20 g) ridge in the center.

Place the ears on either side of the ridge. Place the face between the ears, pointed end up.

Place 1 oz (30 g) of the rice on each side of the face, matching the height of the face *(left)*. Place the whiskers on the face, then the nose *(above)*.

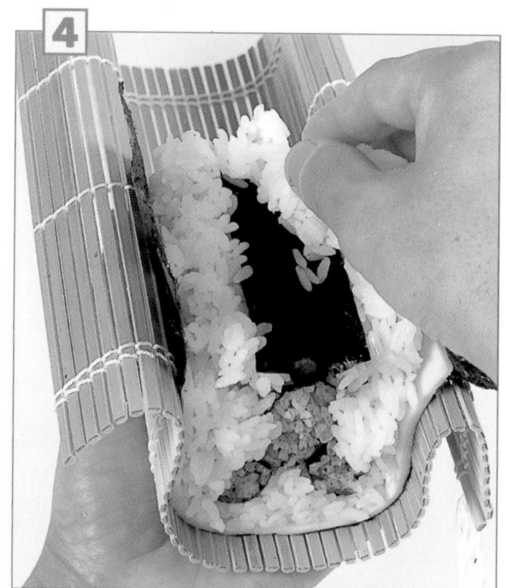

Place the mat in your hand, press the sides together, and spread the remaining 1 $^3/_4$ oz (50 g) of the rice on top. Fold the nori over the rice.

Place the roll seam side down and form into a tunnel shape. Slide the sushi to the ends of the mat to flatten the edges.

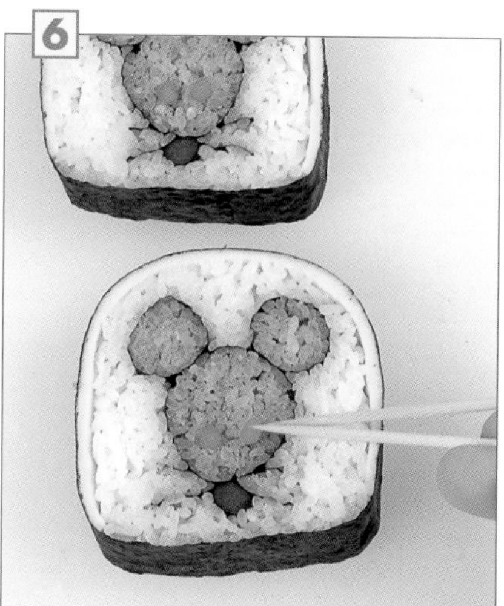

Slice into 4 pieces, wiping the blade with a wet towel after each slice. Slice the yamagobo into thin rounds (eyes) and place them on the faces.

Ox

(for 1 roll)

4 1/3" (11 cm) takuan pickles
4 1/3" (11 cm) kamaboko (fish cake)
1/2" (1.5 cm)-wide omelet
Small piece misozuke yamagobo
1 1/2 Tbsp oboro sprinkles (p. 18)
1 Tbsp ground black sesame seeds
11 oz (310 g) sushi rice (p. 9)
Roasted nori

Setup: Prepare the omelet as on p. 19. Stir the oboro into 3 oz (80 g) of the rice. Stir the sesame seeds into 1 1/2 oz (40 g) of the rice.

Mouth

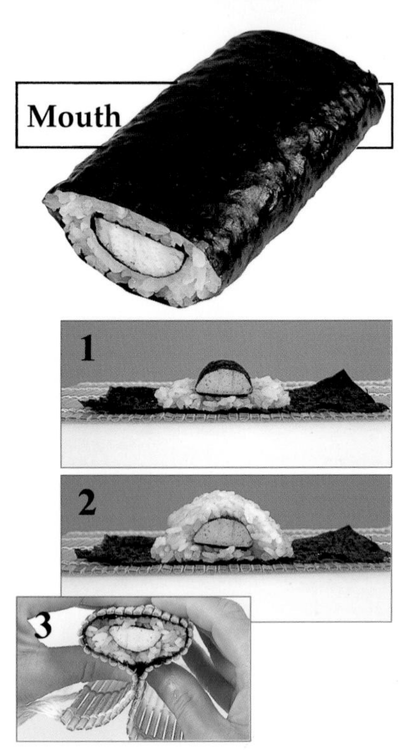

Trim the omelet into a half cylinder and wrap in 1/2 of a halfsheet of nori. Spread half of the pink rice in the center of 2/3 of a halfsheet of nori and place the omelet package on top (Fig. 1). Cover the omelet with the remaining pink rice (Fig. 2), fold the nori over, and form into a half cylinder (Fig. 3).

Head

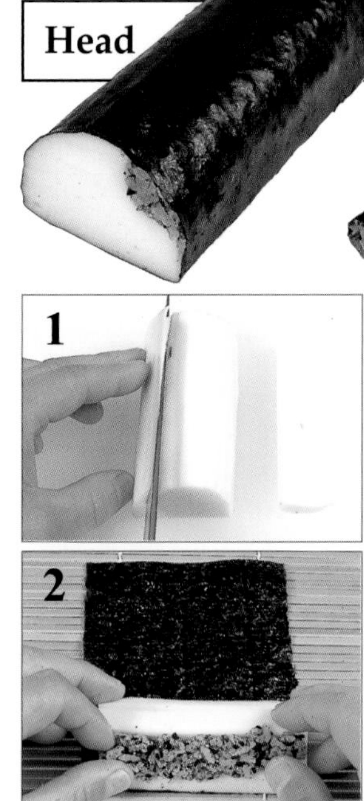

Trim the kamaboko into a half cylinder that is 3/8" (1 cm) narrower than the pink mouth package (Fig. 1). Cut a groove into one side and pack it with around 1/2 oz (15 g) of the black rice (Fig. 2). Wrap in 2/3 of a halfsheet of nori.

Ears

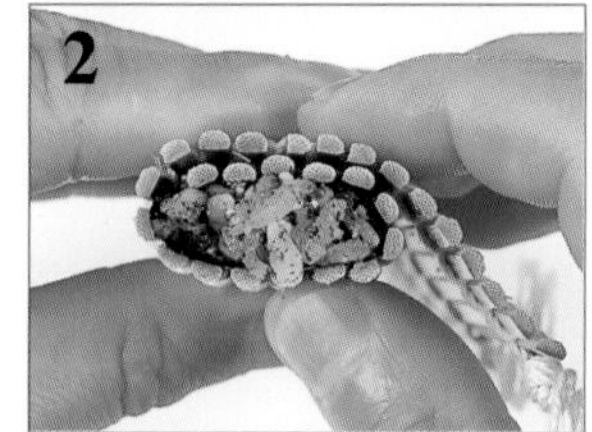

Place the remaining black rice in a cylinder at the center of 1/3 of a halfsheet of nori (Fig. 1). Roll into an oval with the mat (Fig. 2) and cut in half lengthwise.

Horns

Cut the takuan into 2 wedges and place each on 1/4 of a halfsheet of nori (Fig. 1). Wrap by hand (Fig. 2).

1

Using 3 grains of rice, attach $^1/_2$ halfsheet onto 1 halfsheet of nori. Leaving 1" (3 cm) at the top and bottom, spread 3 $^1/_2$ oz (100 g) of the rice on the nori. Leaving $^3/_4$" (2 cm) of rice in the center, make two grooves with a chopstick *(left)*. Place the takuan packages in the grooves, pointed end down *(above)*.

2

Place the ears along the outer edge of each horn, cut sides facing each other. Place the face between the ears, flat side up.

3

Place $^1/_2$ oz (15 g) of the rice on each ear, matching the height of the face. Place the mouth on top of the face, flat side down.

4

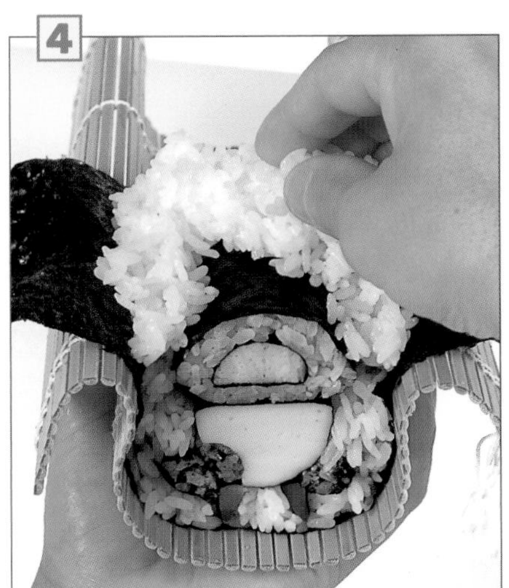

Place the mat in your hand, press the sides together, and spread the remaining 2 oz (60 g) of rice on the sides of the mouth, then on top.

5

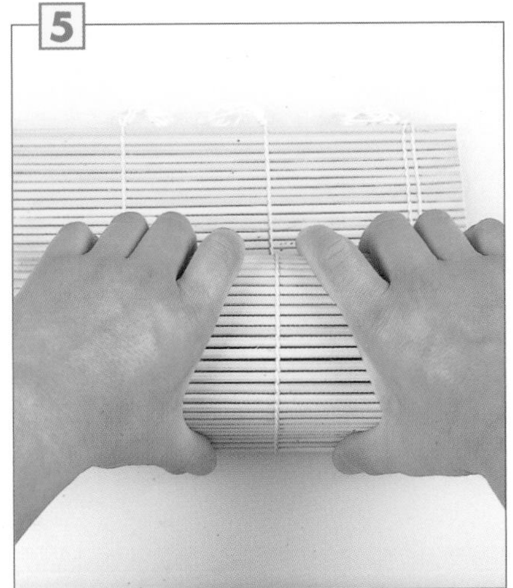

Fold the nori over the rice. Place the roll seam side down and form into a tunnel shape. Flatten the edges.

6

Slice into 4 pieces, wiping the blade with a wet towel after each slice. Slice the yamagobo into thin rounds (eyes) and place them on the faces.

Tiger

(for 1 roll)

39" (99 cm) simmered gourd (p. 17)
1 string bean
Small piece misozuke yamagobo
6 Tbsp egg sprinkles (p. 80)
$^1/_2$ Tbsp ground black sesame seeds
15 oz (420 g) sushi rice (p. 9)
Roasted nori

Setup: Cut the gourd into 9 strips 4 $^1/_3$" (11 cm) long and $^1/_2$" (1.5 cm)-wide. Blanch the green bean and trim to 4 $^1/_3$" (11 cm). Mix the egg sprinkles into 12 $^1/_2$ oz (350 g) of the rice. Mix the sesame seeds into 1 $^1/_2$ oz (40 g) of the rice. There will be 1 oz (30 g) of white rice left.

Forehead Stripes

1. Spread two gourd strips in the center of $^1/_3$ of a half-sheet of nori (Fig. 1). Fold the nori over to wrap. Make two more of these packages.
2. Make a layered stack: $^1/_3$ oz (10 g) yellow rice, gourd package, 1/3 oz (10 g) yellow rice, gourd package, $^2/_3$ oz (20 g) yellow rice (Fig. 2).
3. Slowly cut in half lengthwise (Fig. 3).
4. Insert the third gourd package between the two halves (Fig. 4).

Cheek Stripes

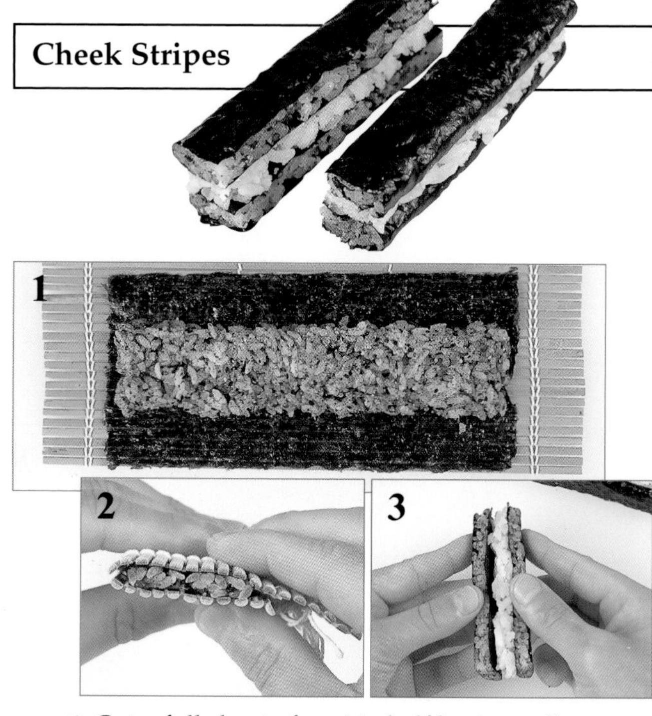

1. Cut a full sheet of nori in half horizontally. Spread the black rice in a 1 $^1/_2$" (4 cm)-wide stripe in the center (Fig. 1).
2. Fold the nori over the rice. Press into a thin layer with the mat (Fig. 2). Cut in half crosswise, then in half lengthwise.
3. Spread $^1/_3$ oz (10 g) of the yellow rice between two of the pieces from step 2 (Fig. 3). Repeat with the other two pieces.

Eyes

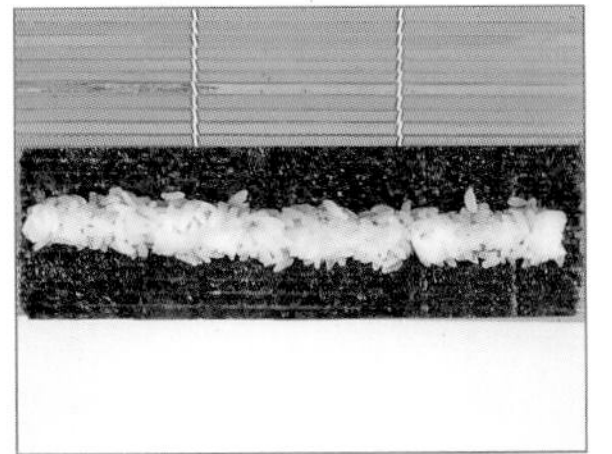

Cut $^{1}/_{3}$ of a full sheet of nori horizontally. Place the 1 oz (30 g) of white rice in the center in a line. Roll into a cylinder and cut half crosswise.

Nose

Place the string bean on $^{1}/_{4}$ of a halfsheet. Roll by hand, sealing the end with 3 grains of rice.

Mouth

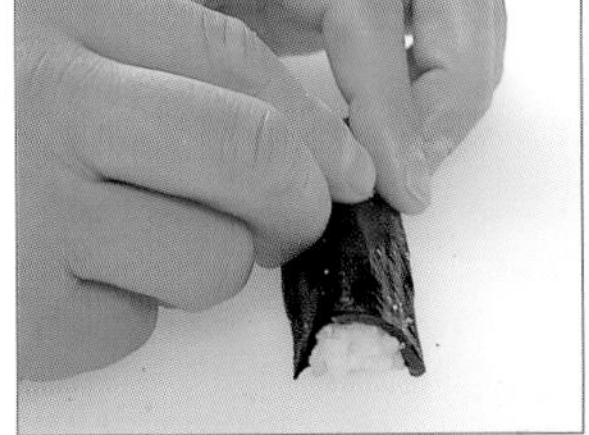

Spread 3 gourd strips on $^{1}/_{3}$ of a halfsheet of nori and fold. Use the gourd package and $^{1}/_{3}$ oz (10 g) yellow rice to make a half cylinder.

Ears

Cut a full sheet of nori in half crosswise. Place 3 oz (80 g) of the yellow rice in the center. Roll into a cylinder and cut into two equal lengths.

1

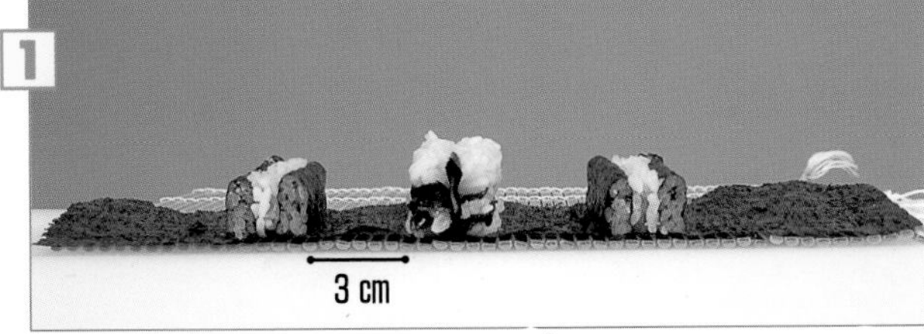

Using 3 grains of rice, attach $^{1}/_{2}$ halfsheet onto 1 half-sheet of nori. Place the forehead package in the center and the cheek packages 1" (3 cm) above and below.

2

Place 1 $^{1}/_{2}$ oz of yellow rice on each side of the forehead and $^{1}/_{3}$ oz (10 g) of the yellow rice above and below the cheeks.

3

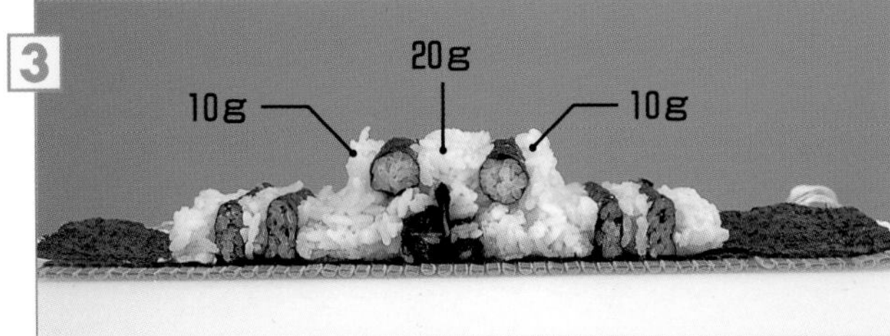

Place $^{2}/_{3}$ oz (20 g) of the yellow rice on top of the forehead. Place the eyes on each side. Place $^{1}/_{3}$ oz (10 g) of the yellow rice on each side of the eyes.

4

Place the nose in the center. Cover the nose and eyes with 1 $^{1}/_{2}$ oz (40 g) of the rice. Place the mouth on top, rice side down.

5

With the mat in your hand, press the sides together and spread the remaining yellow rice on top. Fold the nori over the rice and form into a tunnel shape.

6

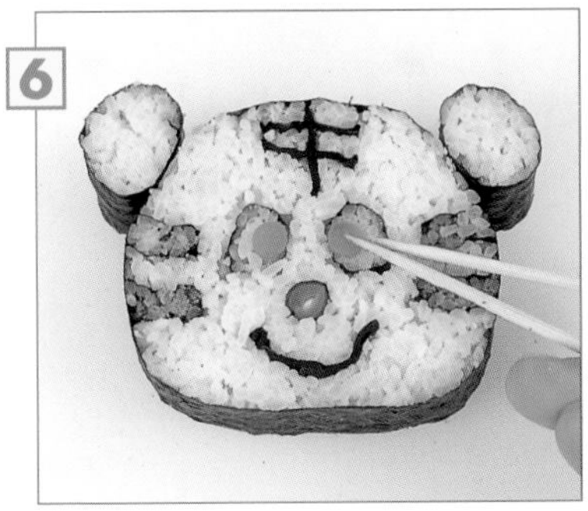

Flatten the edges and slice into 4 pieces. Cut each ear roll into 4 slices and place next to the head. Slice the yamagobo into thin rounds (eyes) and place them on the faces.

Rabbit

(for 1 roll)

$4\,^{1}/_{3}$" (11 cm) nozawana stalk
$4\,^{1}/_{3}$" (11 cm) simmered gourd (p. 17)
2 tsp oboro sprinkles (p. 18)
$^{1}/_{2}$ thickness of an omelet sheet (p. 23)
$9\,^{1}/_{4}$ oz (270 g) sushi rice (p. 9)
Roasted nori

Setup: Trim the omelet sheet to 4 x 7" (10.5 x 18 cm). Mix the oboro sprinkles into 1 oz (30 g) of the rice.

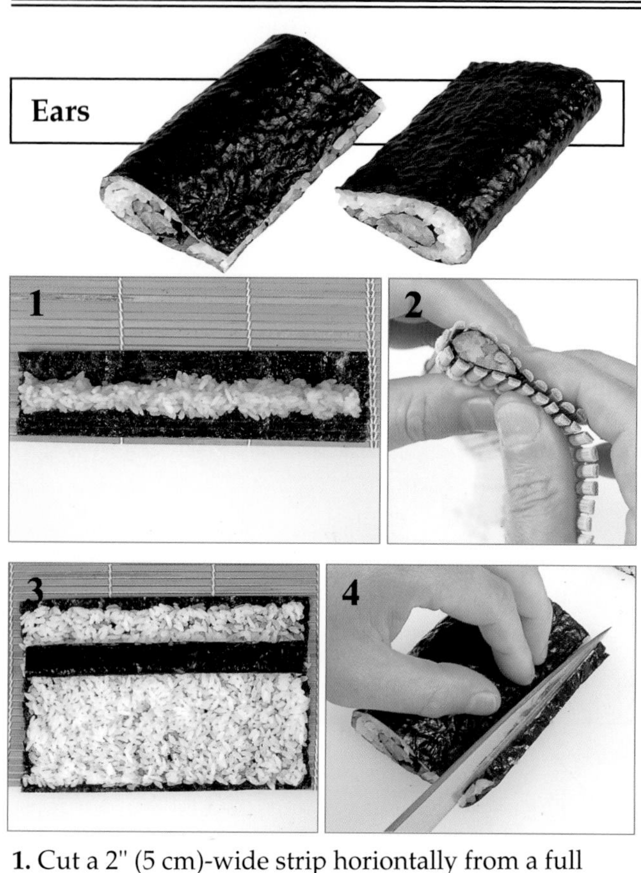

1. Cut a 2" (5 cm)-wide strip horiontally from a full sheet of nori. Place the pink rice in a ridge in the center (Fig. 1). Press the sides together into a teardrop (Fig. 2).
2. Spread $3\,^{1}/_{2}$ oz (100 g) of the white rice on the remaining piece of nori. Place the pink package $^{3}/_{8}$" (1 cm) from the top, pointed end up (Fig. 3). Press the sides together and trim off a bit of the pointed end.

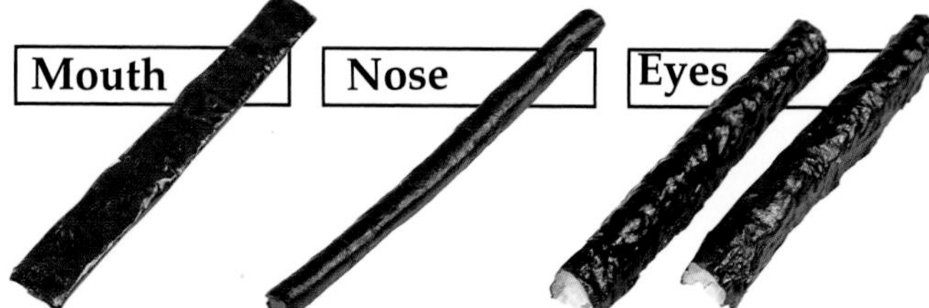

MOUTH
Place the gourd strip in the center of a $1\,^{1}/_{2}$" (4 cm) strip cut from a halfsheet of nori. Fold the nori over the strip.

NOSE
Place the nozawana stalk in the center of a 1" (3 cm) strip cut from a halfsheet of nori. Roll.

EYES
Place $^{2}/_{3}$ oz (20 g) of the rice on $^{1}/_{3}$ of a halfsheet of nori (Fig. 1). Roll into an oval (Fig. 2). Cut the oval in half lengthwise along the flat side.

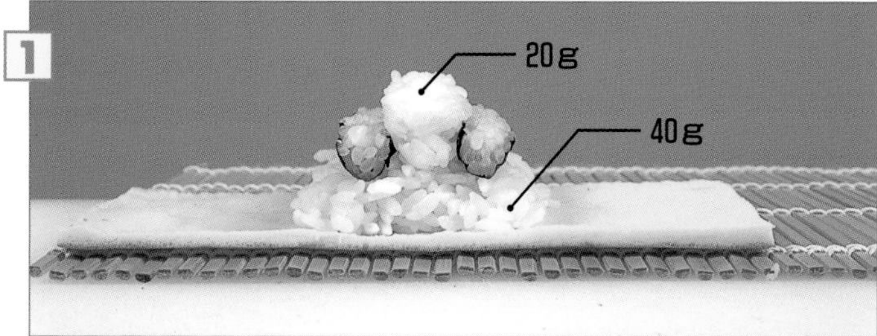

Place the omelet on a rolling mat, short side toward you. Place 1 $^1/_2$ oz (40 g) of the rice in the center, forming a 2 $^3/_4$" (7 cm)-wide strip. Place the eyes on the strip, cut side up, and $^2/_3$ oz (20 g) of the rice between.

Place the nose along the center. Place $^1/_3$ oz (10 g) of rice on the outside of each eye roll to match the height of the eyes, keeping the total width (2 $^3/_4$"; 7 cm) constant.

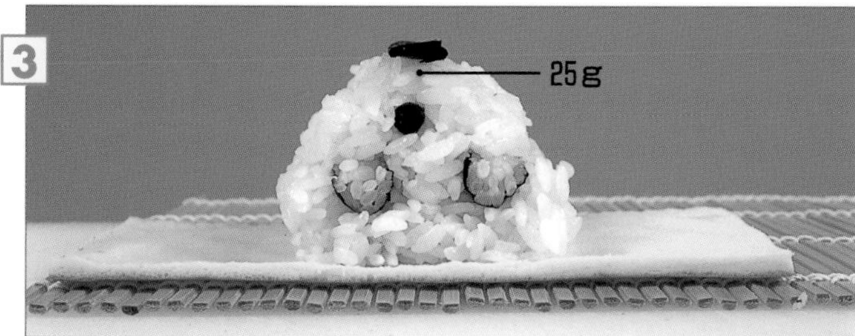

Cover the nose and eyes with $^3/_4$ oz (25 g) of the rice. Place the mouth on top. The overall shape should be close to a half cylinder.

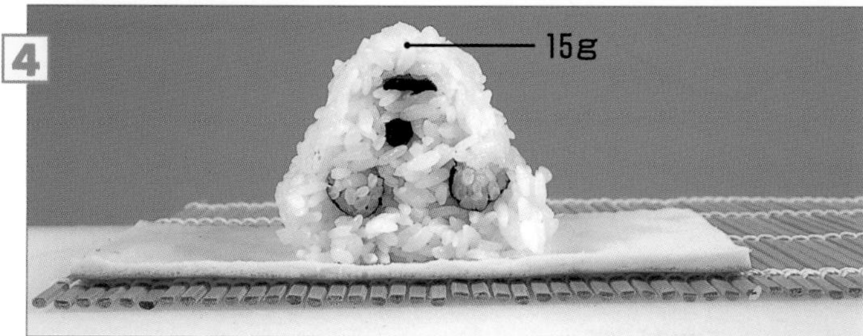

Place $^1/_2$ oz (15 g) of the rice over the mouth. Now the overall shape should be somewhat triangular.

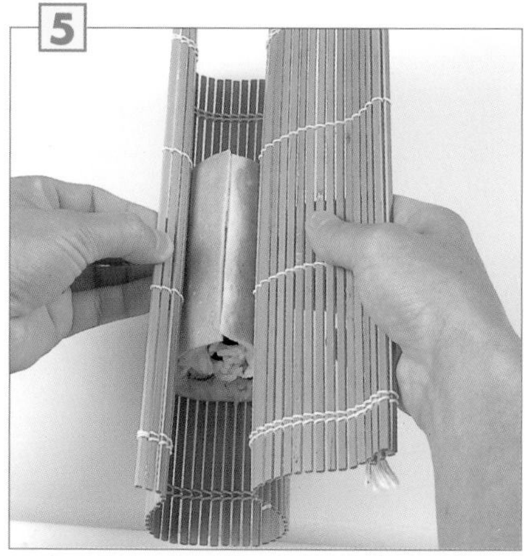

Lift both ends of the mat so that the omelet ends touch. Roll the cylinder up and down in the mat to finish the shape.

Place on a halfsheet of nori and roll by hand. Seal the edge with grains of rice. Roll up and down in the mat to finish the shape. Flatten the ends.

Cut the face and ears into 4 slices of matching thickness. Place the ears next to the faces and serve.

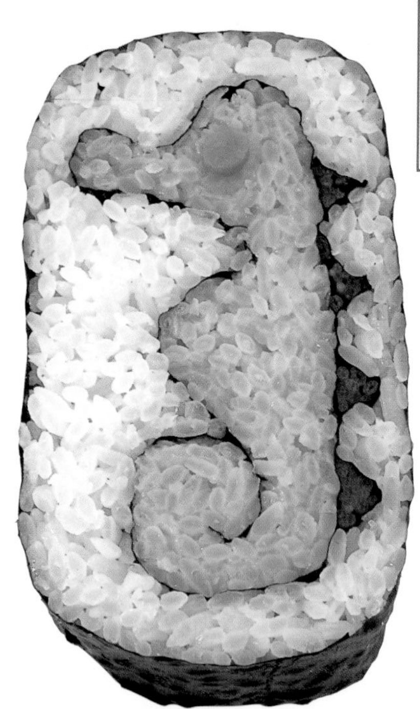

Dragon

(for 1 roll)

$^{1}/_{2}$ bunch mitsuba (honewort)
Small piece misozuke yamagobo
1 $^{1}/_{2}$ oz (40 g) cod roe
11 $^{2}/_{3}$ oz (330 g) sushi rice (p. 9)
Roasted nori

Setup: Blanch the mitsuba, rinse with cold water, and squeeze well. Cut into 4 $^{1}/_{3}$" (11 cm) lengths. Remove the membrane from the cod roe and stir into 4 $^{1}/_{4}$ oz (120 g) of the rice.

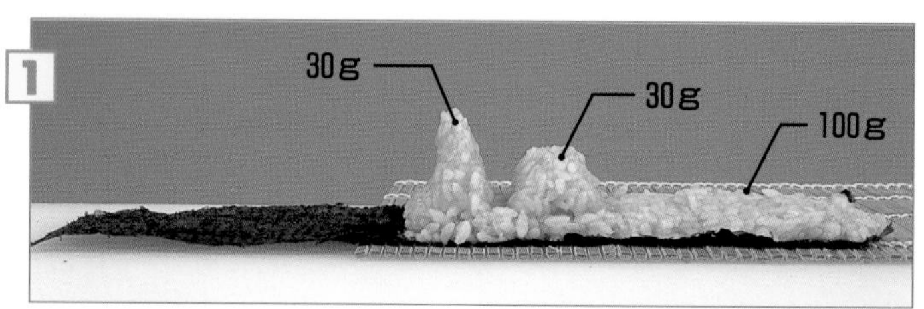

Using 3 grains of rice, attach $^{2}/_{3}$ halfsheet onto 1 half-sheet of nori. Spread 3 $^{1}/_{2}$ oz (100 g) of the red rice on the upper 7" (18 cm) of the nori. Place a 1 oz (30 g) ridge at the bottom edge of the rice (this will be the head). Form the remaining 1 oz (30 g) of red rice into a low hill and place it close to the ridge (this will be the belly).

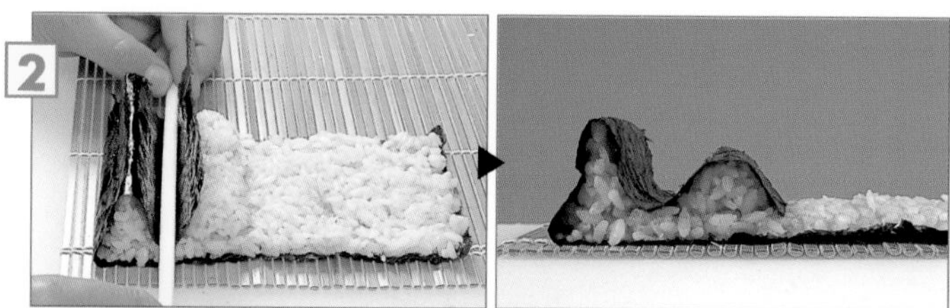

Fold the nori up over the ridge. Press it down into the valley with a chopstick *(far left)*. Curve the remaining rice over the low hill *(left)*.

Pinch the ridge into a snout with a rolling mat *(far left)*. Turn the mat around so that the top edge is now at the bottom. Roll the remaining nori and riceas for a jelly roll (*left*; this will be the tail).

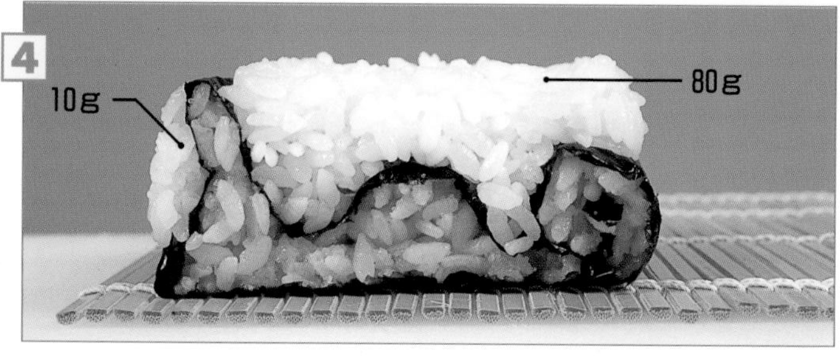

Place $^{1}/_{4}$ oz (10 g) of the rice next to the head. Place 3 oz (80 g) of the rice over the belly and tail, so that the whole forms a rectangular shape.

5

Using 3 grains of rice, attach $^1/_2$ halfsheet onto 1 halfsheet of nori once more. Leaving 2 $^3/_4$" (7 cm) at top and bottom, spread 3 $^1/_2$ oz (100 g) of the rice on the nori. Place $^1/_2$ of a halfsheet just above the midpoint of the rice *(far left)*. Beginning at the bottom of the nori, press a chopstick down in 4 places, pushing the nori toward you to make ripples *(center)*. Place some mitsuba stalks in each of the valleys *(left)*.

6

Place the rectangle shape from step 4 on top.

7

Placing the mat in your hand, press the sides together and spread $^1/_3$ oz (10 g) of the rice over the mouth and the remaining $^1/_3$ oz (10 g) over the tail.

8

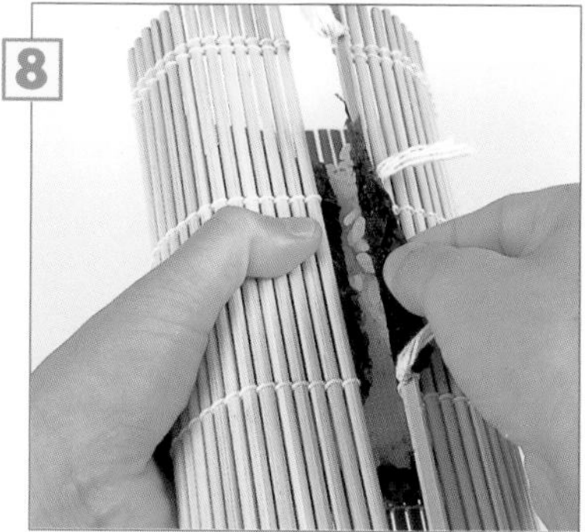

Fold the nori over the rice and close.

9

Place the roll on a board, snout pointing up, and form into a rectangle. (Keep the seam side up in this case, to avoid crushing the snout.) Slide the sushi to the ends of the mat to flatten the edges.

10

Slice into 4 pieces, wiping the blade with a wet towel after each slice. Slice the yamagobo into thin rounds (eyes) and place them on the faces.

Snake

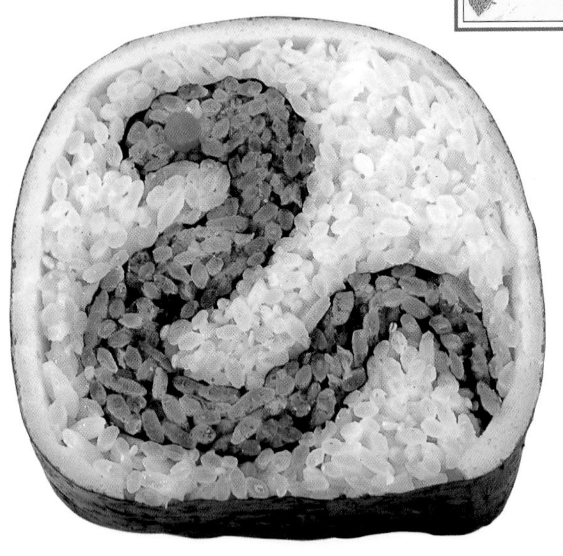

(for 1 roll)

Small piece misozuke yamagobo
1 Tbsp aonori sprinkles
$^1/_3$ oz (10 g) mibuna pickles
1–2 tsp toasted sesame seeds
$^1/_2$ thickness of an omelet sheet (p. 23)
12 $^1/_3$ oz (350 g) sushi rice (p. 9)
Roasted nori

Setup: Trim the omelet sheet to 4 x 7" (10.5 x 18 cm). Mince the mibunazuke (pickled greens; may be substituted with steamed spinach). Mix the mibunazuke and aonori into 3 $^1/_2$ oz (100 g) of the rice. Mix the sesame seeds into the remaining rice.

1

Using 3 grains of rice, attach 1 halfsheet onto another halfsheet of nori *(right)*.

2

Spread the green rice over half of the long nori in a wedge shape, thick end at the center.

3

Fold the nori over the green rice. This package will be the snake. The thicker end is the head.

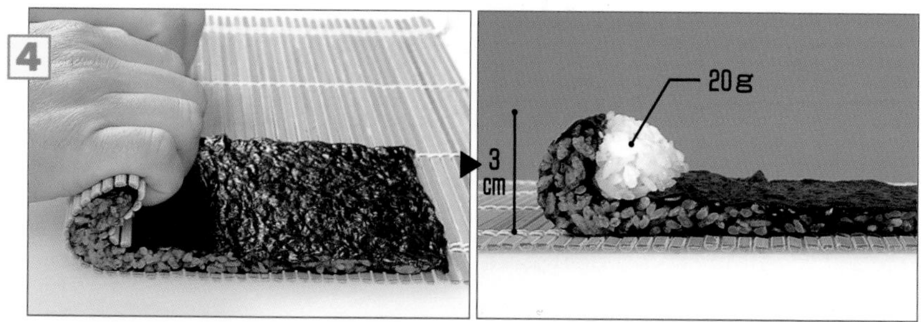

Place the snake package on a rolling mat, head toward you. With the mat, curve the head upward to a 1" (3 cm) height *(far left)*. Form $^2/_3$ oz (20 g) of the sesame rice into a cylinder and place it in the curve *(left)*.

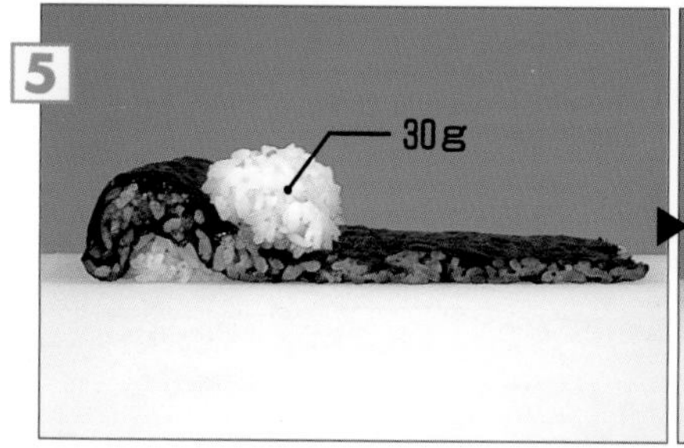

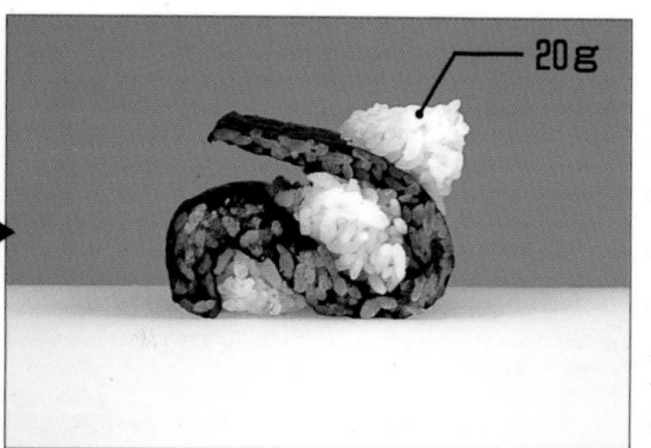

Remove the mat and turn the package over. Form 1 oz (30 g) of the sesame rice into a cylinder and place it on the downhill slope of the curve *(far left)*. Now, curve the tail of the snake back toward the head and place $^2/_3$ oz (20 g) of the sesame rice in another cylinder on top of the tail *(left)*.

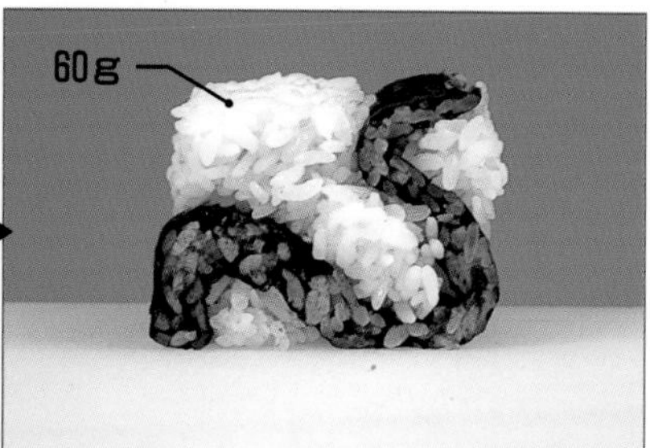

Curve the tail back over the last rice cylinder *(far left)*. Place 2 oz (60 g) of the sesame rice on top of the head curve so that the whole assembly forms a rectangular block *(left)*.

Using 3 grains of rice, attach $^1/_2$ halfsheet onto 1 halfsheet of nori. Place the omelet sheet in the center. Spread 3 oz (80 g) of the sesame rice on the omelet. Place the snake package on the center of the rice, head side down.

Place the mat in your hand, press the sides together, and spread the remaining 1 $^1/_2$ oz (40 g) of the sesame rice on top. Fold the nori over the rice. Place the roll seam side down and form into a tunnel shape.

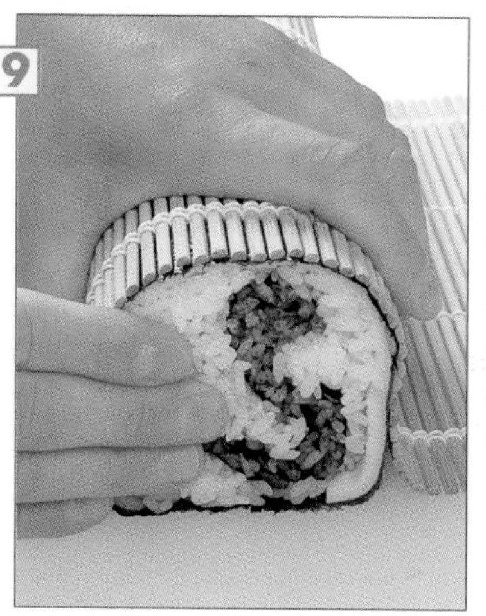

Slide the sushi to the ends of the mat to flatten the edges. Slice into 4 pieces, wiping the blade with a wet towel after each slice. Slice the yamagobo into thin rounds (eyes) and place them on the heads.

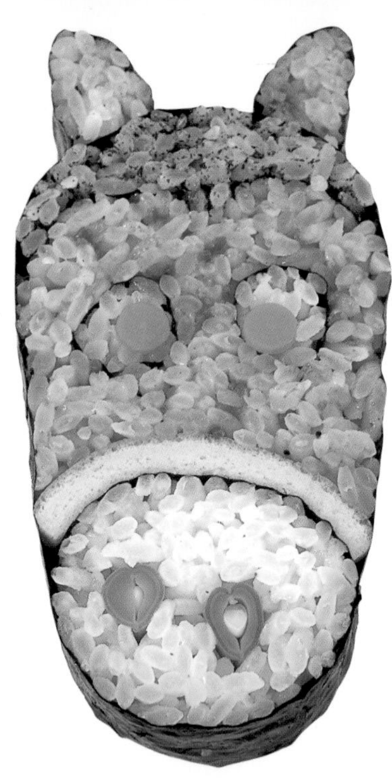

Horse

(for 1 roll)

2 string beans
Small piece misozuke yamagobo
1 tsp ground black sesame seeds
$^3/_4$ oz (20 g) bonito flakes (furikake)
$^1/_2$ thickness of an omelet sheet (p. 23)
10 $^1/_4$ oz (290 g) sushi rice (p. 9)
Roasted nori

Setup: Boil the string beans and trim to 4 $^1/_3$" (11 cm). Trim the omelet sheet to 4 x 1 $^1/_2$" (10.5 x 4 cm). Mix the furikake (substitute with shaved bonito) into 5 oz (140 g) of the rice. Mix the sesame seeds into 1 $^1/_2$ oz (40 g) of the rice.

Eyes

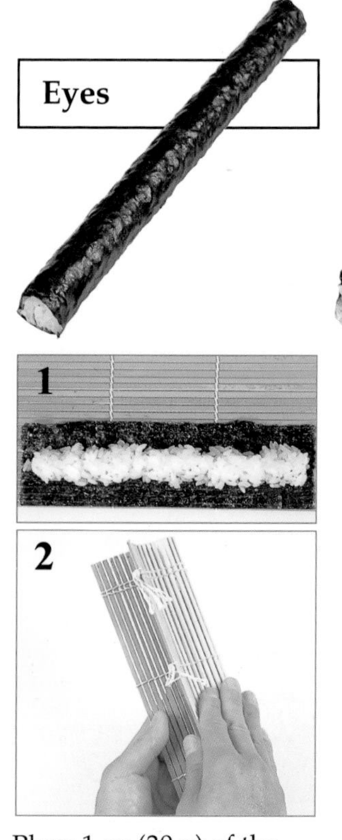

Place 1 oz (30 g) of the white rice in a line on $^1/_3$ of a full sheet of nori (Fig. 1). Roll, rubbing the ends of the mat together to finish the cylinder (Fig. 2).

Ears

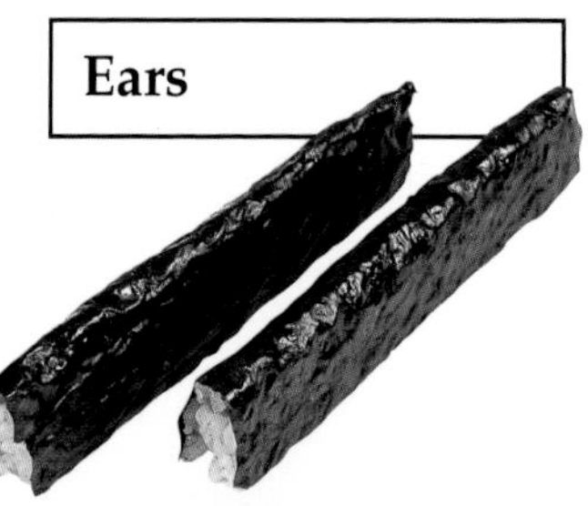

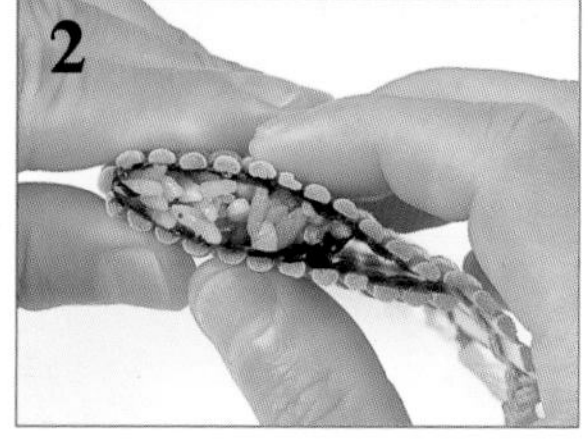

Place 1 oz (30 g) of the brown rice on the upper portion of $^1/_2$ of a halfsheet of nori (Fig. 1). Fold the lower nori over into a thin oval (Fig. 2). Slice in half lengthwise.

Snout

1. Spread 1 $^3/_8$ oz (40 g) of the white rice in a 1 $^1/_2$" (4 cm) strip in the center of 2/3 of a halfsheet of nori. Make 2 grooves with chopsticks (Fig. 1).
2. Place the string beans in the grooves and place 1 $^3/_8$ oz (40 g) of the white rice on top (Fig. 2). This will be the snout.
3. Wrap the nori over the rice and roll, making an oval shape (Fig. 3).

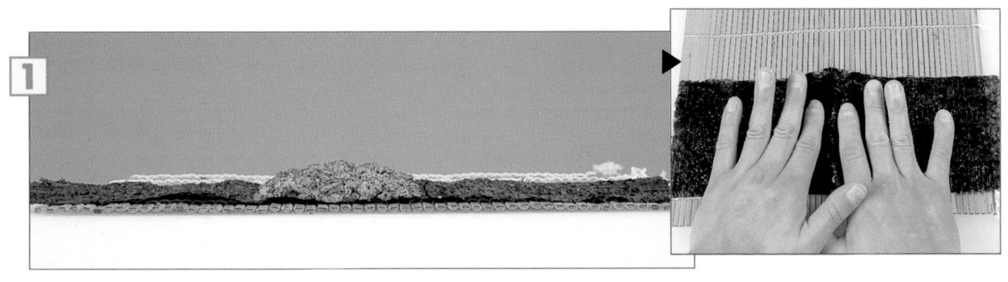
1

Using 3 grains of rice, attach $^{1}/_{2}$ halfsheet onto 1 halfsheet of nori. Spread the black rice in a 2 $^{1}/_{3}$" (6 cm)-wide strip in the center, forming a low triangle *(far left)*. Press $^{1}/_{2}$ of a halfsheet of nori on top of the rice, making a ridge in the center *(left)*.

Spread 1 $^{1}/_{2}$ oz (40 g) of the brown rice on the upper nori, leaving $^{3}/_{8}$" (1 cm) of nori at both edges. Cut the eye cylinder into two lengths and place on top. Place $^{1}/_{3}$ oz (10 g) of the brown rice on each side of the eyes and between them.

3

Spread the remaining brown rice on top of the eyes, matching the width of the rice from step 2. The top should be concave.

4

Place the egg in the concavity and the snout on top, seam side down.

5

Place 3 grains of rice on one edge of the long nori. Lift the mat with both hands and fold the nori over the snout.

6

Form the head into an egg shape, with the top of the head slightly thicker than the snout. Slice the sushi to the ends of the mat and flatten the edges.

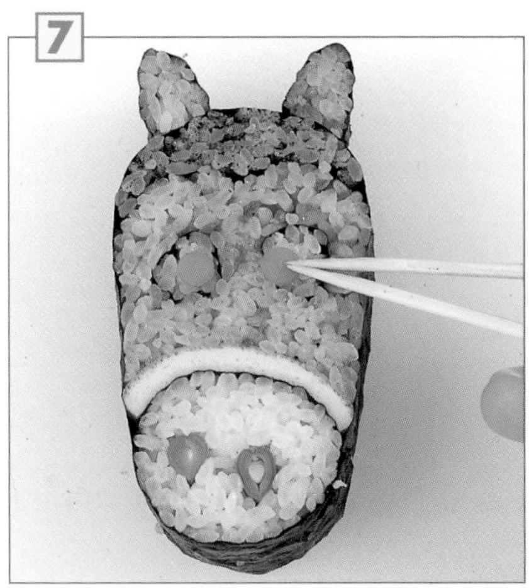
7

Slice the head and ear rolls into 4 slices each. Attach the ears to the heads. Slice the yamagobo into thin rounds (eyes) and place them on the faces.

Ram

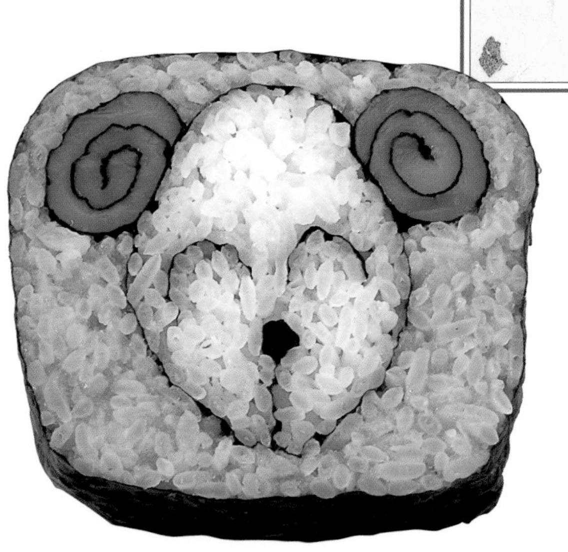

(for 1 roll)
1–2 large squid (ika)
4 $^{1}/_{3}$" (11 cm) nozawana leaves
3 oz (80 g) cod roe sacs
9 $^{1}/_{2}$ oz (270 g) sushi rice (p. 9)
Roasted nori

Setup: Remove the skin from the squid bodies and slice into two 4 x 3" (10.5 x 8 cm) rectangles. Remove the membrane from the cod roe and stir the roe into 4 $^{1}/_{4}$ oz (120 g) of the rice.

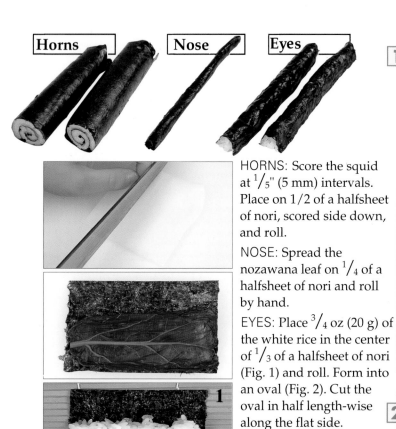

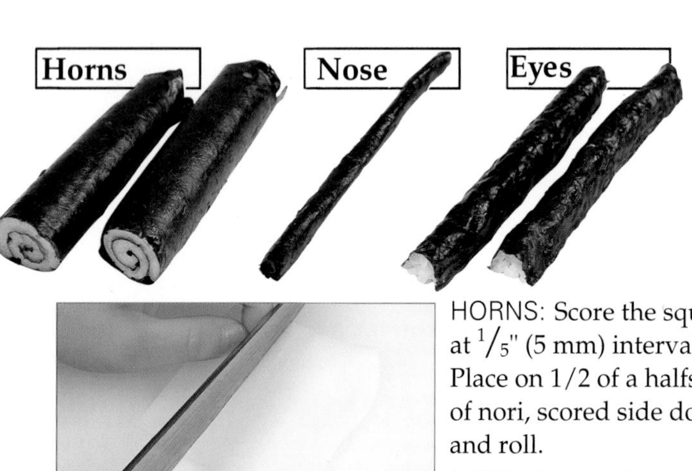

HORNS: Score the squid at $^{1}/_{5}$" (5 mm) intervals. Place on 1/2 of a halfsheet of nori, scored side down, and roll.

NOSE: Spread the nozawana leaf on $^{1}/_{4}$ of a halfsheet of nori and roll by hand.

EYES: Place $^{3}/_{4}$ oz (20 g) of the white rice in the center of $^{1}/_{3}$ of a halfsheet of nori (Fig. 1) and roll. Form into an oval (Fig. 2). Cut the oval in half length-wise along the flat side.

Place a halfsheet of nori on a mat and spread 1 $^{1}/_{2}$ oz (40 g) of the white rice in a 3" (8 cm)-wide strip in the center. Place another $^{2}/_{3}$ oz (20 g) of the white rice on top, in a 1" (3 cm)-wide strip *(above)*. Press a chopstick gently into the upper layer of the rice. *(left)*

Place the nose into the groove made by the chopsick. Place the eyes on top, cut side down. Place $^{1}/_{3}$ oz (10 g) of the rice between the eyes.

3

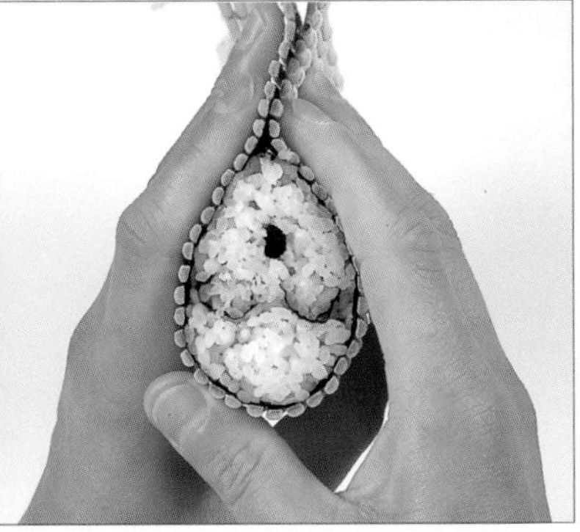

Place the mat in your curved hand and spread the remaining 2 oz (60 g) of white rice to cover the eyes *(far left)*. Press the sides together into a teardrop *(left)*.

4

Slice into the pointed end up to the nose *(far left)*. Cut a $^1/_2$" (1.5 cm)-wide strip from a halfsheet of nori and place it in the opening *(left)* to complete the face.

5

Using 3 grains of rice, attach $^1/_2$ halfsheet onto 1 halfsheet of nori. Leaving 1 $^1/_2$" (4 cm) at the top and bottom, spread 3 oz (80 g) of the red rice on the nori. Place the face in the center, pointed end up. Place the horns on either side.

6

Place 1 $^1/_2$" (40 g) of the red rice on both sides of the face, building it up to match the height of the face and the width of the ears.

7

Place the mat in your hand, press the sides together, and spread the remaining red rice on top. Fold the nori over the rice. Place the roll seam side down and form into a square shape.

8

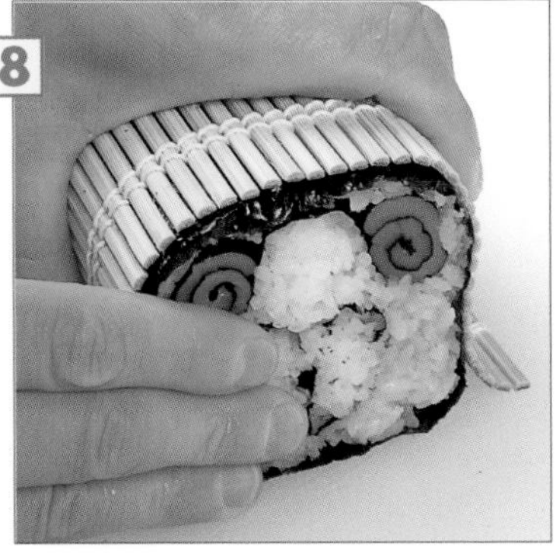

Slide the sushi to the ends of the mat to flatten the edges. Slice into 4 pieces, wiping the blade with a wet towel after each slice.

Monkey

(for 1 roll)

4 1/3" (11 cm) nozawana stalk
17 1/3" (44 cm) simmered gourd
Small piece misozuke yamagobo
3 Tbsp ami tsukudani
2–3 Tbsp oboro sprinkles (p. 18)
11 1/3 oz (320 g) sushi rice (p. 9)
Roasted nori

Setup: Cut the gourd into 4 strips 4 1/3" (11 cm) long and 1/2" (1.5 cm) wide. Mince the ami tsukudani (a sweet soy-flavored topping made with tiny fish) and mix well into 3 3/4 oz (110 g) of the sushi rice. Mix the oboro into another 6 1/3 oz (180 g) of the sushi rice.

Mouth

1

2

Place the 4 gourd strips in two stacks on 1/2 of a halfsheet of nori (Fig. 1). Wrap with the nori. Place 1/3 oz (10 g) of the pink rice in a line on a board. Cover with the gourd package and press into a half cylinder (Fig. 2).

Brow

Spread 1/3 oz (10 g) of the pink rice on each of two 1" (3 cm)-wide strips of a halfsheet of nori. Stack.

Nose

Eyes

Ears

1

2

NOSE: Roll the nozawana stalk by hand in 1/4 of a halfsheet of nori.
EYES: Place 1 1/4 oz (30 g) of the white rice on 1/3 of a full sheet of nori and roll (see p. 144).
Cut into 2 lengths.
EARS: Place 1 3/4 oz (50 g) of the brown rice on 1/3 of a full sheet of nori (Fig. 1) and roll,. Press into a narrow tunnel shape (Fig. 2) and cut into two lengths.

1

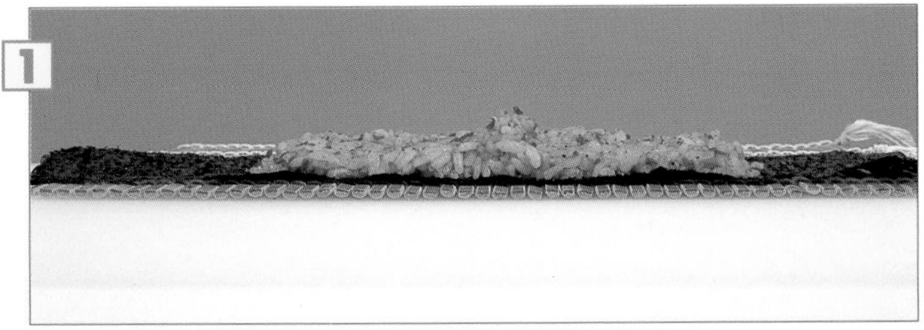

Using 3 grains of rice, attach $^{1}/_{2}$ halfsheet onto 1 halfsheet of nori. Leaving 2 $^{1}/_{3}$" (6 cm) at both ends, spread the remaining brown rice so that there is a slight peak in the center.

2

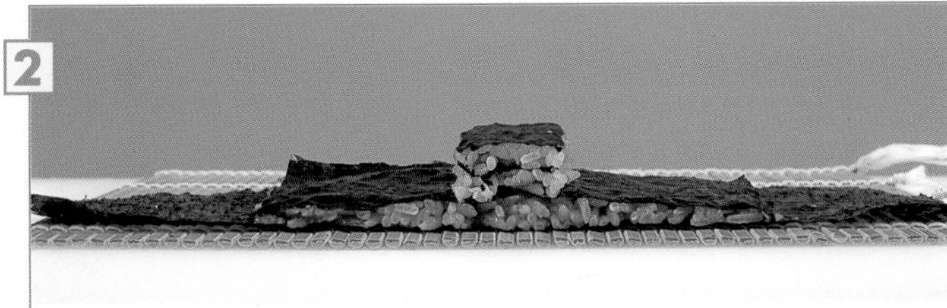

Cover the brown rice with $^{3}/_{4}$ of a halfsheet of nori. Place the brow layers on top, nori side up.

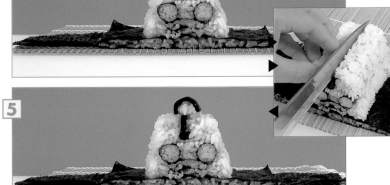

3

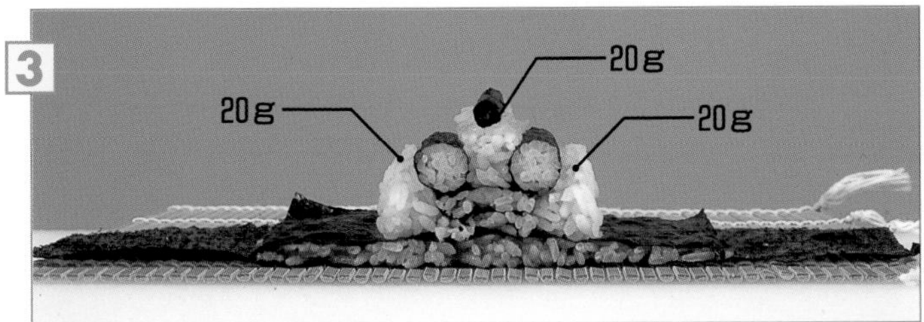

Place $^{3}/_{4}$ oz (20 g) of the pink rice on each side of the brow. Place the eyes on top of the brow. Mound another $^{3}/_{4}$ oz (20 g) of the pink rice between the eyes, slightly higher than the level of the eyes. Place the nose on top.

4

Surround the nose with 2 oz (60 g) of the pink rice. (A third of the rice goes on each side of the nose and the final third goes on top). The assembly should now look like a trapezoid.

5

Make an incision in the rice up to the nose. Cut a $^{3}/_{4}$" (2 cm)-wide strip from a halfsheet of nori, fold it in half, and place it in the opening. Place the mouth on top, rice side down.

6

Bring the sides of the mat together in your hand and place the remaining pink rice on top *(left)*. Fold the nori over and close, pressing in just below the eyes *(below)*.

7

Flatten the ends and slice the face and ears into 4 pieces each. Slice the yamagobo into thin rounds (eyes) and place them on the faces. Place two ears next to each face.

Rooster

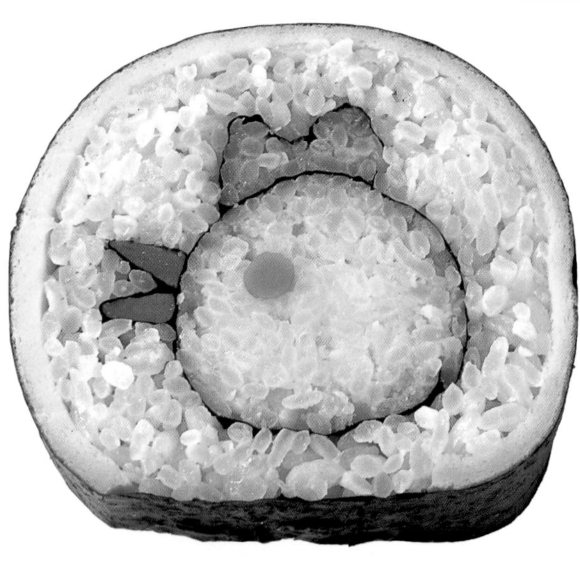

(for 1 roll)
4 1/3" (11 cm) takuan pickles
Small piece misozuke yamagobo
1 tsp oboro sprinkles (p. 18)
3 Tbsp egg sprinkles (p. 80)
1/2 thickness of an omelet sheet (p. 23)
10 1/4 oz (290 g) sushi rice (p. 9)
Roasted nori

Setup: Cut the takuan into narrow triangles 3/8" (1 cm) tall. Trim the omelet sheet to 4 x 7" (10.5 x 18 cm). Stir the oboro into 3/4 oz (20 g) of the rice. Stir the egg sprinkles into another 3 oz (80 g) of the rice. Cooked carrot may be substituted for the misozuke yamagobo.

Face

Form the yellow rice into a cylinder and place it on 2/3 of a halfsheet of nori (Fig. 1). Roll (Fig. 2) and finish the cylinder by rubbing the ends of the mat together.

Beak

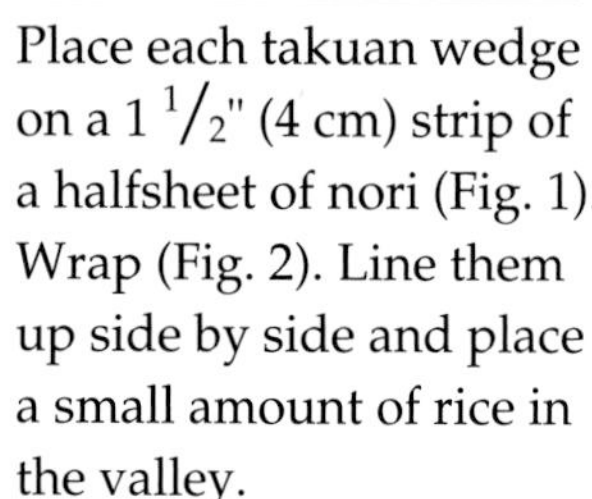

Place each takuan wedge on a 1 1/2" (4 cm) strip of a halfsheet of nori (Fig. 1). Wrap (Fig. 2). Line them up side by side and place a small amount of rice in the valley.

Comb

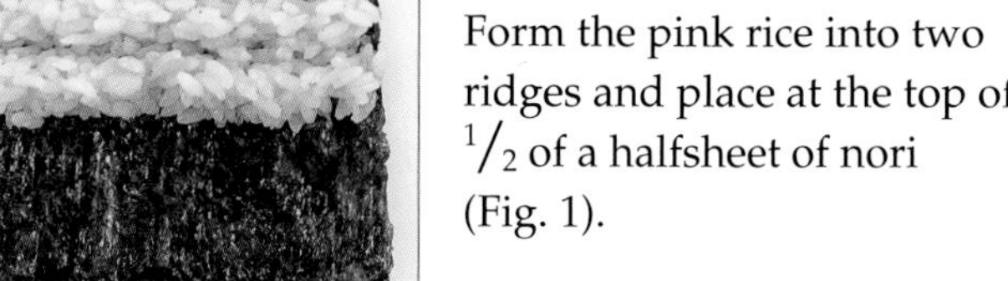

Form the pink rice into two ridges and place at the top of 1/2 of a halfsheet of nori (Fig. 1).

Fold the nori over the first ridge and press into the valley with a chopstick. Next, fold the nori over the second ridge and seal the end under the ridge (Fig. 2).

Place 1/3 oz (10 g) of the white rice in the valley between the ridges (Fig.3).

Using 3 grains of rice, attach $^{1}/_{2}$ halfsheet onto 1 halfsheet of nori. Place the omelet sheet in the center. Spread 3 oz (80 g) of the rice all over the omelet sheet. Place the cockscomb package in the center, ridges pointing down. Place the beak about $^{3}/_{4}$" (2 cm) below the cockscomb, ridges pointing down.

Place 2 oz (60 g) of the rice on top, tapering down toward the top and bottom. (The rice between the cockscomb and the beak should match their height.)

Place the face on top of the cockscomb.

Place the mat in your hand, press the sides together, and spread the remaining rice around and on top of the face. Fold the nori over the rice.

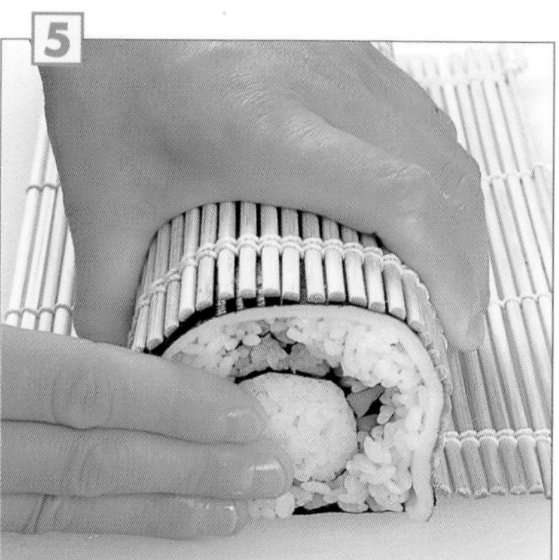

Place the roll seam side down and form into a tunnel shape. Slide the sushi to the ends of the mat to flatten the edges.

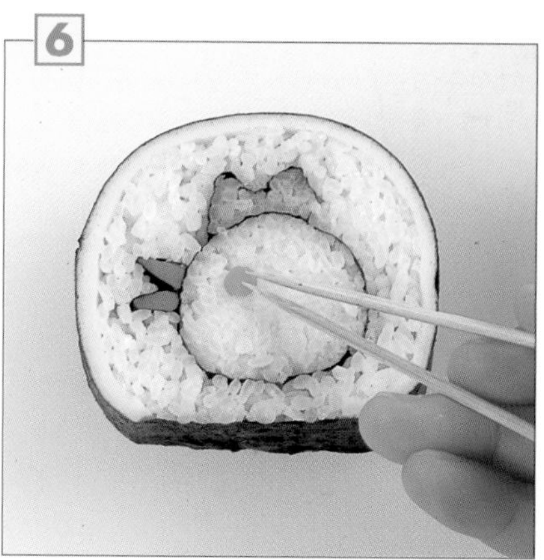

Slice into 4 pieces, wiping the blade with a wet towel after each slice. Slice the yamagobo into thin rounds (eyes) and place them on the faces.

Dog

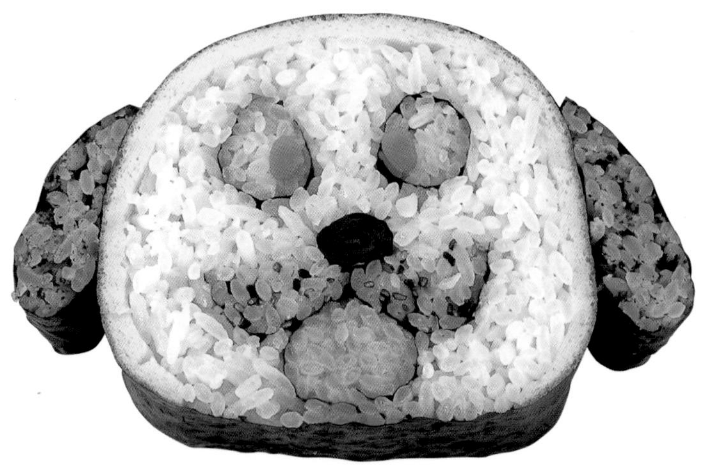

(for 1 roll)

13" (33 cm) simmered gourd (p. 17)
Small piece misozuke yamagobo
$^1/_3$ oz (10 g) cod roe
1 tsp black sesame seeds
1 Tbsp ground black sesame seeds
$^1/_2$ thickness of an omelet sheet (p. 23)
13 oz (365 g) sushi rice (p. 9)
Roasted nori

Setup: Cut the gourd into three equal lengths. Trim the omelet sheet to 4 x 7" (10.5 x 18 cm).
Remove the membrane from the cod roe and stir into $^1/_2$ oz (15 g) of the rice.

Eyes

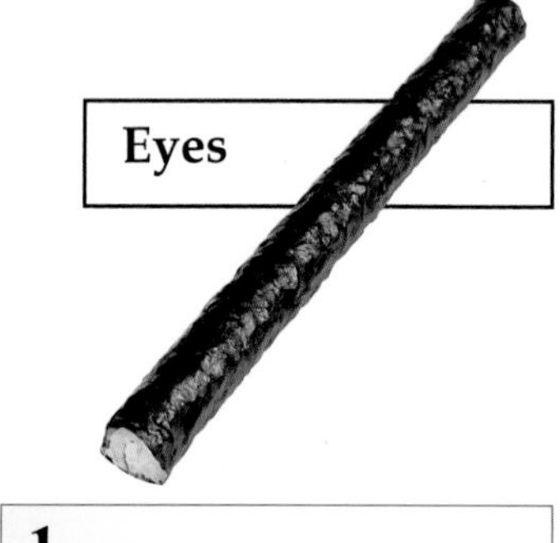

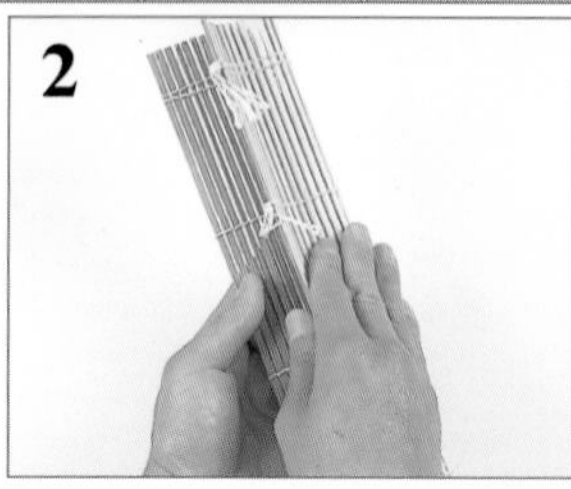

Place 1 oz (30 g) of the white rice on $^1/_3$ of a full sheet of nori (Fig. 1). Roll, finishing the cylinder by rubbing the ends of the mat together.

Nose

Place the gourd strips side by side on $^1/_2$ of a halfsheet of nori (Fig. 1). Roll tightly by hand, as for a jelly roll (Fig. 2).

Chops

Stir the whole black sesame seeds into 1 $^1/_2$ oz (40 g) of the white rice. Form into a cylinder and place on $^1/_2$ of a halfsheet of nori (Fig. 1). Roll, then slice in half lengthwise (Fig. 2).

Tongue

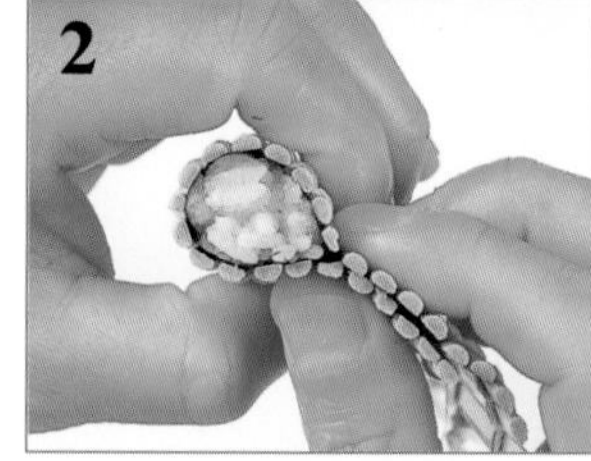

Form the pink rice into a cylinder and place on $^1/_3$ of a halfsheet of nori (Fig. 1). Roll with the mat into a teardrop shape (Fig. 2).

Ears

Stir the ground black sesame seeds into 2 oz (60 g) of the white rice. Cut $^{1}/_{3}$ of a halfsheet of nori. Leaving $^{1}/_{2}$" (1.5 cm) of nori at the bottom, place the black rice in a wedge that tapers toward the top (Figs. 1, 2). Curve the nori over the rice (Fig. 3). Turn over and press into a half-heart shape (Fig. 4).

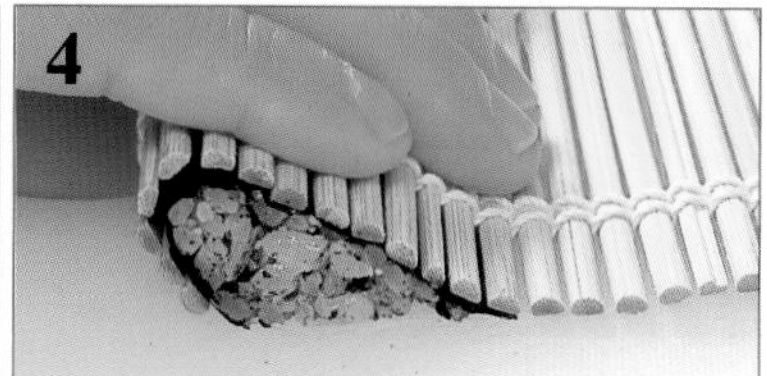

1

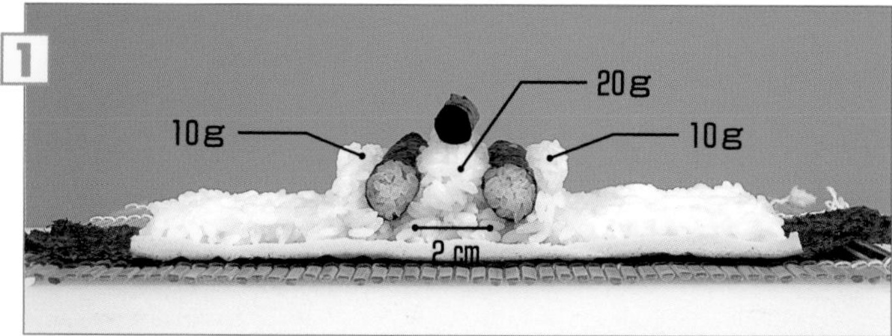

Using 3 grains of rice, attach $^{1}/_{2}$ halfsheet onto 1 halfsheet of nori. Place the omelet sheet in the center and spread with 3 $^{1}/_{2}$ oz (100 g) of the white rice. Cut the ear roll into two lengths and place in the center, $^{3}/_{4}$" (2 cm) apart. Place $^{1}/_{3}$ oz (10 g) on either side of the eyes and $^{3}/_{4}$ oz (20 g) between them, mounding it up slightly in the middle. Place the nose on top.

2

Place $^{3}/_{4}$ oz (20 g) of the rice on each side of the nose, matching the height of the nose.

3

Place the cheeks on the nose, rice side down. Place the tongue on top, pointed end down.

4

Place the mat in your hand, press the sides together, and spread the remaining 1 $^{1}/_{2}$ oz (40 g) of the white rice around the tongue. Fold the nori over the rice. Place the roll seam side down and form into a tunnel shape.

5

Flatten the edges and slice into 4 pieces, wiping the blade with a wet towel after each slice. Slice the yamagobo into thin rounds (eyes) and place them on the faces. Slice the ear wedge into 8 pieces and place next to the faces.

Boar

(for 1 roll)
4 1/3" (11 cm) takuan pickle
Small piece misozuke yamagobo
3/4 oz (20 g) bonito flakes
1/2 thickness of an omelet sheet (p. 23)
11 1/3 oz (320 g) sushi rice
Roasted nori

Setup: Trim the omelet sheet to 4 x 7" (10.5 x 18 cm). Mix the bonito flakes into 3 1/2 oz (100 g) of the rice. Shaved bonito moistened with soy sauce can be used instead of the bonito flakes; raw carrot can be used instead of the yamagobo.

Tusks

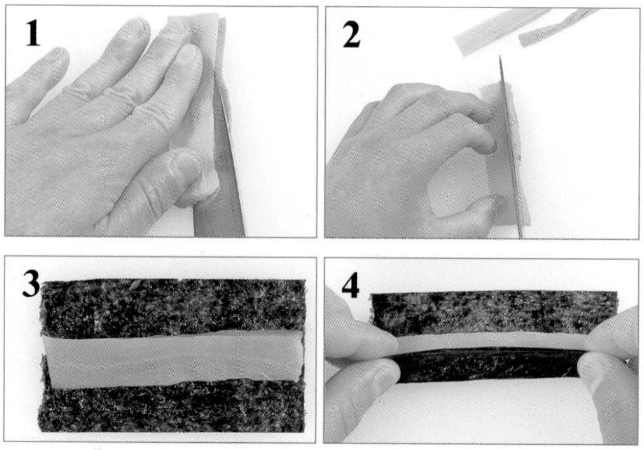

1. Cut two wedge shapes from the takuan (Fig. 1). Trim off the outer skin (Fig. 2) and cut so that the wedges are about 1/2" (1.5 cm)-wide.
2. Place each wedge on 1/3 of a halfsheet of nori (Fig. 3) and wrap (Fig. 4).

Ears

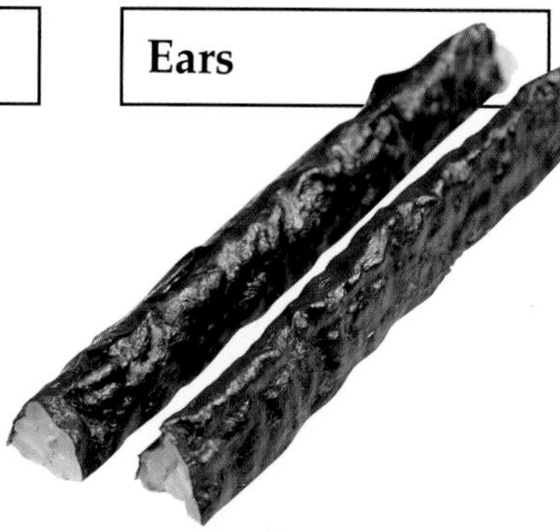

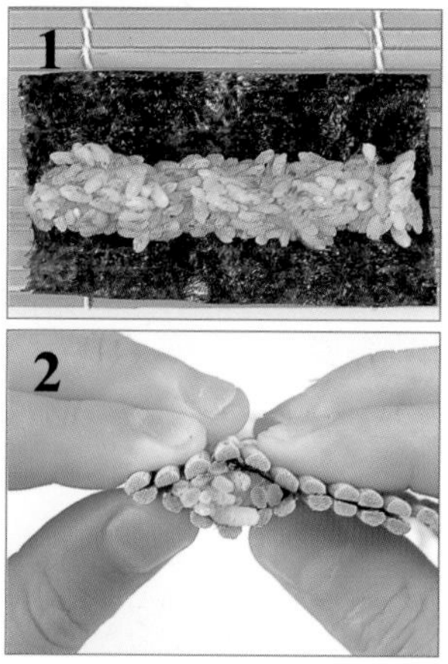

Place 1/3 oz (10 g) of the brown rice on 1/3 of a halfsheet (Fig. 1). Press into a diamond shape (Fig. 2) and slice in half lengthwise.

Face

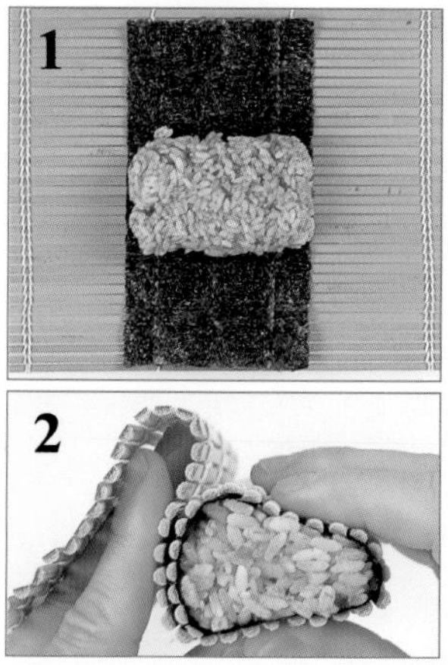

Place the remaining brown rice in a cylinder on a halfsheet of nori (Fig. 1). Roll with the mat and form into an egg shape (Fig. 2).

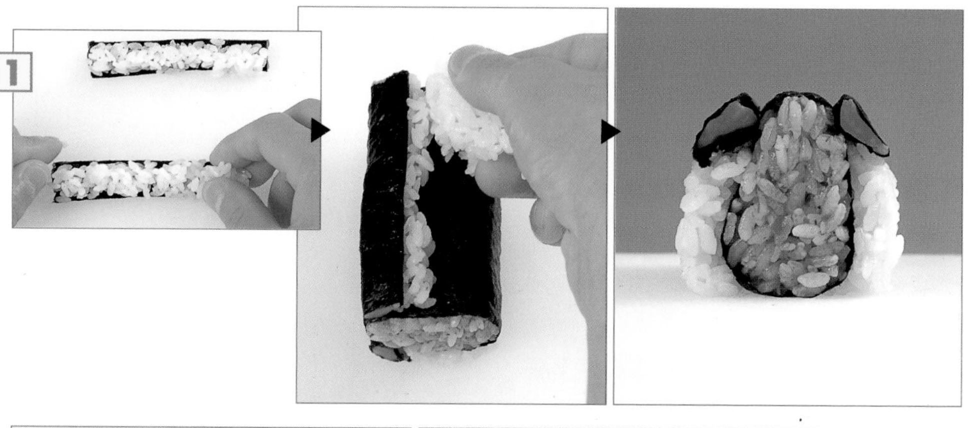

Place $^{1}/_{3}$ oz (10 g) of the white rice on each of the tusk packages *(far left)* . Place one tusk along each side of the narrow end of the face, with the white rice toward the face *(left center)*. Place an additional $^{3}/_{4}$ oz (20 g) of the white rice on each side of the face *(left)*.

Using 3 grains of rice, attach $^{1}/_{2}$ halfsheet onto 1 halfsheet of nori. Place the omelet sheet in the center. Leaving $^{3}/_{4}$" (2 cm) at the top and bottom, spread 4 $^{1}/_{4}$ oz (120 g) of white rice on the omelet sheet. Using a chopstick, make two grooves in the center about $^{3}/_{4}$" (2 cm) apart *(far left)*. Place the ears into the grooves, pointed ends down *(left)*.

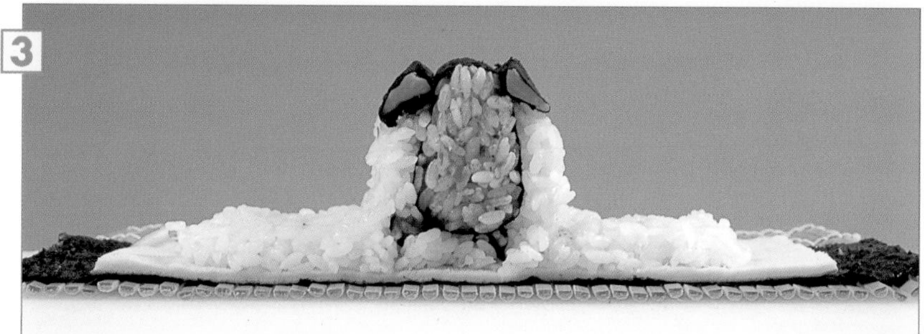

Place the face on the ears, tusk end up.

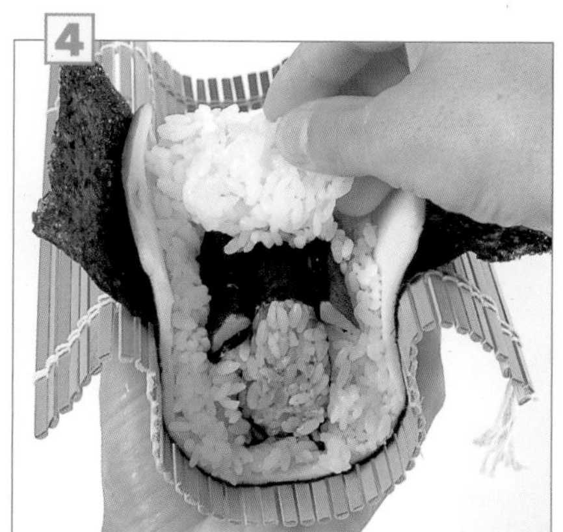

Place the mat in your hand, press the sides together, and spread the remaining 1 $^{1}/_{2}$ oz (40 g) of the rice on top. Fold the nori over the rice.

Place the roll seam side down and form into a tunnel shape. Slide the sushi to the ends of the mat to flatten the edges. Slice into 4 pieces.

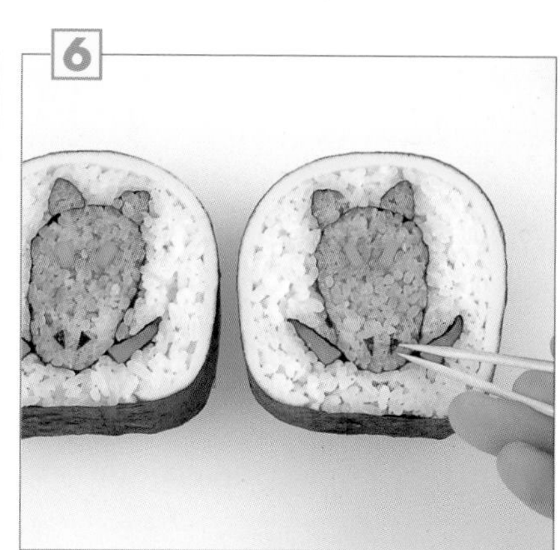

Slice the yamagobo into short matchsticks (eyes) and place them on the faces. Use small triangles of nori for nostrils.

Alphabet Sushi

Spell any message with decorative sushi rolls for every letter.

HAPPY
BIRTHDAY
LOVE

Fundamentals of Alphabet Sushi

• Making the Letters

All the letters are formed from simmered gourd (p. 17) and roasted nori.

1. Cut the gourd into 4 $^1/_3$" (11 cm) lengths. Remove all excess liquid by patting with paper towels.

2. In order to cover the gourd, the nori must be twice as long as the width of the gourd stripe plus 3/8" (1 cm) (see below: a 1 $^1/_2$" (4 cm)-wide gourd stripe requires a 3 $^1/_2$" (9 cm)-long piece of nori).

3. Spread out the gourd strips completely before placing on the nori. If the gourd is thin, use two layers; for thick gourd, one layer is sufficient. Begin with the bottom edge of the nori.

• If left too long after rolling, the nori will absorb liquid from the gourd and begin to shrink.

• M, N, W, and X use a full sheet of nori. The gourd strips are 8 $^2/_3$" (22 cm) long.

• If gourd is unavailable, use any thin, flexible, dark-colored material, such as aburage (tofu puffs).

• Shaping the Rice

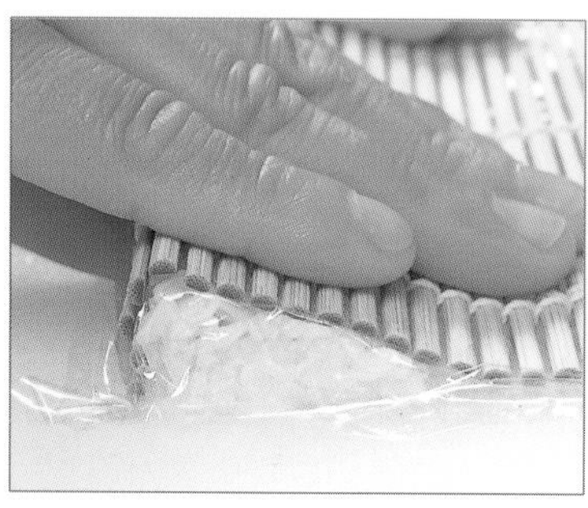

To shape rice by itself, drape it with plastic wrap so that the rice will not stick to the mat. When slicing, leave the wrap on, which will help preserve the shape.

• For Right Angles

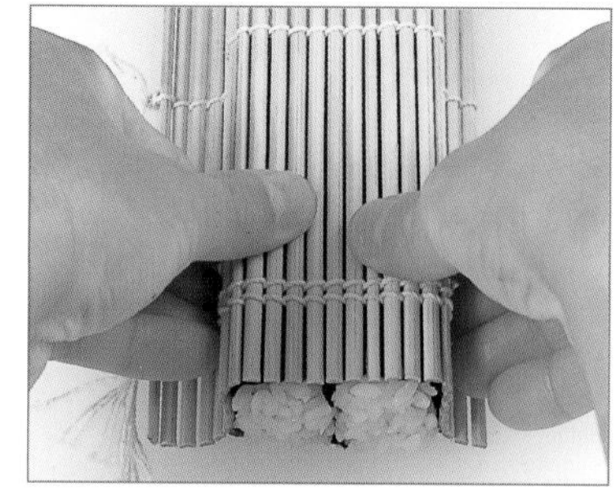

When any right-angled letter (such as E) is formed, use a mat to finish the square edges. Cover any exposed rice with plastic wrap before using the mat.

• For Curves

For rounded letters (such as C), tuck some rice along both sides of the bottom of the letter. This will help preserve the shape when you roll.

• Finishing the Roll

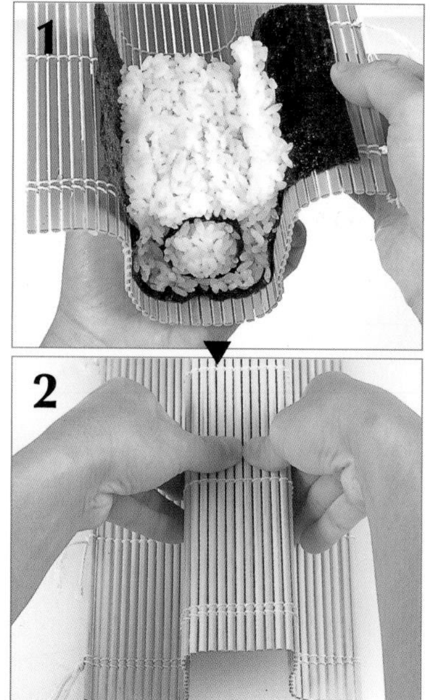

For ease of combining the letters, all rolls in this section are square.

1. Place the letter in the center of the sushi rice. Place the mat in your hand, press the sides together (Fig. 1), and fold the nori over the rice.

2. Place the roll seam side down and form into a square (Fig. 2).

3. Slide the sushi to the ends of the mat to flatten the edges.

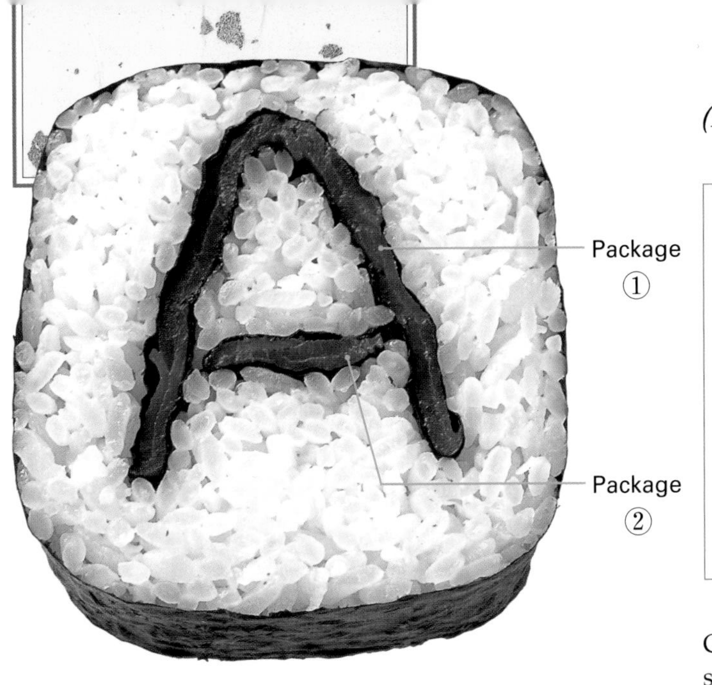

(*for 1 roll*) **9 1/2 oz (270 g) sushi rice** (p. 9)
Simmered gourd (p.17), **Roasted nori**

Cut the nori and gourd to produce two packages as shown (see facing page).

1 Form 1 1/2 oz (40 g) of the rice into a trapezoid matching the length of package 2. The top of the trapezoid should be 3/4" (2 cm) wide *(far left)*. Place package 2 on top. Form a triangle with 1 oz (30 g) of the rice and place it on top. Cover with package 1 and finish the triangle with a rolling mat *(left)*.

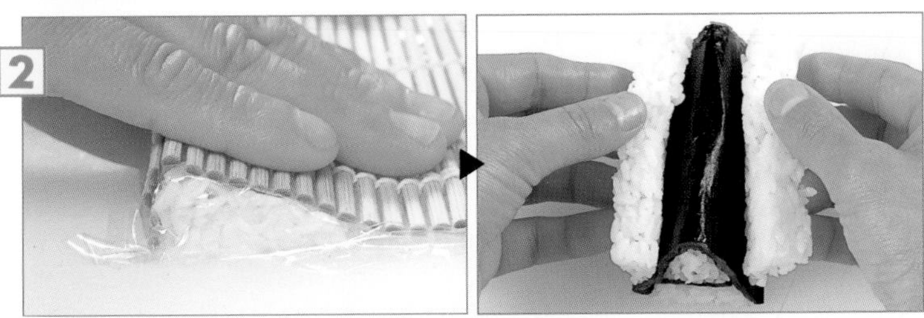

2 Spread 2 oz (60 g) of the rice in a line 8 1/4" (21 cm)-long. Using the mat, shape into a right triangle *(far left)*. Cut in half crosswise. Place the triangles on top of the letter *(left)*, thick end up and right angle outward.

3 Using 3 grains of rice, attach 1/3 halfsheet onto 1 halfsheet of nori. Leaving 1" (3 cm) at top and bottom, spread 4 1/4 oz (120 g) of the rice evenly on the nori. Place the letter in the center, pointed end down.

4 Place the remaining 3/4 oz (20 g) of the rice on top of the letter block. Place the mat in your hand, press the sides together, and fold the nori over. Place the roll seam side down and form into a square. Push the sushi to the ends of the mat to flatten the edges. Slice into 4 pieces, wiping the blade with a wet towel.

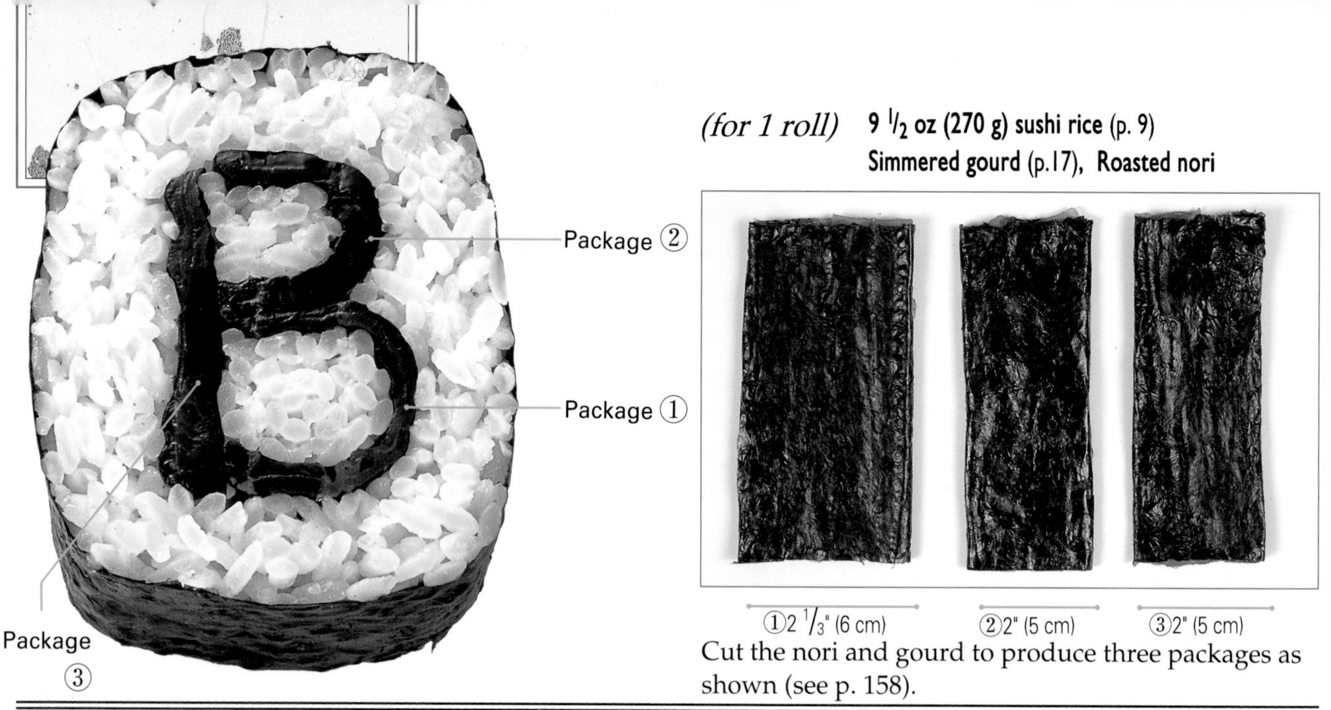

(for 1 roll) **9 $^{1}/_{2}$ oz (270 g) sushi rice** (p. 9)
Simmered gourd (p.17), **Roasted nori**

Cut the nori and gourd to produce three packages as shown (see p. 158).

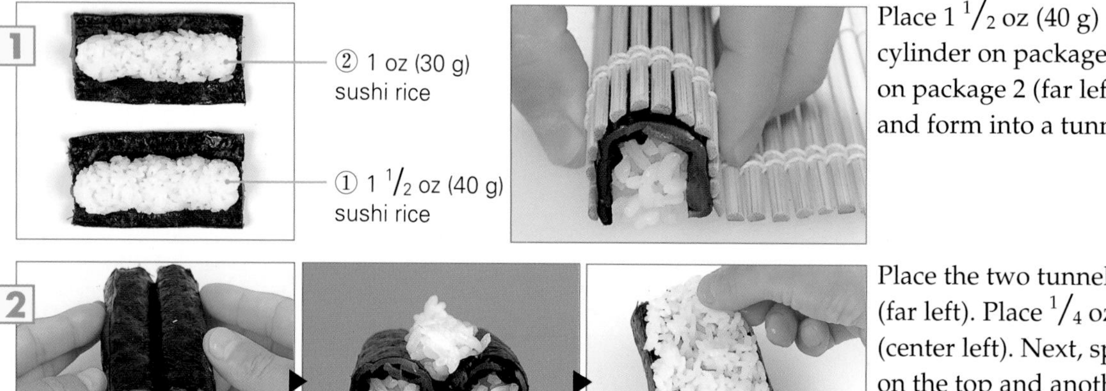

Place 1 $^{1}/_{2}$ oz (40 g) sushi rice in a cylinder on package 1 and 1 oz (30 g) on package 2 (far left). Turn both over and form into a tunnel shape (left).

Place the two tunnels on package 3 (far left). Place $^{1}/_{4}$ oz (10 g) on top (center left). Next, spread $^{3}/_{4}$ oz (20 g) on the top and another $^{3}/_{4}$ oz (20 g) on the bottom (left).

Using 3 grains of rice, attach $^{1}/_{3}$ halfsheet onto 1 halfsheet of nori. Leaving 1" (3 cm) at top and bottom,.spread 4 $^{1}/_{4}$ oz (120 g) of the rice evenly on the nori. Place the letter in the center.

Place the remaining 1 oz (30 g) of rice on top of the letter block. Place the mat in your hand, press the sides together, and fold the nori over. Place the roll seam side down and form into a square. Push the sushi to the ends of the mat to flatten the edges. Slice into 4 pieces, wiping the blade with a wet towel.

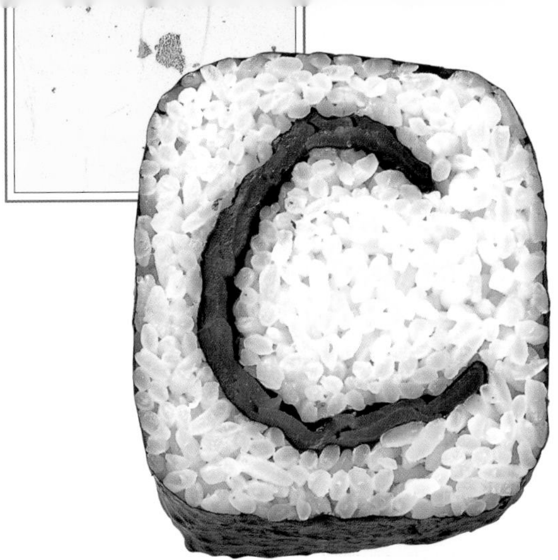

(for 1 roll)

9 $^1/_2$ oz (270 g) sushi rice (p.9)
Simmered gourd (p.17)
Roasted nori

Cut the nori and gourd to produce one package as shown (see p.158).

4 $^3/_4$" (12 cm)

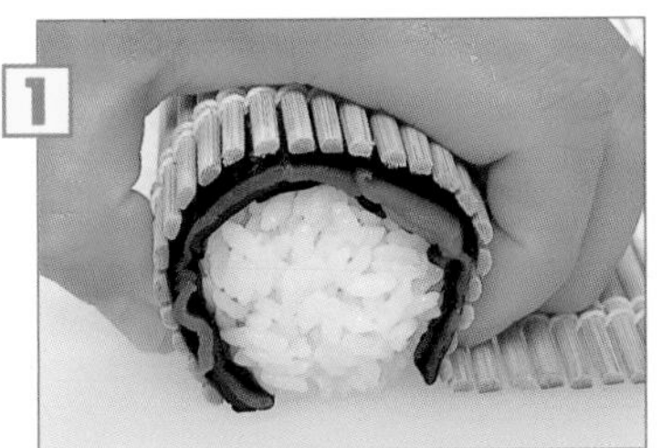

1

Gather 3 $^1/_2$ oz (100 g) of the rice in a cylinder and place on the package. Turn over and press into a C *(left)*.

2

Attach $^1/_3$ halfsheet onto 1 halfsheet of nori. Leaving 1" (3 cm) at top and bottom, spread with 4 $^1/_4$ oz (120 g) of the rice. Place the letter in the center and tuck $^1/_3$ oz (10 g) on each side.

3

Place the remaining rice on top of the letter block. Place the mat in your hand, press the sides together, and fold the nori over. Place the roll seam side down and form into a square. Flatten the edges and slice into 4 pieces.

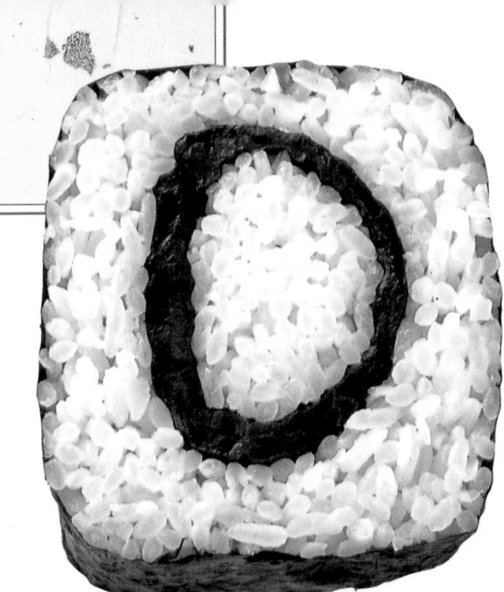

(for 1 roll)

9 $^1/_2$ oz (270 g) sushi rice (p.9)
Simmered gourd (p.17)
Roasted nori

Cut the nori and gourd to produce one package as shown (see p. 158).

6" (15 cm)

1

Form 3 oz (80 g) of the rice in a cylinder and wrap the gourd package around it. Press into shape with the mat *(left)*.

2

Spread $^3/_4$ oz (20 g) in a thin layer on the top and repeat on the bottom (flat side). Drape with plastic wrap and press into a square.

3

Attach $^1/_3$ halfsheet to 1 halfsheet of nori. Leaving 1" (3 cm) at top and bottom, spread with 4 $^1/_4$ oz (120 g) of the rice. Place the letter in the center and spread 1 oz (30 g) of the rice on top. Press the sides together, fold the nori over, and form into a square. Flatten the edges and slice into 4 pieces.

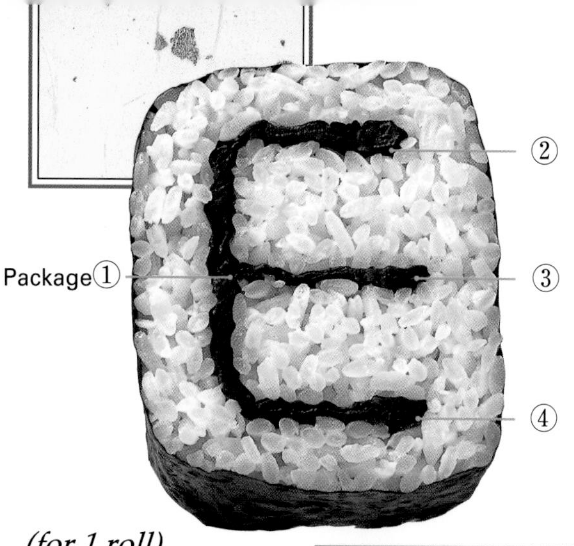

(for 1 roll)

9 $^1/_2$ oz (270 g) sushi rice (p. 9)
Simmered gourd (p. 17)
Roasted nori

Cut the nori and gourd to produce four packages as shown (see p. 158).

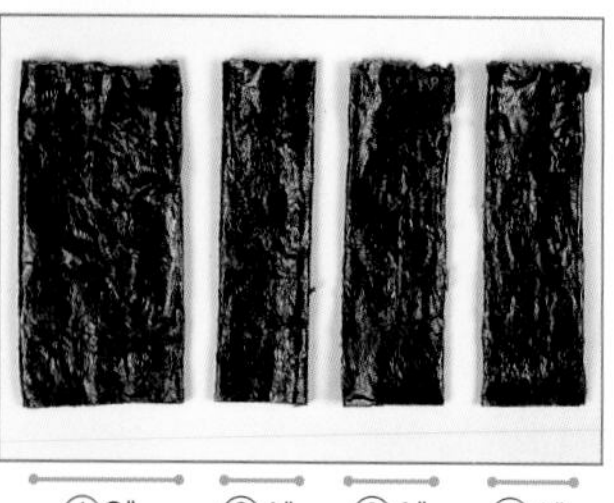

Place 4 $^1/_4$ oz (120 g) of the rice on package 1. With plastic wrap and a rolling mat, form into a block 1" (3 cm) high. Slice in half, almost all the way through.

Place package 2 in the incision. Place the other two packages on the sides.

Attach $^1/_3$ halfsheet onto 1 halfsheet of nori. Leaving 1" (3 cm) at top and bottom, spread with 4 $^1/_4$ oz (120 g) of the rice. Place the letter in the center. Place the remaining 1 oz (30 g) of rice on top. Fold the nori over. Place the roll seam side down and form into a square. Flatten the edges and slice into 4 pieces.

(for 1 roll)

9 $^1/_2$ oz (270 g) sushi rice (p. 9)
Simmered gourd (p. 17)
Roasted nori

Cut the nori and gourd to produce three packages as shown (see p.158).

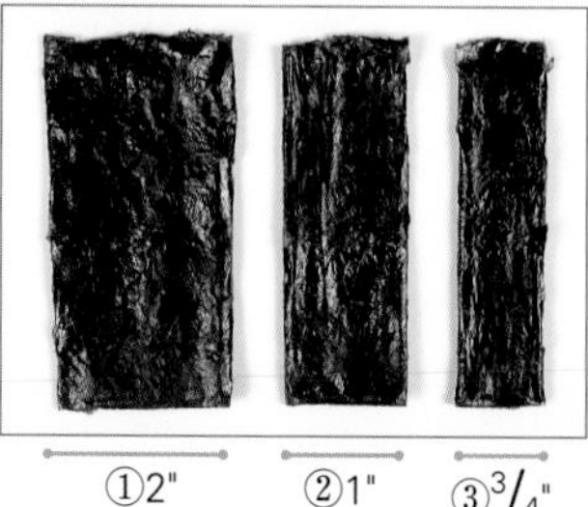

Place 4 $^1/_4$ oz (120 g) of the rice on package 1. With plastic wrap and a rolling mat, form into a block 1" (3 cm) high. Slice in half, almost all the way through.

Place package 3 in the incision and package 2 on one side.

Attach $^1/_3$ halfsheet onto 1 halfsheet of nori. Leaving 1" (3 cm) at top and bottom, spread with 4 $^1/_4$ oz (120 g) of the rice. Place the letter in the center. Place the remaining 1 oz (30 g) of rice on top. Fold the nori over. Place the roll seam side down and form into a square. Flatten the edges and slice into 4 pieces.

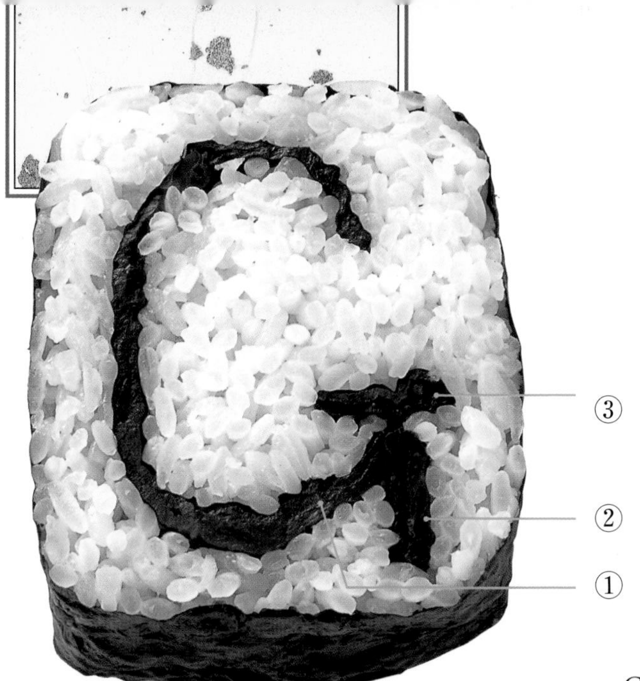

(for 1 roll) **9 $\frac{1}{2}$ oz (270 g) sushi rice (p.9)**
Simmered gourd (p.17), Roasted nori

Cut the nori and gourd to produce three packages as shown.

1

Form 3 $^{1}/_{4}$ oz (90 g) of the rice into a cylinder and place on package 1. Turn over and press with the mat into a C shape *(far left)*. Make a $^{3}/_{8}$" (1 cm) incision into the bottom of the exposed portion *(left)*.

2

Place package 3 in the incision.

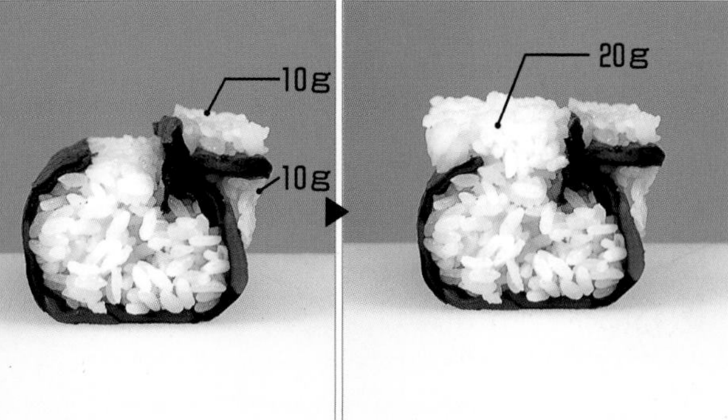

Spread $^{1}/_{3}$ oz (10 g) of the rice on the bottom edge of package 1. Spread another $^{1}/_{3}$ oz (10 g) on package 2 and place it at right angles with package 3.

Place $^{3}/_{4}$ oz (20 g) of the rice to the left of package 3.

3

Attach $^{1}/_{3}$ halfsheet onto 1 halfsheet of nori. Leaving 1" (3 cm) at top and bottom, spread with 3 $^{1}/_{2}$ oz (100 g) of the rice. Place the letter in the center, tucking 1/3 oz (10 g) of the rice on the rounded side as shown. Place the remaining 1 oz (30 g) of rice on top. Fold the nori over. Place the roll seam side down and form into a square. Flatten the edges and slice into 4 pieces.

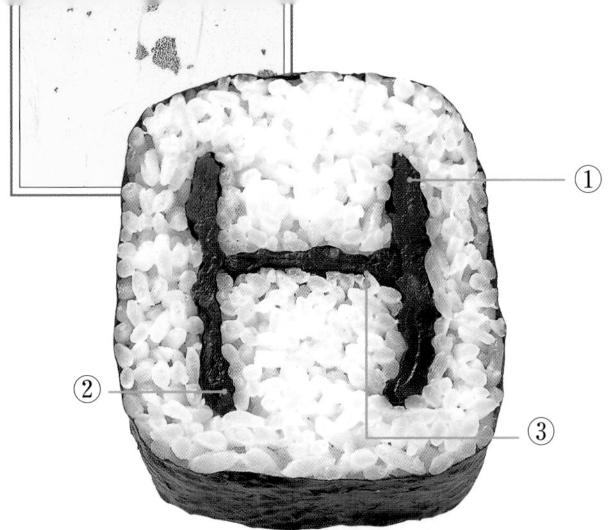

(for 1 roll)

9 $^1/_2$ oz (270 g) sushi rice (p.9)
Simmered gourd (p.17)
Roasted nori

Cut the nori and gourd to produce three packages as shown (see p. 158).

Place 4 $^1/_4$ oz (120 g) of the rice on package 1. With plastic wrap and a rolling mat, form into a block 1" (3 cm) high. Slice in half, almost all the way through.

Place package 3 in the incision. Cover with package 2.

Attach $^1/_3$ halfsheet onto 1 halfsheet of nori. Leaving 1" (3 cm) at top and bottom, spread with 4 $^1/_4$ oz (120 g) of the rice. Place the letter in the center. Place the remaining 1 oz (30 g) of the rice on top. Fold the nori over. Form into a square, flatten the edges, and slice into 4 pieces.

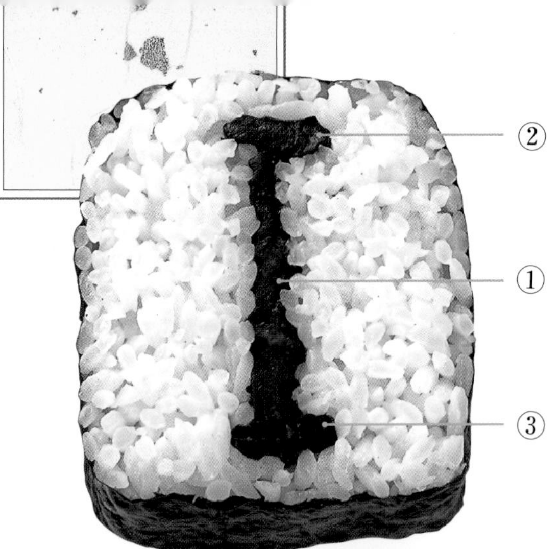

(for 1 roll)

9 $^1/_2$ oz (270 g) sushi rice (p.9)
Simmered gourd (p.17)
Roasted nori

Cut the nori and gourd to produce three packages as shown (see p. 158).

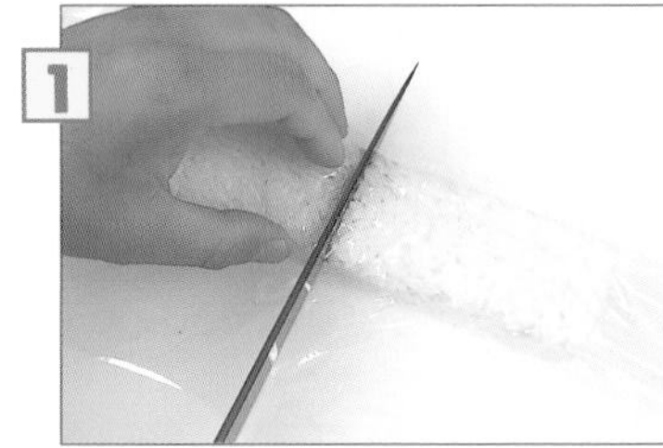

Gather 4 $^1/_4$ oz (120 g) of the rice into a long block. Drape with plastic wrap and use a mat to form into a 2 x 8 $^1/_4$ x $^1/_2$" (5 x 21 x 1.5 cm) rectangle. Cut in half crosswise.

Place package 1 between the blocks. Place the other two packages along the sides.

Attach $^1/_3$ halfsheet onto 1 halfsheet of nori. Leaving 1" (3 cm) at top and bottom, spread with 4 $^1/_4$ oz (120 g) of the rice. Place the letter in the center. Place the remaining 1 oz (30 g) of the rice on top. Fold the nori over. Form into a square, flatten the edges, and slice into 4 pieces.

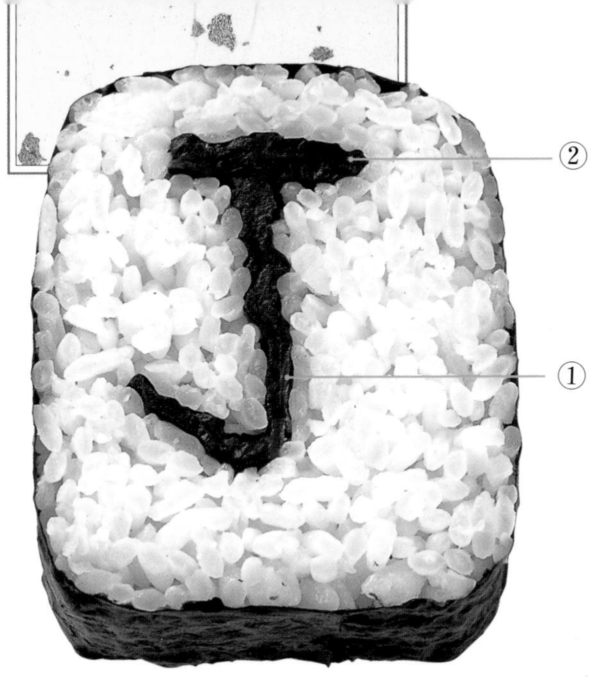

(for 1 roll) **9 1/2 oz (270 g) sushi rice (p.9)**
Simmered gourd (p.17), Roasted nori

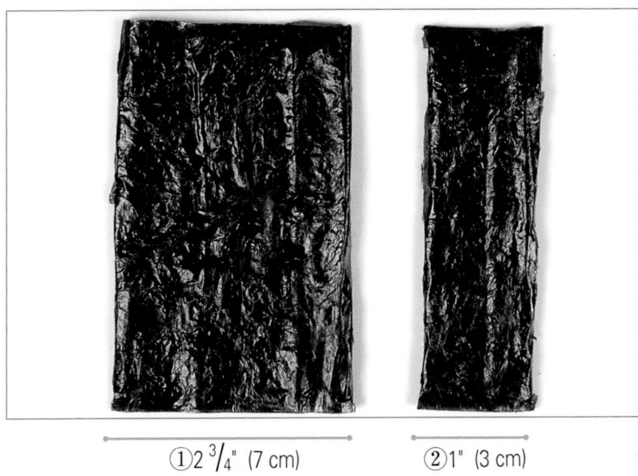

Cut the nori and gourd to produce two packages as shown.

Gather 1 3/4 oz (50 g) of the rice into a rectangle 4 1/2 x 1 3/4" (11 x 4.5 cm) and place on the far end of package 1 *(far left)*. Roll the front end up to cover the front edge of the rice *(left)*.

Place 1/3 oz (10 g) of the rice on top of the turned-up end *(far left, middle left)*. Turn over and spread 2 oz (60 g) of the rice on the back of the package *(left)*.

Using 3 grains of rice, attach 1/3 halfsheet onto 1 halfsheet of nori. Leaving 1" (3 cm) at top and bottom, spread 4 1/4 oz (120 g) of the rice evenly on the nori. Place package 2 on top of the letter, then place the letter in the center.

Place the remaining 1 oz (30 g) of rice on top of the letter block. Place the mat in your hand, press the sides together, and fold the nori over. Place the roll seam side down and form into a square. Push the sushi to the ends of the mat to flatten the edges. Slice into 4 pieces, wiping the blade with a wet towel.

(for 1 roll) **9 $^{1}/_{2}$ oz (270 g) sushi rice** (p.9)
Simmered gourd (p.17), **Roasted nori**

Cut the nori and gourd to produce three packages as shown.

Spread 1 $^{1}/_{2}$ oz (40 g) of the rice in a line along the front edge of package 1. With plastic wrap and a rolling mat, press into a right triangle about 1 $^{1}/_{3}$" (3.5 cm)-high *(far left)*. Place package 2 on the slope, then press 1 oz (30 g) of the rice on the bottom and cover the new rice with package 3 *(left)*.

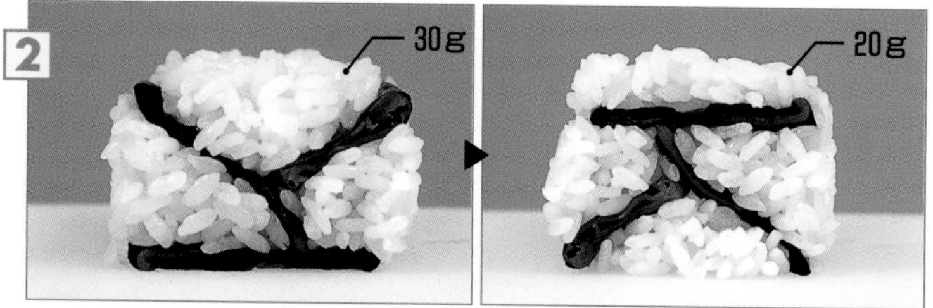

Place another 1 oz (30 g) of the rice on top *(far left)*. Turn over and spread $^{3}/_{4}$ oz (20 g) of the rice on the flat side *(left)*. Drape with plastic wrap and form into a block with a rolling mat.

Using 3 grains of rice, attach $^{1}/_{3}$ halfsheet onto 1 halfsheet of nori. Leaving 1" (3 cm) at top and bottom, spread 4 $^{1}/_{4}$ oz (120 g) of the rice evenly on the nori. Place the letter in the center.

Place the remaining 1 oz (30 g) of rice on top of the letter block. Place the mat in your hand, press the sides together, and fold the nori over. Place the roll seam side down and form into a square. Push the sushi to the ends of the mat to flatten the edges. Slice into 4 pieces, wiping the blade with a wet towel.

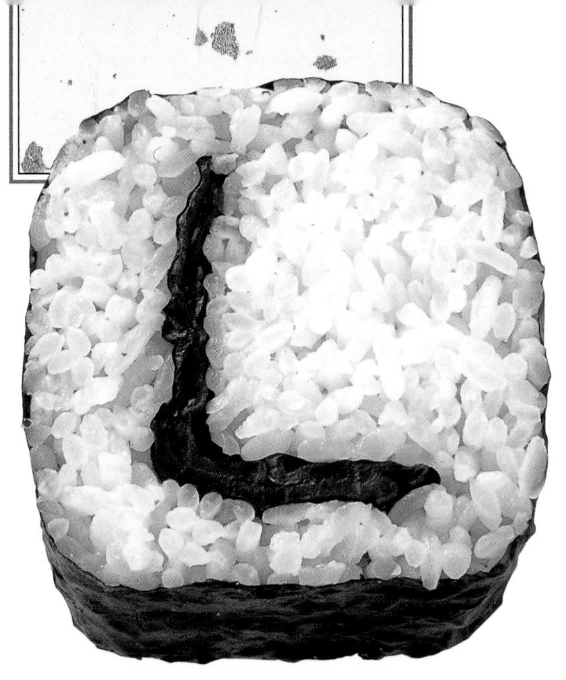

(for 1 roll) **$9\frac{1}{2}$ oz (270 g) sushi rice** (p.9)
Simmered gourd (p.17), **Roasted nori**

Cut the nori and gourd to produce one package as shown.

1

Place $3\frac{1}{2}$ oz (100 g) of the rice in a mound approximately 4 1/3" (11 cm)-long. Drape with plastic wrap and use a rolling mat to form into a 1 x 2 x $4\frac{1}{3}$" (3 x 5 x 11 cm) rectangular block *(far left)*. Place the block on the far edge of the gourd package *(left)*.

2

Lift the front edge of the gourd package and press it onto the side *(far left)*. Turn over and spread $\frac{3}{4}$ oz (20 g) on the long side of the gourd package *(left)*.

3

Using 3 grains of rice, attach $\frac{1}{3}$ halfsheet onto 1 halfsheet of nori. Leaving 1" (3 cm) at top and bottom, spread $4\frac{1}{4}$ oz (120 g) of the rice evenly on the nori. Place the letter in the center.

4

Place the remaining 1 oz (30 g) of rice on top of the letter block. Place the mat in your hand, press the sides together, and fold the nori over. Place the roll seam side down and form into a square. Push the sushi to the ends of the mat to flatten the edges. Slice into 4 pieces, wiping the blade with a wet towel.

(for 1 roll) **9 ½ oz (270 g) sushi rice** (p.9)
Simmered gourd (p.17), **Roasted nori**

Cut a 6" (15 cm) strip horizontally from a full sheet of nori. Cut the gourd strips to 8 ⅔" (22 cm) lengths. Spread the gourd strips on the nori and wrap to the size shown above.

1 Leaving ¾" (2 cm) at the near edge, spread 3 ½ oz (100 g) of the rice on the gourd package (far left). Fold the remaining gourd to a 45-degree angle over the front edge of the rice (left).

2 Cut the block in half crosswise. Place the rice sides together (far left). Tuck ¾ oz (20 g) of the rice in the indentation (left).

3 Using 3 grains of rice, attach ⅓ halfsheet onto 1 halfsheet of nori. Leaving 1" (3 cm) at top and bottom, spread 4 ¼ oz (120 g) of the rice evenly on the nori. Place the letter in the center, pointed end down.

4 Place the remaining 1 oz (30 g) of the rice on top of the letter block. Place the mat in your hand, press the sides together, and fold the nori over. Place the roll seam side down and form into a square. Push the sushi to the ends of the mat to flatten the edges. Slice into 4 pieces, wiping the blade with a wet towel.

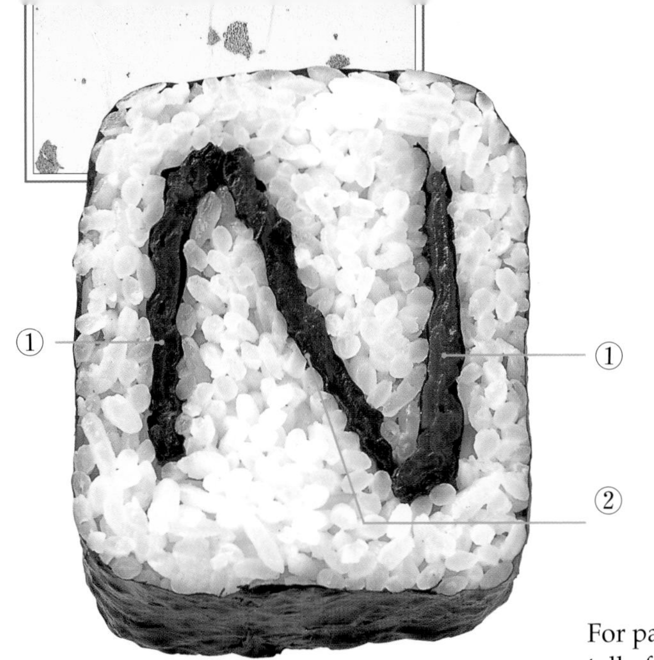

(for 1 roll) **9 1/2 oz (270 g) sushi rice** (p. 9)
Simmered gourd (p.17), **Roasted nori**

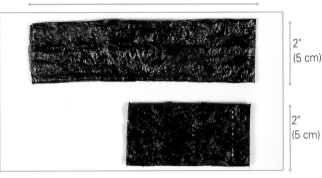

For package 1, the nori is a 4 1/3" (11 cm)-wide strip cut horizontally from a full sheet and the gourd strips are 8 2/3" (22 cm)-long.

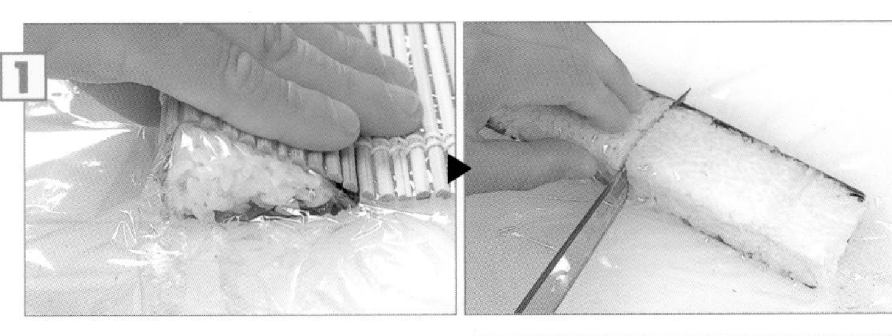

Place 4 1/4 oz (120 g) of the rice on package 1. Drape with plastic wrap and form into a right triangle with a rolling mat (far left). Cut in half crosswise (left).

Place the two sides together with package 2 between them.

Using 3 grains of rice, attach 1/3 halfsheet onto 1 halfsheet of nori. Leaving 1" (3 cm) at top and bottom, spread 4 1/4 oz (120 g) of the rice evenly on the nori. Place the letter in the center.

Place the remaining 1 oz (30 g) of rice on top of the letter block. Place the mat in your hand, press the sides together, and fold the nori over. Place the roll seam side down and form into a square. Push the sushi to the ends of the mat to flatten the edges. Slice into 4 pieces, wiping the blade with a wet towel.

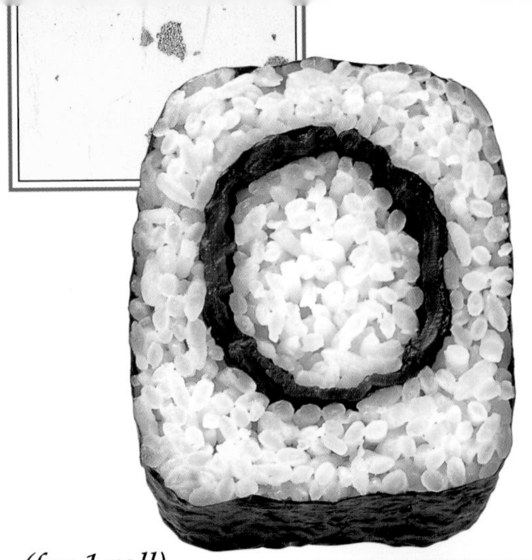

(for 1 roll)

9 $^{1}/_{2}$ oz (270 g) sushi rice (p. 9)
Simmered gourd (p.17)
Roasted nori

Cut the nori and gourd to produce one package as shown (see p. 158).

1. Gather 3 $^{1}/_{2}$ oz (100 g) of the rice in a cylinder and place on the gourd package. Roll into an oval with a rolling mat.

2. Attach $^{1}/_{3}$ halfsheet onto 1 halfsheet of nori. Leaving 1" (3 cm) at top and bottom, spread 4 $^{1}/_{4}$ oz (120 g) of the rice on the nori. Place the letter in the center, tucking $^{1}/_{8}$ oz (5 g) of the rice along each side.

3. Place the remaining 1 $^{1}/_{2}$ oz (40 g) of rice on top of the letter block. Place the mat in your hand and fold the nori over. Place the roll seam side down and form into a square. Flatten the edges. and slice into 4 pieces.

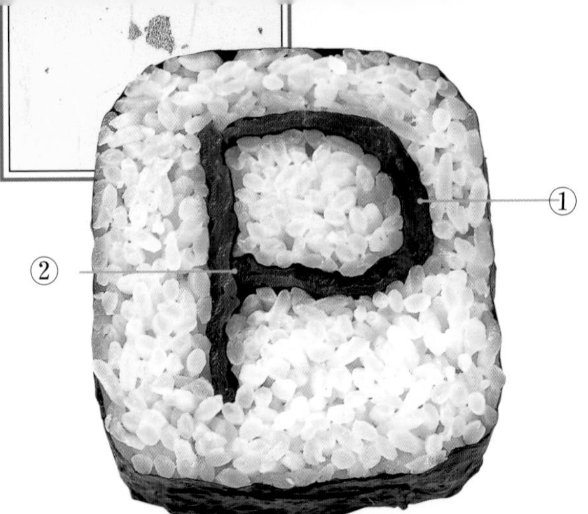

(for 1 roll)

9 $^{1}/_{2}$ oz (270 g) sushi rice (p. 9)
Simmered gourd (p. 17)
Roasted nori

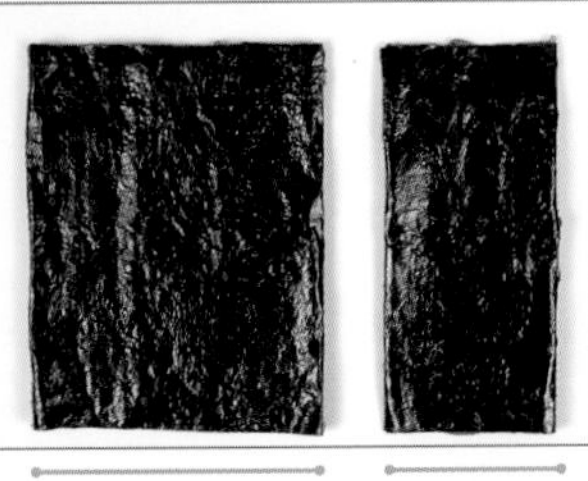

Cut the nori and gourd to produce two packages as shown (see p. 158).

1. Place 1 $^{3}/_{4}$ oz (50 g) of the rice in a line on package 1. Turn it over and form into a tunnel with a rolling mat.

2. Place package 2 as shown, putting another 1 $^{3}/_{4}$ oz (50 g) of the rice in the space next to the tunnel. Press into a block with plastic wrap and the mat. Spread an additional $^{3}/_{4}$ oz (20 g) on the long side of the letter.

3. Attach $^{1}/_{3}$ halfsheet onto 1 halfsheet of nori. Leaving 1" (3 cm) at top and bottom, spread with 4 $^{1}/_{4}$ oz (120 g) of the rice. Place the letter in the center. Place the remaining 1 oz (30 g) of the rice on top. Fold the nori over. Form into a square, flatten the edges, and slice into 4 pieces.

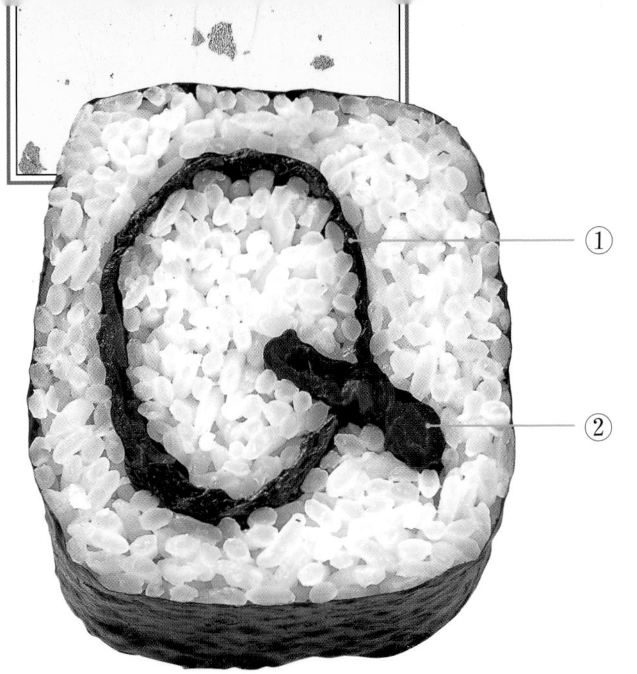

(for 1 roll) **9 $^1/_2$ oz (270 g) sushi rice (p. 9)**
Simmered gourd (p.17), Roasted nori

Cut the nori and gourd to produce two packages as shown.

Form 3 oz (80 g) of the rice into a cylinder and place it on package 1 *(far left)*. Roll with a mat into an oval shape. Where the two ends meet, slice into the rice to a depth of about $^1/_2$" (1.5 cm) *(left)*.

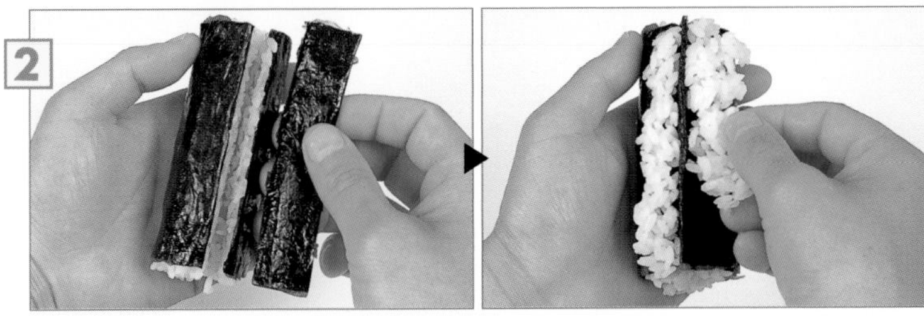

Place package 2 in the incision *(far left)*. Use 1 oz (30 g) of the rice to cover package 2, beginning with the sides *(left)* and continuing with a thin layer to hide the edge.

Attach $^1/_3$ halfsheet onto 1 halfsheet of nori. Leaving 1" (3 cm) at top and bottom, spread with 4 $^1/_4$ oz (120 g) of the rice. Place the letter in the center, tucking $^1/_8$ oz (5 g) of the rice along each side.

Place the remaining 1 oz (30 g) of rice on top of the letter block. Place the mat in your hand and fold the nori over. Place the roll seam side down and form into a square. Flatten the edges and slice into 4 pieces.

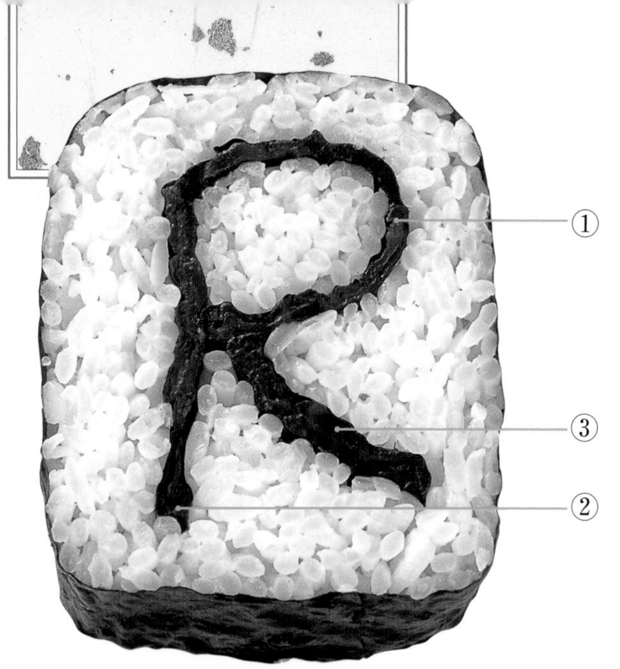

(for 1 roll) **9 $^{1}/_{2}$ oz (270 g) sushi rice** (p. 9)
Simmered gourd (p.17), **Roasted nori**

①2 $^{3}/_{4}$" (7 cm) ②2" (5 cm) ③1" (3 cm)

Cut the nori and gourd to produce three packages as shown.

Gather 1 $^{1}/_{2}$ oz (40 g) of the rice into a cylilnder and place on package 1 *(far left)*. Turn over and press into a tunnel shape with a rolling mat *(left)*.

Spread another 1 $^{1}/_{2}$ oz (40 g) in a line. Drape with plastic wrap and press into a right triangle *(far left)*. Place the tunnel and the triangle on package 2 *(left)*.

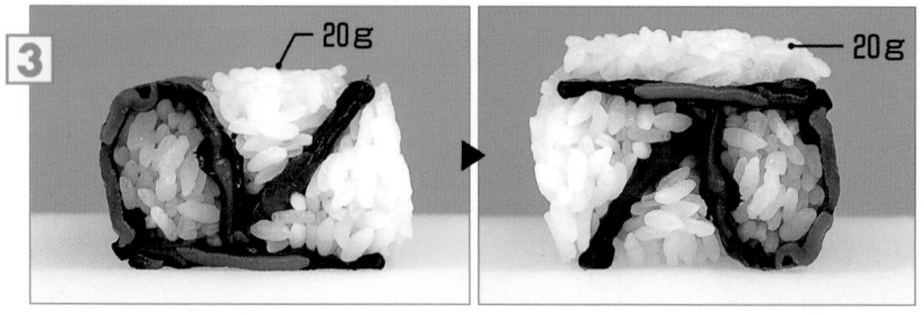

Place package 3 on the sloping rice. Cover with $^{3}/_{4}$ oz (20 g) of the rice *(far left)*. Turn over and cover the long side with another $^{3}/_{4}$ oz (20 g) of the rice *(left)*.

Attach $^{1}/_{3}$ halfsheet onto 1 halfsheet of nori. Leaving 1" (3 cm) at top and bottom, spread with 4 $^{1}/_{4}$ oz (120 g) of the rice. Place the letter in the center. Place the remaining $^{3}/_{4}$ oz (30 g) of the rice on top. Fold the nori over. Form into a square, flatten the edges, and slice into 4 pieces.

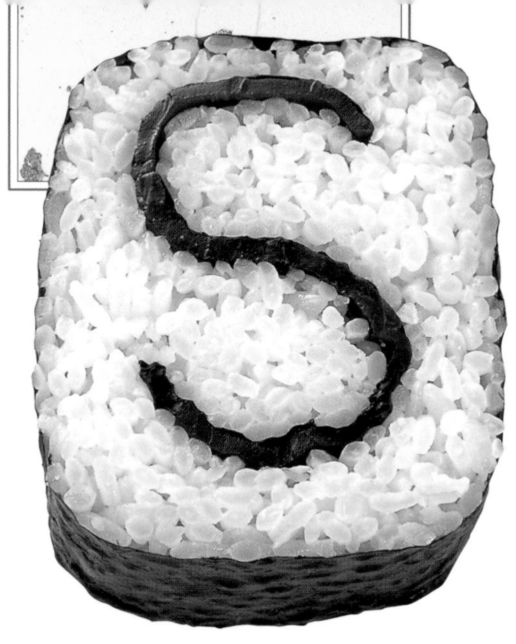

(for 1 roll) **9 1/2 oz (270 g) sushi rice** (p. 9)
Simmered gourd (p.17), **Roasted nori**

5 1/2" (14 cm)

Cut the nori and gourd to produce one package as shown.

1 Form 1 1/2 oz (40 g) of the rice into a cylinder and place at the front end of the gourd package *(far left)*. Roll one quarter turn *(left)* and press the gourd into position.

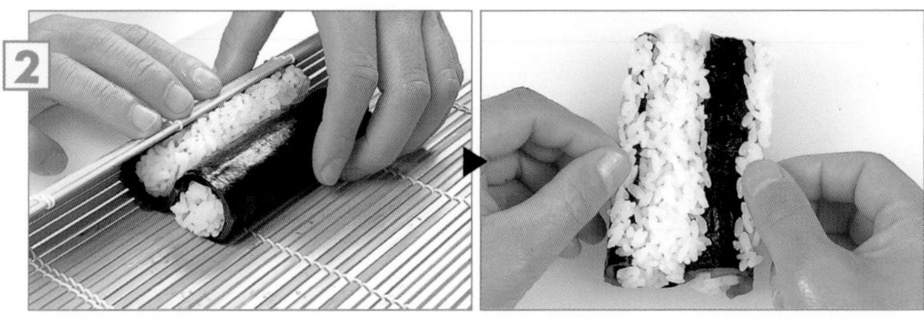

2 Turn over. Place another 1 1/2 oz (40 g) of the rice at the front end and roll another quarter turn *(far left)*. Use 3/4 oz (20 g) to form lines of rice along the center and along both sides of the top surface *(left)*. Turn over and repeat with another 3/4 oz (20 g). Drape with plastic wrap and form into a block with the mat.

3 Using 3 grains of rice, attach 1/3 halfsheet onto 1 halfsheet of nori. Leaving 1" (3 cm) at top and bottom, spread 4 1/4 oz (120 g) of the rice evenly on the nori. Place the letter in the center.

4 Place the remaining 3/4 oz (30 g) of the rice on top of the letter block. Place the mat in your hand and fold the nori over. Place the roll seam side down and form into a square. Push the sushi to the ends of the mat to flatten the edges. Slice into 4 pieces, wiping the blade with a wet towel.

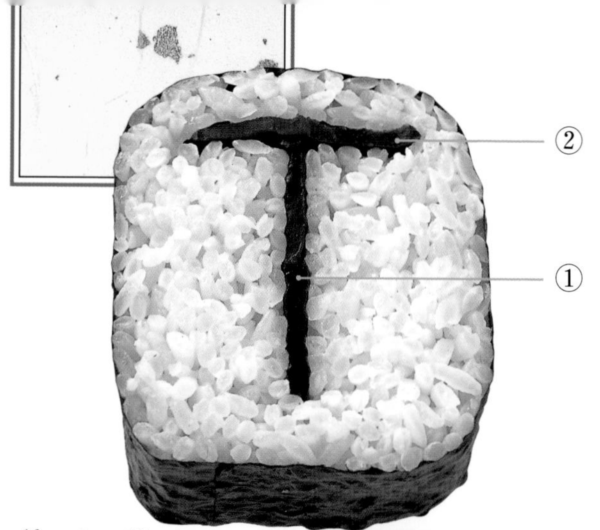

(for 1 roll)

9 $^1/_2$ oz (270 g) sushi rice (p. 9)
Simmered gourd (p.17)
Roasted nori

Cut the nori and gourd to produce two packages as shown (see p. 158).

Spread 4 $^1/_4$ oz (120 g) of the rice in a line about 8" (20 cm)-long. Drape with plastic wrap and use a rolling mat to shape into a block 2 x 8 $^1/_4$" and slightly less than $^3/_4$" (5 x 21 x 2 cm)-tall. Cut into 2 equal lengths.

Place the blocks together with package 1 between. Place package 2 on top.

Attach $^1/_3$ halfsheet onto 1 halfsheet of nori. Leaving 1" (3 cm) at top and bottom, spread with 4 $^1/_4$ oz (120 g) of the rice. Place the letter in the center. Place the remaining 1 oz (30 g) of rice on top. Fold the nori over. Form into a square, flatten the edges, and slice into 4 pieces.

(for 1 roll)

9 $^1/_2$ oz (270 g) sushi rice (p. 9)
Simmered gourd (p.17)
Roasted nori

Cut the nori and gourd to produce one package as shown (see p. 158).

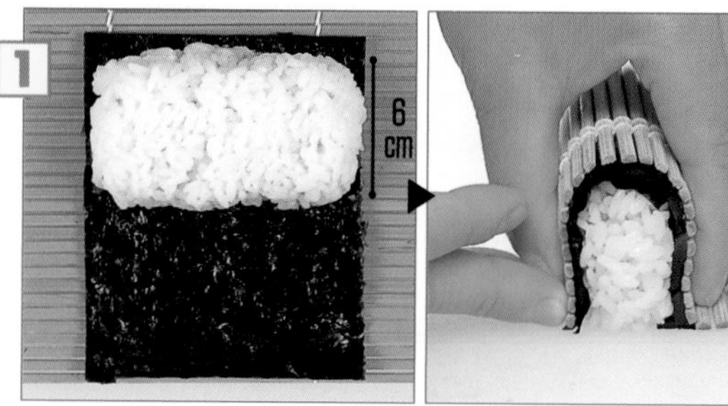

Form 3 $^1/_2$ oz (100 g) of the rice into a block 2 $^1/_3$" (6 cm) wide. Place on the far end of the gourd package *(above left)*. Fold the gourd over. Place the rice side down and form into a narrow tunnel shape (above right).

Attach $^1/_3$ halfsheet onto 1 halfsheet of nori. Leaving 1" (3 cm) at top and bottom, spread with 4 $^1/_4$ oz (120 g) of the rice. Place the letter in the center. Place the remaining 1 $^3/_4$ oz (50 g) of rice on top. Fold the nori over. Form into a square, flatten the edges, and slice into 4 pieces.

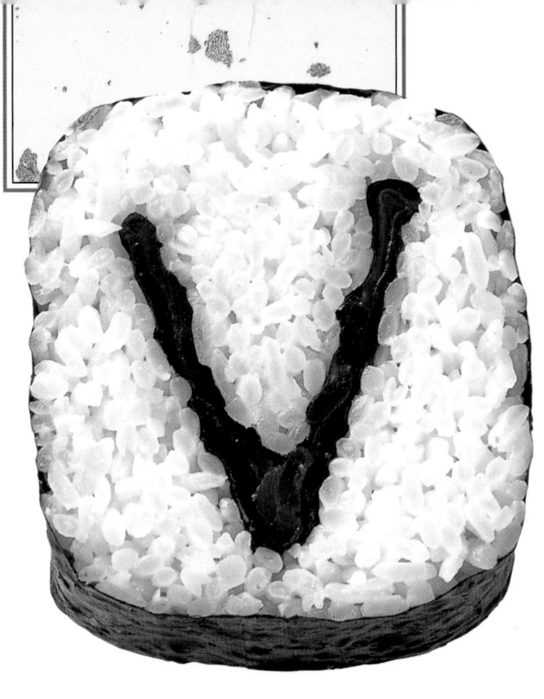

(for 1 roll) **9 $^{1}/_{2}$ oz (270 g) sushi rice** (p. 9)
Simmered gourd (p.17), **Roasted nori**

Cut the nori and gourd to produce one package as shown.

Form 2 oz (60 g) of the rice into a wedge at the far end of the gourd package, so that the high point is at the back *(far left)*. Fold the gourd package over the rice, turn the assembly rice side down, and press into a triangle *(left)*.

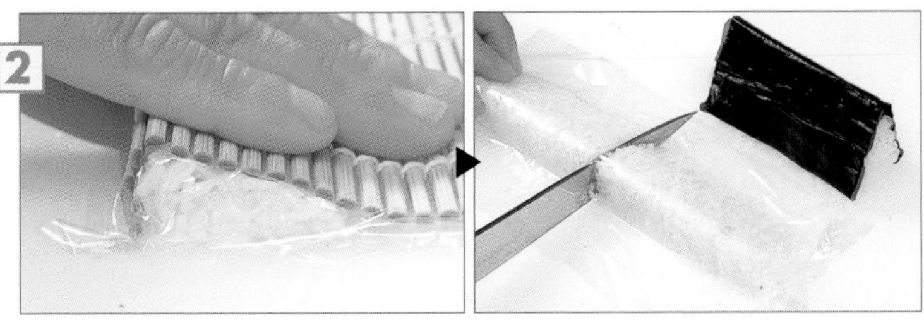

Place 2 oz (60 g) of the rice in an 8 $^{1}/_{4}$" (21 cm) line. Drape with plastic wrap and press into a right triangle with the mat *(far left)*. Cut into two equal lengths and place on the V.

Using 3 grains of rice, attach $^{1}/_{3}$ halfsheet onto 1 halfsheet of nori. Leaving 1" (3 cm) at top and bottom, spread 4 $^{1}/_{4}$ oz (120 g) of the rice evenly on the nori. Place the letter in the center.

Place the remaining 1 $^{1}/_{4}$ oz (30 g) of rice on top of the letter block. Place the mat in your hand, press the sides together, and fold the nori over. Place the roll seam side down and form into a square. Push the sushi to the ends of the mat to flatten the edges. Slice into 4 pieces, wiping the blade with a wet towel.

(for 1 roll) **9 1/2 oz (270 g) sushi rice** (p. 9)
Simmered gourd (p. 17), **Roasted nori**

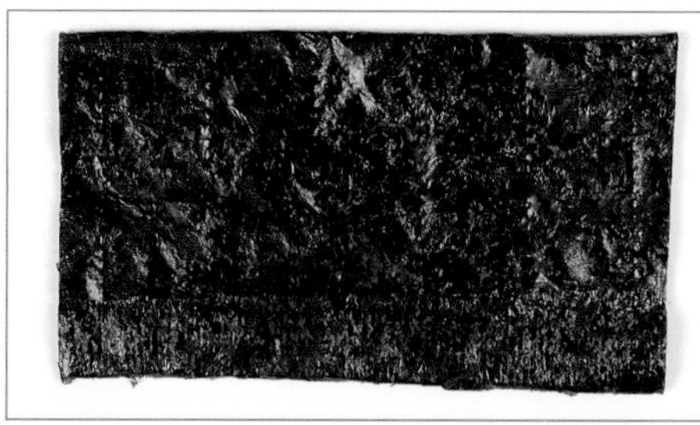

Use a full sheet of nori horizontally. Cut the gourd into 8 2/3" (22 cm) strips. As shown on p. 158, trim the nori, place the gourd strips on it, and wrap to the dimensions shown.

Spread 2 oz (60 g) of the rice on the far half of the gourd package so that the near end is slightly thinner than the far end *(far left)*. Fold the gourd package over and press into shape (left).

Place the package down on a board with the pointed end toward you. Leaving 1/2" (1.5 cm) at the top, spread 1 oz (30 g) of the rice on each side.

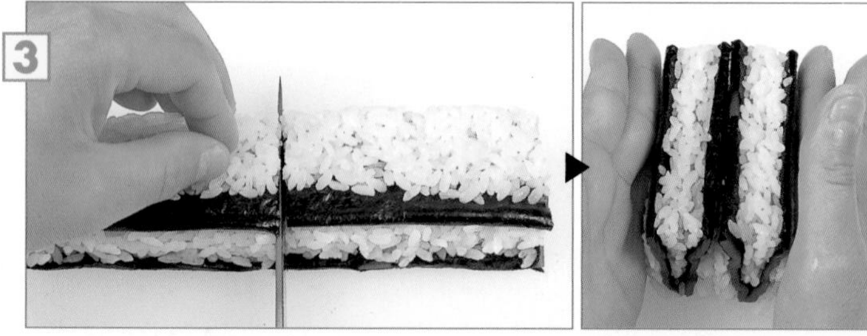

Cut into two equal lengths *(far left)* and place them together *(left)*. Drape with plastic wrap and press into a rectangular block.

Attach 1/3 halfsheet onto 1 halfsheet of nori. Leaving 1" (3 cm) at top and bottom, spread with 4 1/4 oz (120 g) of the rice. Place the letter in the center. Place the remaining 1 1/4 oz (30 g) of rice on top. Fold the nori over. Form into a square, flatten the edges, and slice into 4 pieces.

(for 1 roll) **9 $^1/_2$ oz (270 g) sushi rice** (p. 9)
Simmered gourd (p.17), **Roasted nori**

Cut a 6" (15 cm) strip horizontally from a full sheet of nori. Cut the gourd into 8 $^2/_3$" (22 cm) strips. As shown on p. 158, trim the nori, place the gourd strips on it, and wrap to the dimensions shown.

1

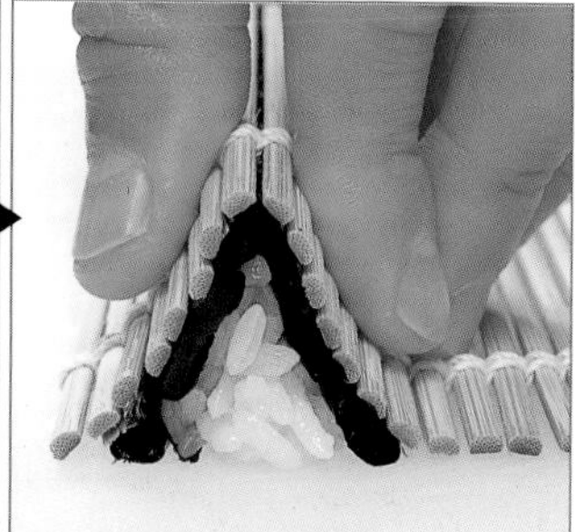

Form 1 $^1/_2$ oz (40 g) of the rice into a wedge on the far half of the gourd package so that the high point is at the back *(far left)*. Fold the gourd package over the rice and turn rice side down. Press into a triangle with the rolling mat *(left)*.

2

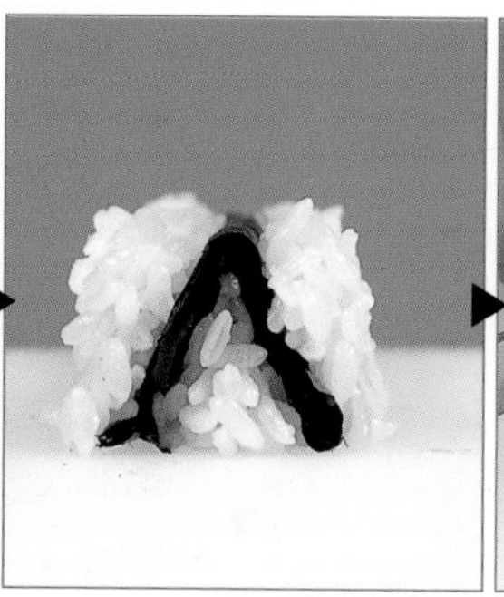

Place 1 $^1/_2$ oz (40 g) of the rice on each side with the upper edge thicker than the lower edge so that the whole assembly forms a square *(far left, center left)*. Cut into two equal lengths *(left)*.

3

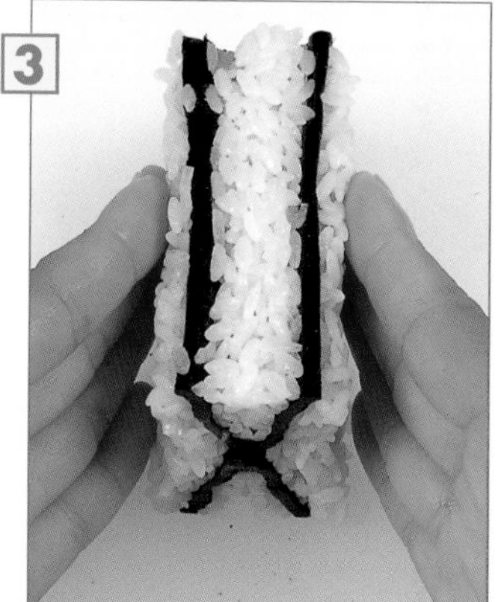

Place one length on top of the other. Drape with plastic wrap and form into a rectangular block.

4

Attach $^1/_3$ halfsheet onto 1 halfsheet of nori. Leaving 1" (3 cm) at top and bottom, spread with 4 $^1/_4$ oz (120 g) of the rice. Place the letter in the center. Place the remaining $^3/_4$ oz (30 g) of the rice on top. Fold the nori over. Form into a square, flatten the edges, and slice into 4 pieces.

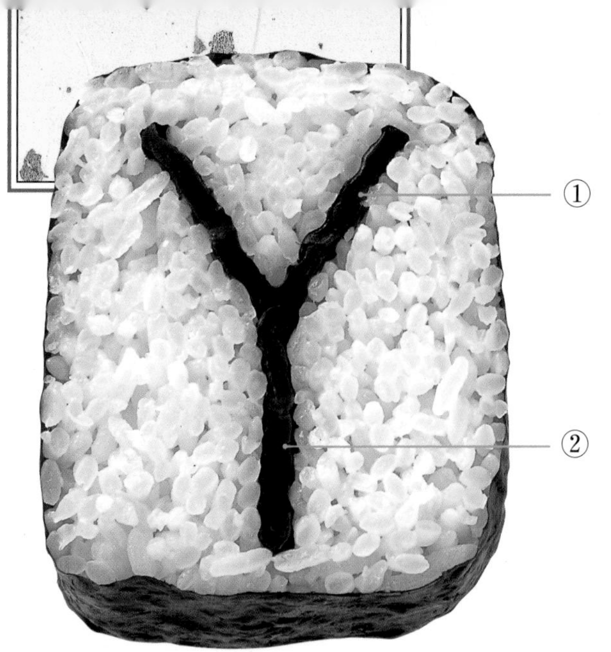

(for 1 roll) **9 $^{1}/_{2}$ oz (270 g) sushi rice** (p. 9)
Simmered gourd (p.17), **Roasted nori**

Cut the nori and gourd to produce two packages as shown.

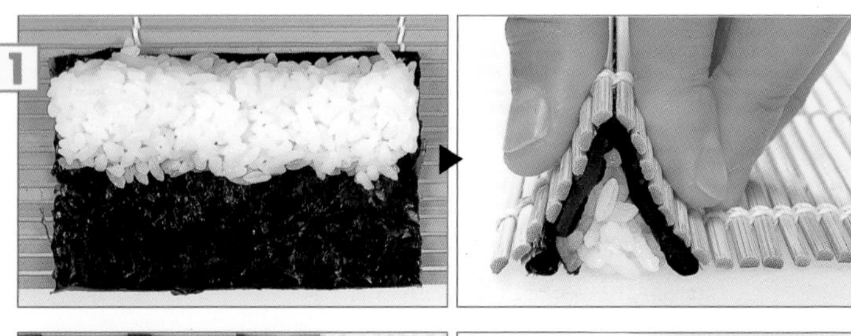

1. Form 1 oz (30 g) of the rice into a wedge on the far half of package 1 with the high point in back. Fold the package over the rice. Turn rice side down and press into a triangle with the rolling mat.

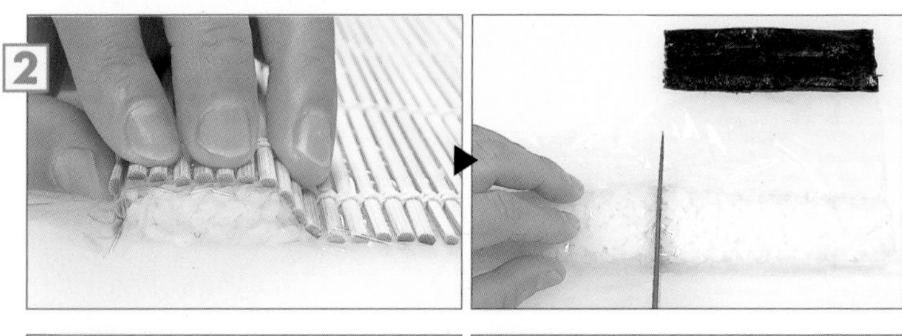

2. Spread 3 $^{1}/_{4}$ oz (90 g) of the rice in a line 8 $^{1}/_{4}$" (21 cm)-long. Drape with plastic wrap and form into a modified trapezoid where one side is square with the top and bottom and the other side is at an angle. The bottom edge should be 1 $^{1}/_{2}$" (4 cm) and the top edge should be just under 1" (3 cm) *(far left)*. Cut into two equal lengths *(left)*.

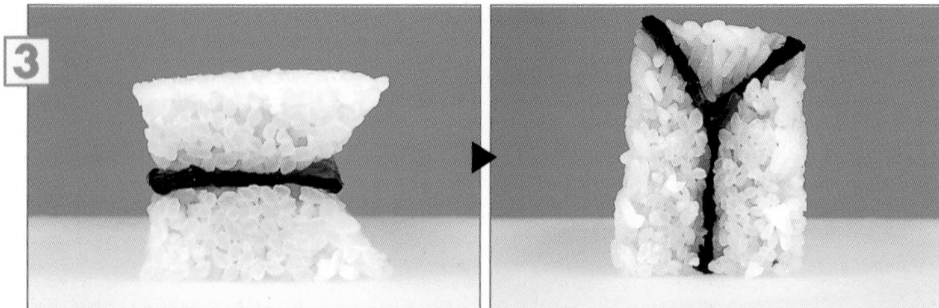

3. Place the lengths together with package 2 between *(far left)*. Place the V (from step 1) on top *(left)*.

4. Attach $^{1}/_{3}$ halfsheet onto 1 halfsheet of nori. Leaving 1" (3 cm) at top and bottom, spread with 4 $^{1}/_{4}$ oz (120 g) of the rice. Place the letter in the center. Place the remaining 1 oz (30 g) of rice on top. Fold the nori over. Form into a square, flatten the edges, and slice into 4 pieces.

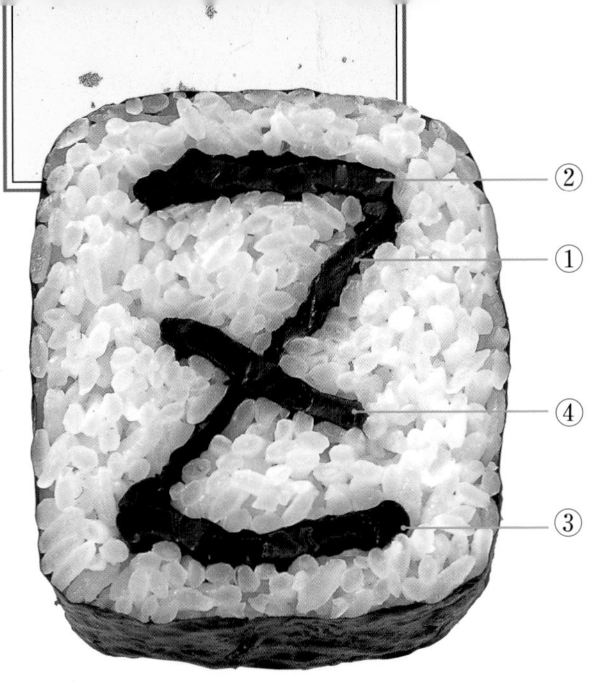

(for 1 roll) **9 $^1/_2$ oz (270 g) sushi rice** (p. 9)
Simmered gourd (p.17), **Roasted nori**

①2 $^1/_3$" (6 cm) ②1 $^1/_2$"(4 cm) ③1 $^1/_2$"(4 cm) ④$^3/_4$" (2 cm)

Cut the nori and gourd to produce four packages as shown.

1 Spread 4 $^1/_4$ oz (120 g) of the rice in a line about 8" (20 cm)-long. Drape with plastic wrap and press into a right triangle whose long side is 2 $^1/_3$" (6 cm) *(far left)*. Cut into two equal lengths and place the lengths together with package 1 between *(center left)*. Place packages 2 and 3 on the sides *(left)*.

2 Slice in half on the diagonal, cutting through package 1 *(far left)*. Place package 4 between the halves and press them back together *(center left, left)*.

3 Using 3 grains of rice, attach $^1/_3$ halfsheet onto 1 halfsheet of nori. Leaving 1" (3 cm) at top and bottom, spread 4 $^1/_4$ oz (120 g) of the rice evenly on the nori. Place the letter in the center.

4 Place the remaining 1 oz (30 g) of rice on top of the letter block. Place the mat in your hand, press the sides together, and fold the nori over. Place the roll seam side down and form into a square. Push the sushi to the ends of the mat to flatten the edges. Slice into 4 pieces, wiping the blade with a wet towel.

Celebration (Iwai)

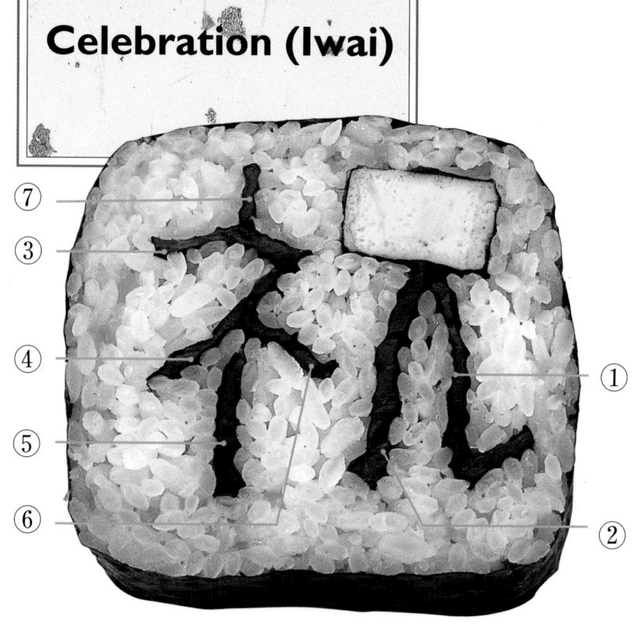

(for 1 roll) **10 $^1/_2$ oz (300 g) sushi rice** (p. 9)
1 omelet block,
$^3/_8$ x $^3/_4$ x 4 $^1/_3$" (1 x 2 x 11 cm) (p.19)
3 Tbsp oboro sprinkles (p.18)
Simmered gourd (p.17)
Roasted nori

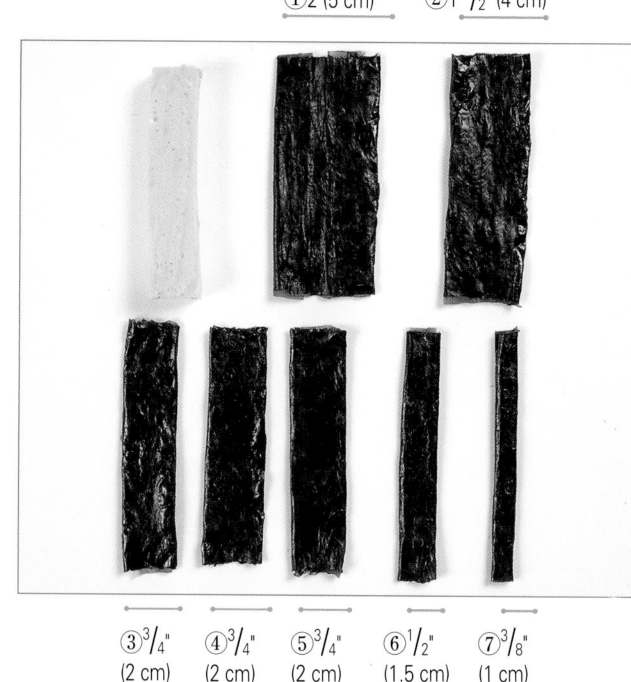

Cut the nori and gourd to produce seven packages as shown.

Shape 1 oz (30 g) of sushi into a block $^3/_8$ x $^3/_4$ x 4 $^1/_3$" (1 x 2 x 11 cm). Cut in half lengthwise *(far left)*. Place package 7 between the halves and cover with package 3 *(middle left)*. Form 2/3 oz (20 g) of the rice into a right triangle and place on top. Place package 4 on the slope *(left)*.

Shape $^1/_3$ oz (10 g) of the rice into a triangle on package 6 *(far left)*. Turn over and place on package 4 *(middle left, left)*.

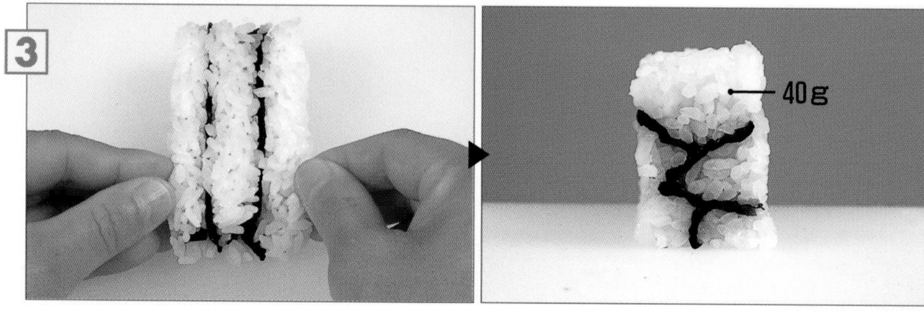

Lay the assembly on its side and place $1^1/_2$ oz (40 g) of the rice on (to the right of) packages 4 and 6. Press into a rectangular block with a rolling mat and set the assembly upright (far left, left).

Make an incision into the top layer of rice, stopping when you reach the gourd package *(far left)*. Place package 5 in the incision *(middle left)*. Wrap the omelet in nori and place next to the assembly *(left)*.

Spread $^2/_3$ oz (20 g) of the rice on one surface of package 2 so that one end is thinner than the other *(far left)*. Place on top of the omelet package, rice side in, with the thinner end facing up *(middle left, left)*.

Leaving $^3/_8$" (1 cm) on the near edge, spread $^2/_3$ oz (20 g) of the rice on one surface of package 1 *(far left)*. Curve the gourd up over the front edge of rice *(middle left)*. Place $^2/_3$ oz (20 g) of the rice on in a wedge on the other surface, thick end toward the curved part *(left)*.

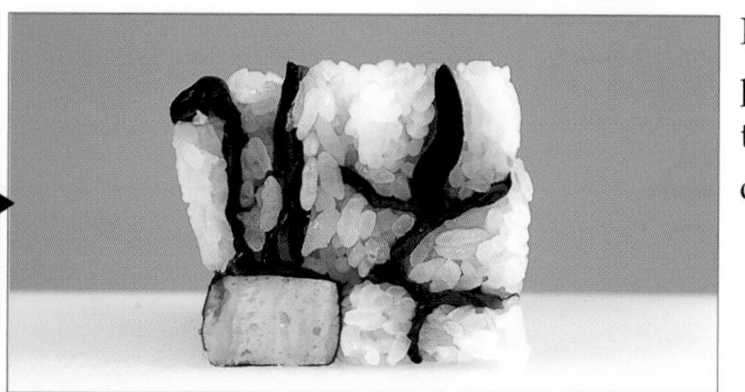

Place on the omelet so that the curve points outward and press both sides toward the center *(far left)*. The character is now complete *(left)*.

Stir the oboro sprinkles into 5 oz (140 g) of the rice. Attach $^1/_2$ halfsheet onto 1 halfsheet of nori with 3 grains of rice. Leaving 1" (3 cm) at top and bottom, spread 3 $^1/_2$ oz (100 g) of the pink rice evenly on the nori. Place the character in the center. Place the remaining pink rice on top of the character block. Place the mat in your hand, press the sides together, and fold the nori over. Form into a square and flatten the edges.

Slice into 4 pieces, wiping the blade with a damp cloth. For this and other character patterns, slice off a thin piece from the right-reading end so that all pieces will display clear-cut forms.

Felicitations (Kotobuki)

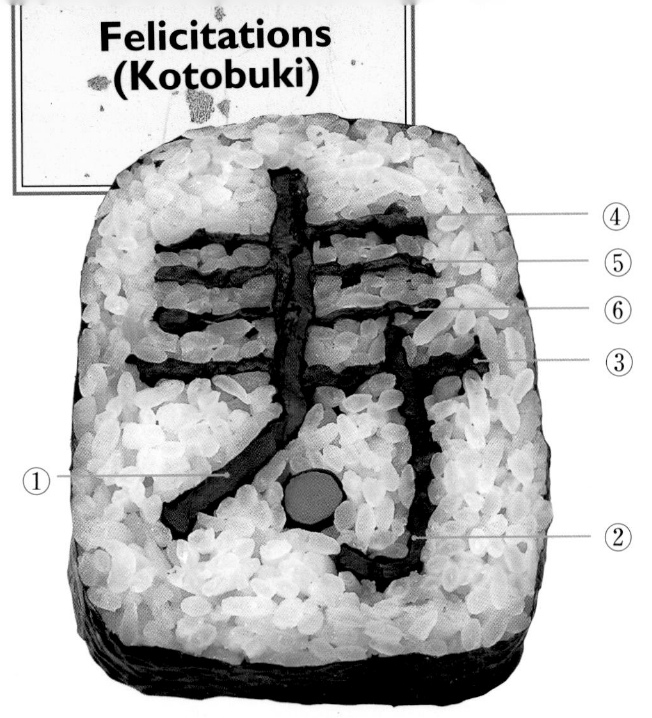

(for 1 roll) **9 $^1/_2$ oz (270 g) sushi rice (p. 9)**
4 $^1/_3$" (11 cm) misozuke yamagobo
3 Tbsp oboro sprinkles (p.18)
Simmered gourd (p.17)
Roasted nori

Cut the nori and gourd to produce six packages as shown.

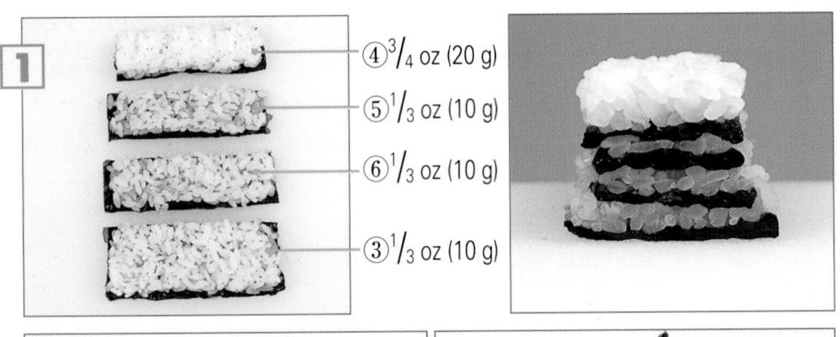

Spread $^3/_4$ oz (20 g) of the white rice on package 4 and $^1/_3$ oz (10 g) on each of packages 5, 6, and 3 *(far left)*. Place package 3 on the bottom, then layer packages 6, 5, and 4 on top, in that order *(left)*.

Carefully slice the assembly in half lengthwise *(far left)*. Because of the multiple layers of package, cut a small amount at a time to avoid crushing the assembly. Place package 1 between the halves and press the halves back together *(left)*.

Curve the exposed end of package 1 to the right. Place $^3/_4$ oz (20 g) of the rice under the curve *(far left, left)*.

Spread $^{3}/_{4}$ oz (20 g) of the sushi rice in the center of package 2 *(far left)*. Curve the far edge of the package up over the edge of the rice *(middle left)*. Place $^{3}/_{4}$ oz (20 g) on the other side of the package, in a wedge that begins at the curve and tapers down to a point 1" (3 cm) below the curve.

On the left side of the 4-layer assembly, slice through the first layer *(far left)*. Place the assembly from step 4 in the incision, curved end up *(left)*.

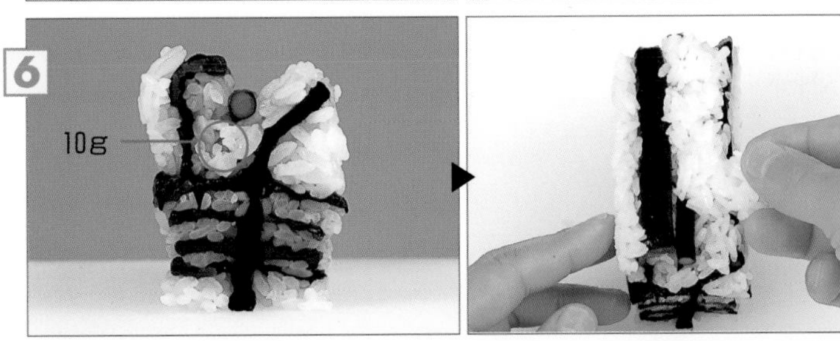

Tuck an additional $^{1}/_{3}$ oz (10 g) of the rice into the space next to the curved piece as shown *(far left)*. Wrap the yamagobo in nori and place on top. Place $^{3}/_{4}$ oz (20 g) in the valley above the yamagobo *(left)*. Drape with plastic wrap and use the mat to form into a rectangular block.

Mix the oboro into the remaining 4 $^{1}/_{2}$ oz (130 g) of the rice. Using 3 grains of rice, attach $^{1}/_{2}$ halfsheet onto 1 half-sheet of nori. Leaving 1" (3 cm) at top and bottom, spread 3 $^{1}/_{2}$ oz (100 g) of the pink rice evenly on the nori. Place the character in the center.

Place the remaining pink rice on top of the character block. Place the mat in your hand, press the sides together, and fold the nori over. Place the roll seam side down and form into a square. Push the sushi to the ends of the mat to flatten the edges. Slice into 4 pieces, wiping the blade with a damp cloth.

Sho (First)

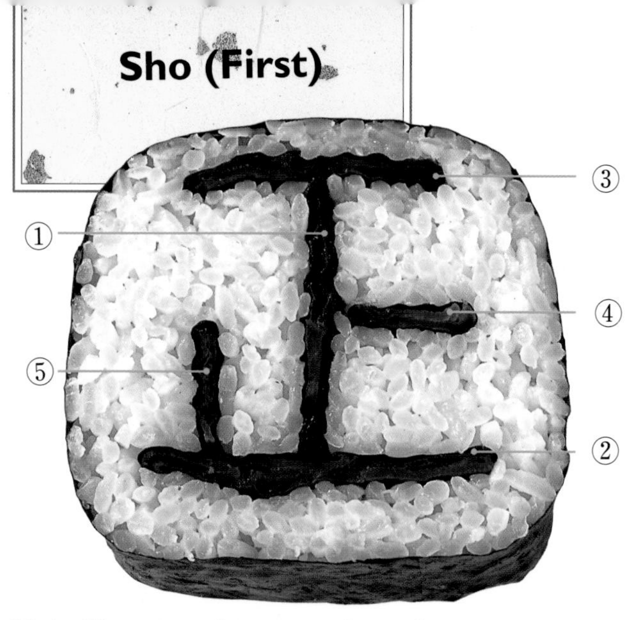

(for 1 roll) **11 1/3 oz (320 g) sushi rice (p. 9)**
Simmered gourd (p.17), Roasted nori

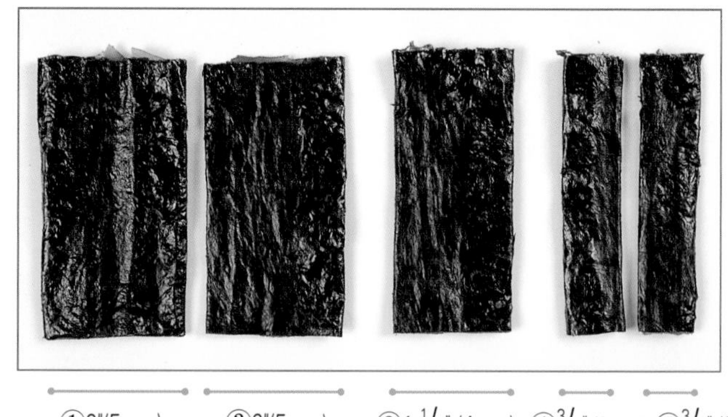

Cut the nori and gourd to produce five packages as shown.

Note: These two characters, sho and gatsu, combine to make "New Year's."

Spread 2 $^{3}/_{4}$ oz (80 g) of the rice on package 1 and use a rolling mat to form into a $^{3}/_{4}$" (2 cm)-high rectangular block *(far left)*. Slice into the rice lengthwise, stopping before you cut the gourd *(middle left)*. Place package 4 in the incision *(left)*.

On a board, form another block with 1 $^{1}/_{2}$ oz (40 g) of the rice to match the shape of package 1 *(far left)*. Place on the exposed side of package 1 and place package 5 along one end *(left)*.

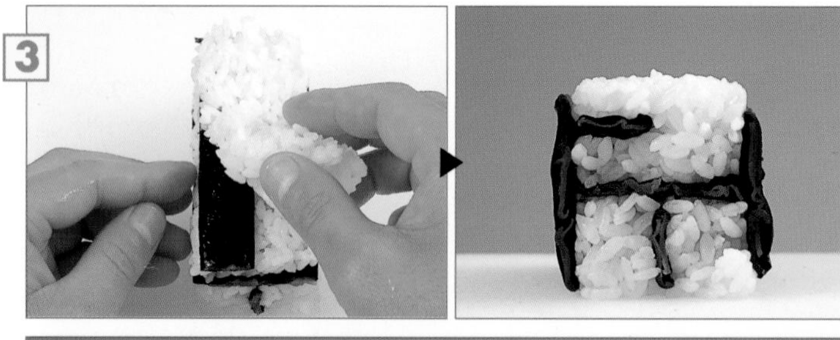

Form another 1 $^{1}/_{2}$ oz (40 g) rectangular block and place on top of the assembly *(far left)*. Drape with plastic wrap and use the mat to form into a square block. Place package 2 along the left side and package 3 along the right side *(left)*.

Attach $^{1}/_{2}$ halfsheet onto 1 halfsheet of nori. Leaving 1" (3 cm) at top and bottom, spread with 4 $^{1}/_{4}$ oz (120 g) of the rice. Place the character in the center. Place the remaining 1 $^{1}/_{3}$ oz (40 g) of rice on top. Fold the nori over. Place the roll seam side down and form into a square. Flatten the edges and slice into 4 pieces.

Gatsu (Month)

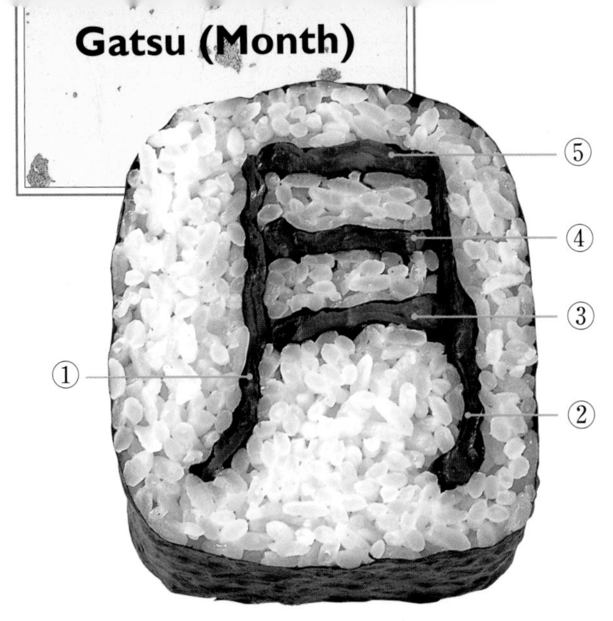

(for 1 roll) **11 $^1/_3$ oz (320 g) sushi rice (p. 9)**
Simmered gourd (p.17), Roasted nori

①2 $^1/_3$" (6 cm) ②2 $^1/_3$" (6 cm) ③1" (3 cm) ④1" (3 cm) ⑤1" (3 cm)

Cut the nori and gourd to produce five package as shown.

1 Spread $^3/_4$ oz (25 g) of the rice on each of packages 3 and 4 *(far left)*. Top with package 5 *(left)*.

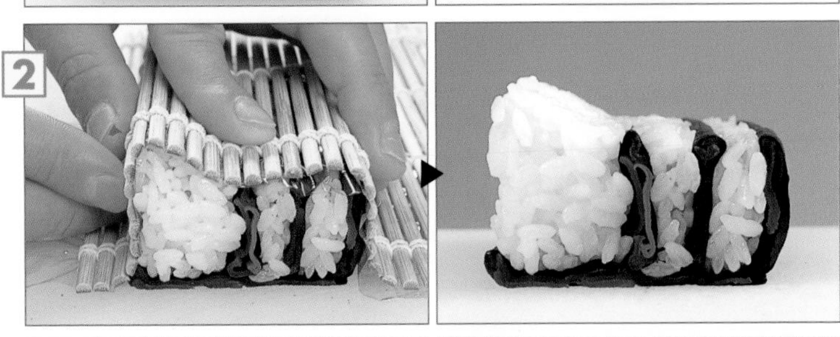

2 Place package 2 horizontally in front of you. Place the layered assembly from step 1 along the back of package 2. Place 2 $^1/_3$ oz (60 g) of the rice in a block in front of the assembly, with the front edge slightly higher than the rest. Drape with plastic wrap and press into shape with a rolling mat *(far left)*. The finished form will be flat along the layered portion and angled upward in front *(left)*.

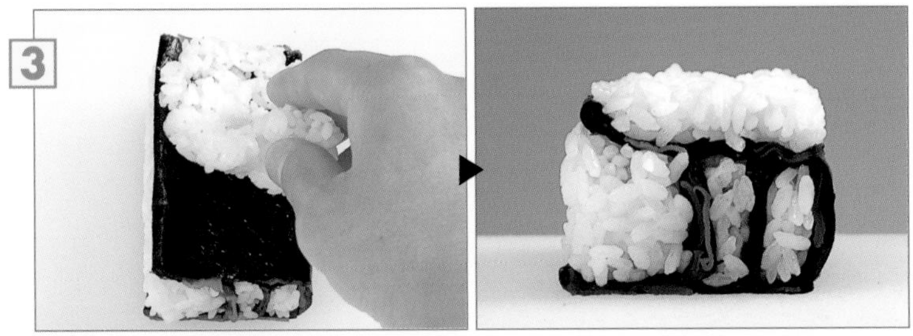

3 Place package 1 on the top, curving it to match the angled surface, and cover with 1 $^1/_2$ oz (40 g) of the rice *(far left)*. Because package 1 is curved, this rice layer will be thin in front and thick in back *(left)*.

4 Attach $^1/_2$ halfsheet onto 1 halfsheet of nori. Leaving 1" (3 cm) at top and bottom, spread with 5 oz (140 g) of the rice. Place the letter in the center. Place the remaining 1 oz (30 g) of the rice on top. Fold the nori over. Place the roll seam side down and form into a square. Flatten the edges and slice into 4 pieces.

Festive Platters with Decorative Sushi

Bell

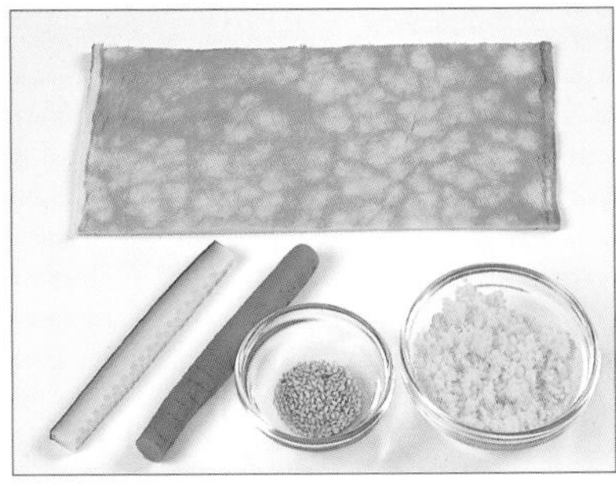

(for 1 roll)

4 1/3" (11 cm) cucumber
4 1/3" (11 cm) misozuke yamagobo
3 Tbsp egg sprinkles (p.80)
1 tsp roasted sesame seeds
1/2 thickness of an omelet sheet (p.23)
11 1/4 oz (320 g) sushi rice (p. 9)
Roasted nori

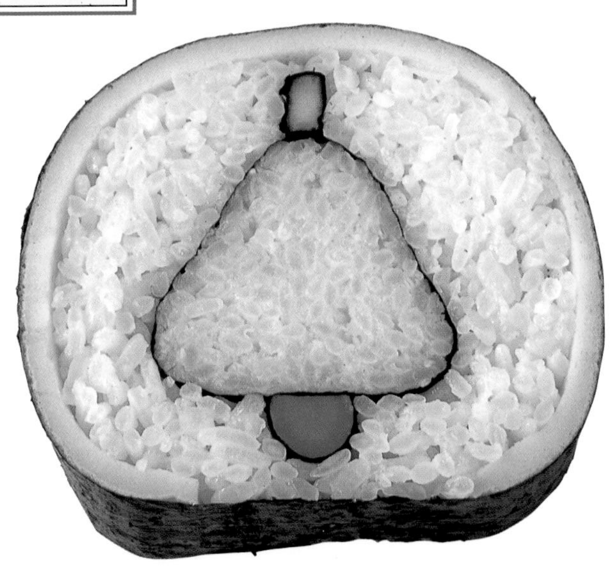

Setup: Trim the cucumber to a strip 1/5 x 3/8" (5 mm x 1 cm). Trim the omelet sheet to 4 x 7" (10.5 x 18 cm). Stir the egg sprinkles and sesame seeds into 3 1/2 oz (100 g) of the rice.

1

Trim off about 1/3 of the yamagobo, lengthwise *(above left)*. Place the yamagobo and the cucumber each on 1/4 of a halfsheet of nori *(above right)* and roll.

2

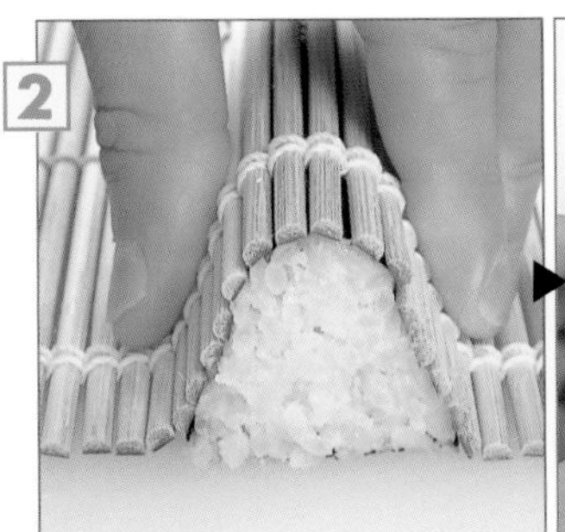

Place the yellow rice in a cylinder on 3/4 of a halfsheet of nori. Roll into a cylinder with a rolling mat, ending with the seam side down. Press into a bell shape *(above left)*. With plastic wrap and a mat, form 2 oz (60 g) of the white rice into a 9" (22 cm)-long right triangle (see p.175, step 2). Cut in half and place along the bell *(above right)*.

3

Attach 1/2 halfsheet onto 1 halfsheet of nori. Place the omelet sheet in the center. Leaving 3/4" (2 cm) at the top and bottom, spread with 4 1/4 oz (120 g) of the rice. Make a groove in the center with a chopstick *(left)*. Place the cucumber package in the groove and place the bell assembly on top *(below)*.

4

Place the yamagobo package in the center. Cover with 1 1/2 oz (40 g) of the rice. Place the mat in your hand, press the sides together, and fold the nori over the rice. Form into a square, flatten the edges, and slice into 4 pieces, wiping the blade with a damp cloth.

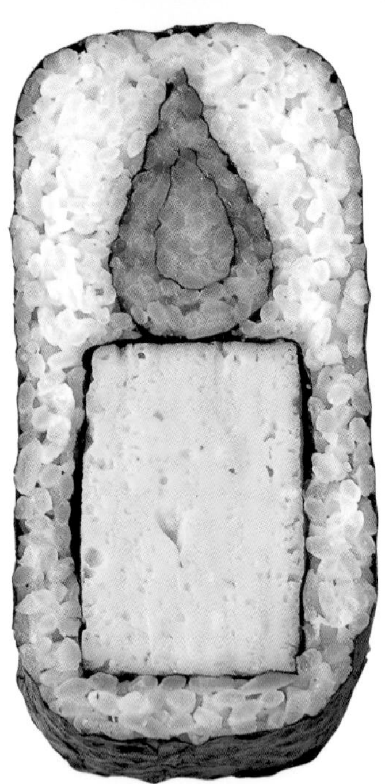

Candle

(for 1 roll)

1 omelet block (p.19)
$^{1}/_{3}$ oz (10 g) flying fish roe
1 tsp oboro sprinkles (p.18)
9 oz (250 g) sushi rice (p. 9)
Roasted nori

Setup: Trim the omelet to 2" (5 cm)-wide. Mix the roe into 1 oz (30 g) of the rice. Mix the oboro into $^{3}/_{4}$ oz (20 g) of the rice.

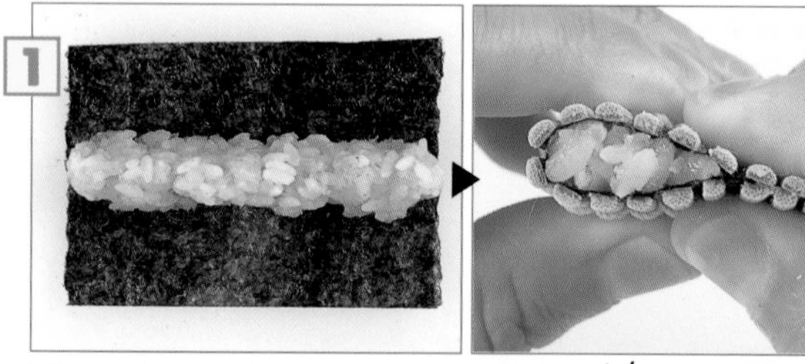

Place the pink rice in the center of $^{1}/_{3}$ of a halfsheet of nori *(above left)*. Fold in half and press into an elongated teardrop *(above right)*.

Leaving $^{3}/_{8}$" (1 cm) at the top and bottom, spread the orange rice evenly on $^{3}/_{2}$ of a halfsheet of nori *(above left)*. Place the pink teardrop about $^{3}/_{8}$" (1 cm) from the far edge of the rice. Fold and press into a teardrop shape *(above right)*.

Place the omelet block on 1 halfsheet of nori. Wrap.

Place 1 oz (30 g) of the rice on each side of the teardrop, more at the pointed end and less at the rounded end *(above left)*. The final form should be a square *(above right)*.

Attach $^{1}/_{2}$ halfsheet onto 1 halfsheet of nori. Leaving 1" (3 cm) at the top and bottom, spread with 4 $^{1}/_{2}$ oz (120 g) of the rice. Place the flame in the center with the omelet package on top. Place the mat in your hand and press the sides together. Cover the omelet package with the remaining $^{3}/_{4}$ oz (20 g) of rice. Close the nori, place the roll seam side down, and press into a rectan-gular block. Flatten the ends and slice into 4 pieces.

Stocking

(for 1 roll)

4 $^{1}/_{3}$" (11 cm) misozuke yamagobo
1 $^{1}/_{2}$ Tbsp egg sprinkles (p.80)
1 $^{1}/_{2}$ Tbsp oboro sprinkles (p.18)
$^{1}/_{2}$ thickness of an omelet sheet (p.23)
10 $^{1}/_{2}$ oz (300 g) sushi rice (p. 9)
Roasted nori

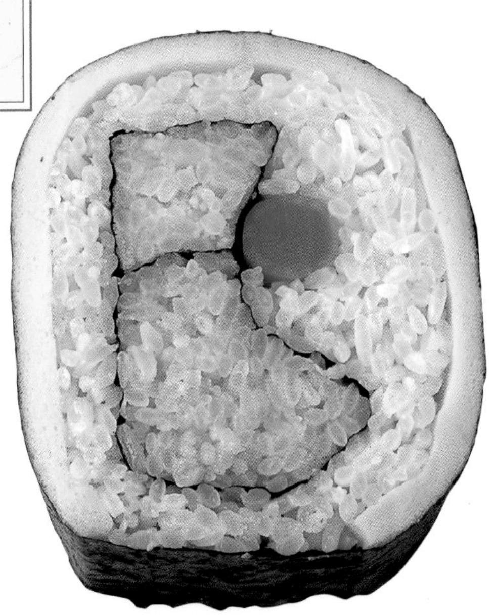

Setup: Trim the omelet sheet to 4 x 7" (10.5 x 18 cm). Mix the egg sprinkles into 1 oz (30 g) of the rice. Mix the oboro into 3 oz (80 g) of the rice. Substitute a cooked carrot, trimmed to an even thickness, for the yamagobo.

1

Place the yellow and pink rice in blocks at the far end of a halfsheet of nori as shown above. Between the two blocks, place a $^{3}/_{4}$" (2 cm) strip cut from a halfsheet of nori.

2

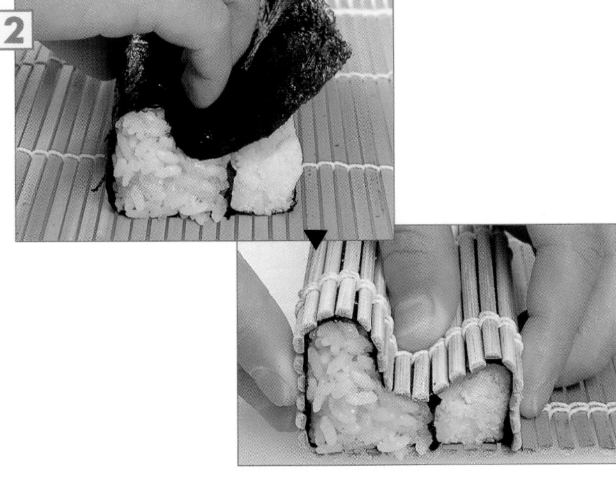

Cover the blocks with the nori, following the outline *(top)*. Press into shape with the mat *(bottom)*.

3

Place the yamagobo as shown, then cover it with 2 oz (60 g) of the white rice. Drape with plastic wrap and press into a rectangular block with the mat.

4

Attach $^{1}/_{2}$ halfsheet onto 1 halfsheet of nori and place the omelet sheet in the center. Leaving 1 $^{1}/_{2}$" (4 cm) at the top and bottom, spread with 3 $^{1}/_{2}$ oz (100 g) of the rice. Place the stocking assembly in the center *(top)*. Place 1 oz (30 g) of the rice on the assembly *(bottom)*. Place the mat in your hand and close the nori. Press into a square, flatten the edges, and slice into 4 pieces.

Meadow

For this floral theme, colorful roses, tulips, and dandelions are surrounded by lively butterflies and ladybugs.

Tulip (p. 80)
Dandelion (p. 82)
Rose (p. 83)
Butterfly (p. 96)
Ladybug (p. 104)

Ocean

Three boats sail in the breeze along an ocean filled with fish, seahorses, and crabs. The blue glass of the platter heightens the effect.

Boat (p. 110)
Fish (p. 106)
Dragon (p. 140)
Crab (p. 98)

Common Problems and How to Fix Them

•Rice sticks to fingers

Before handling rice, prepare a dish of water with a dash of vinegar. Wash your hands and dry well, then dip your fingertips in the water dish and spread the water on your palms. (Conversely, too much water leads to soggy rice.)

•The roll is uneven; the fillings are off center

Both of these problems can be corrected by spreading the rice differently.

(1) As shown at left, if the rice and/or the filling is thicker on one side than the other, then the roll will be thicker at one end also.

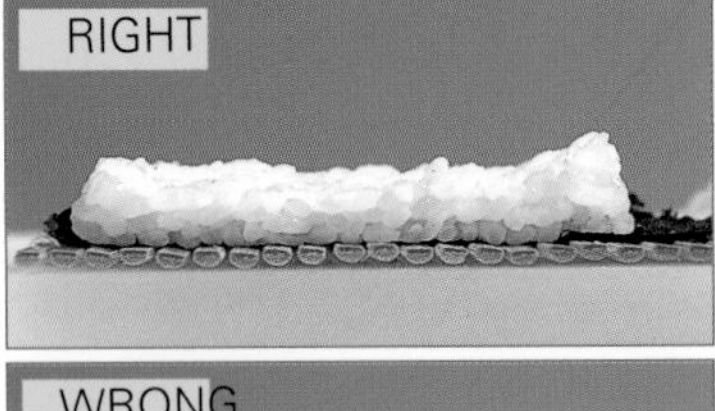

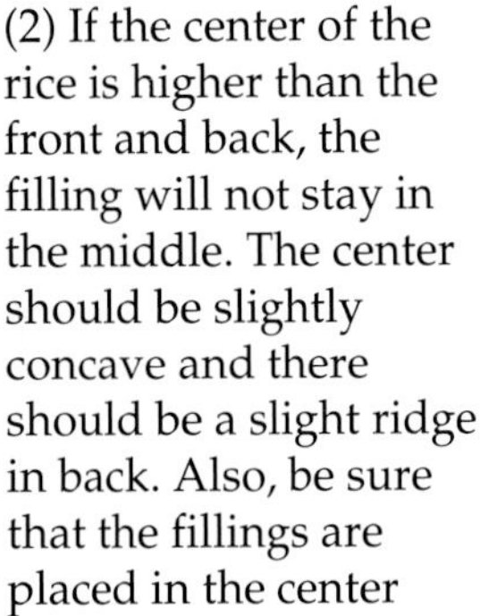

(2) If the center of the rice is higher than the front and back, the filling will not stay in the middle. The center should be slightly concave and there should be a slight ridge in back. Also, be sure that the fillings are placed in the center

(3) Be sure to place the nori squarely along the front edge of the rolling mat. If placed at an angle as shown at left, the sushi will not roll properly. If placed behind the front edge, the rolling will be difficult.

•The sushi bursts at the seam

Splitting or bursting has three possible causes.

(1) There was too much filling for the rice. For a hosomaki, the filling should be no more than 1 oz (30 g); for futomaki, $3\,{}^{1}/_{2}$ oz (100 g).

(2) The rice was spread too close to the far edge. Over time, the nori will shrink, and the seam then opens.

(3) Liquid seeped out of the filling. Be sure to squeeze all excess fluid from such fillings as simmered gourd and freeze-dried tofu.

•The filling scatters when rolling

Oboro, minced takuan, and other loose fillings can scatter when the mat is lifted, mixing with the other ingredients and interfering with the seal. To avoid this problem, make a ridge as shown on p.20, step 6.

•The fillings are loose in the roll

If the fillings are difficult to keep together when picking up the sushi, the rolling was not finished properly. Be sure to press the roll in with your fingertips when the front edge meets the back edge (p.21, step 9; p 43, step 3).